The U.S. Military's "Don't Ask, Don't Tell" Policy

The U.S. Military's "Don't Ask, Don't Tell" Policy

A Reference Handbook

Melissa Sheridan Embser-Herbert

Foreword by Lawrence J. Korb

Contemporary Military, Strategic, and Security Issues

PRAEGER SECURITY INTERNATIONAL
Westport, Connecticut • London

Library of Congress Cataloging-in-Publication Data

Embser-Herbert, Melissa Sheridan.
   The U.S. military's "don't ask, don't tell" policy : a reference handbook / Melissa
Sheridan Embser-Herbert ; foreword by Lawrence J. Korb.
       p. cm. — (Contemporary military, strategic, and security issues, ISSN 1932–295X)
    Includes bibliographical references and index.
    ISBN 978–0–275–99191–3 (alk. paper)
    1. Gays in the military—Government policy—United States.   2. Gays in the
    military—Legal status, laws, etc.—United States.   3. United States—Military policy.
    I. Title.   II. Title: US military's "don't ask, don't tell" policy.   III. Title: United
    States military's "don't ask, don't tell" policy.
    UB418.G38E53   2007
    355.3'3086640973—dc22   2007028017

British Library Cataloguing in Publication Data is available.

Library of Congress Catalog Card Number: 2007028017
ISBN: 978–0–275–99191–3
ISSN: 1932–295X

First published in 2007

Praeger Security International, 88 Post Road West, Westport, CT 06881
An imprint of Greenwood Publishing Group, Inc.
www.praeger.com

Printed in the United States of America

The paper used in this book complies with the
Permanent Paper Standard issued by the National
Information Standards Organization (Z39.48–1984).

10 9 8 7 6 5 4 3 2 1

Contents

Foreword

The subject of this volume is Title 10, Section 654 of the U.S. Code, "Policy Concerning Homosexuality in the Armed Forces," popularly known as, "Don't Ask, Don't Tell." The author, Melissa Sheridan Embser-Herbert, served in the U. S. Army and Army Reserve under the two policies that directly preceded "Don't Ask, Don't Tell." She was a member of the Army Reserve when "Don't Ask, Don't Tell" was implemented in 1993. As a lesbian veteran, a sociologist, and an attorney, she brings a breadth of experience and a special insight to the issue.

The publication of this volume comes at a critical time. Former Chair of the Joint Chiefs of Staff, General John Shalikashvili, has called for a reexamination of the policy, as has former Secretary of Defense, William Cohen. Taking a different position, the Chair of the Joint Chiefs, as of this writing, General Peter Pace, has openly stated his personal opposition to the open military service of gays and lesbians. Veterans of past wars as well as veterans of Operation Enduring Freedom in Afghanistan and Operation Iraqi Freedom have "come out" and asked that their service as a gay or lesbian service member be honored by the repeal of "Don't Ask, Don't Tell." For example, Eric Alva, a gay Marine veteran who lost his leg on the first day of combat in Iraq, has recently become a spokesperson for the elimination of the policy. He has said, " . . . We're losing probably thousands of men and women that are skilled at certain types of jobs, from air traffic controllers to linguists, because of this broken policy." Representative Martin Meehan (D-MA) has, along with 126 cosponsors in the House, introduced a bill to repeal the policy. In the First Circuit of the United States Court of Appeals, we await a decision in *Cook v. Gates*, formerly *Cook v. Rumsfeld*, a challenge to the constitutionality of the policy. Major newspapers across the country continue to publish editorials calling for an end to the policy. Support for a reexamination of the policy, at a minimum, is being called for by both Democratic and Republican members of Congress, such as Senators Collins and Snowe of Maine. Never, since the very first ban on the military service of gay men and lesbians, has discussion of the policy been so much a part of the public discourse.

This volume aims to explain the origins, implementation, and implications of the federal law/military policy concerning the military service of gays, lesbians, and bisexuals. As such, it addresses an issue about which many have strong opinions. Now is the time for a comprehensive and accessible book about the policy to be read by all those concerned about the issue, regardless of opinion. Embser-Herbert, though clearly believing that the time has come for the policy to be eliminated, approaches the discussion as objectively as possible. She is careful to let the words of the people and documents tell the story. She begins by introducing the reader to the issue, addressing the tension between a call for equal rights and claims about the needs of the military. The first chapter also describes what happened during the first months of the Clinton administration, leading to the creation of the law. Embser-Herbert then describes how the military has implemented the policy. By drawing on military sources, the reader gets a firsthand look at the difficulties of understanding and enforcing the policy. In turning to an examination of how the policy impacts both the institution of the military and the individual service member, Embser-Herbert is able to provide the reader with a sense of those effects that are measurable, such as discharges under the policy. Acknowledging that international comparisons are themselves contentious, Embser-Herbert, along with coauthor and expert Dr. Aaron Belkin, discusses the Canadian, Australian, and British policies on gays and lesbians in the military. Although it's still too early to know for certain, there is a good chance that 9/11 and the United States' presence in Afghanistan and Iraq will come to be recognized as having a significant impact on the future of "Don't Ask, Don't Tell." In her fifth chapter, Embser-Herbert discusses this potential relationship, focusing on the experiences of gay and lesbian service members in these regions. Finally, the volume concludes with a look at where things currently stand.

There are a number of good books that address this issue, though none, to my knowledge, provide as comprehensive and accessible an overview of the topic in the form of a monograph. Most are edited volumes reflecting a particular viewpoint, article/thesis length treatments, or auto/biographical accounts. As such, this volume provides the unfamiliar reader with an understanding of how the law came to be and what it means for the U.S. military. Yet, one of the difficulties in writing such a volume now is that things are changing so quickly. By the time you read this, something significant will likely have occurred. Nonetheless, the historical and contemporary overviews that Embser-Herbert provides remain useful to anyone seeking to understand the creation of the policy and its impact on both the military and individuals within the military.

Lawrence J. Korb
Senior Fellow at the Center for American Progress,
Senior Adviser to the Center for Defense Information,
and former Assistant Secretary of Defense
(Manpower, Reserve Affairs, Installations and Logistics, 1981–1985)

Preface

In 1993, days after the inauguration of President William Jefferson Clinton, the United States became embroiled in a national debate over whether gays and lesbians would be permitted to serve openly in the U.S. military. The answer was a resounding, "No." Enacted in 1993 as Public Law 103-160 and codified as Section 654 under Title 10 of the U.S. Code, the current "policy concerning homosexuality in the armed forces" eventually became known as "Don't Ask, Don't Tell, Don't Pursue, Don't Harass," or "Don't Ask, Don't Tell" for short.

When first approached about writing a book about this policy, I was skeptical. I feel very strongly about the issue and the notion of crafting an objective, neutral account of a discriminatory policy seemed overwhelming. Everyone agrees that the policy is discriminatory. The disagreement is over whether the discrimination is justified. I couldn't imagine writing something that might be seen as providing justification for the policy. Nor did I think it appropriate to have a hidden—or not so hidden—agenda of convincing the reader, through selective discussion of the issues, to see things "my way." What I decided was that I would accept the challenge, doing my best to let the legislative, historical, and public records speak for themselves. Hopefully you will conclude that I have done so.

This volume provides the reader with an overview of the enactment, implementation, and impact of the policy. The chapters provide the narrative. The first chapter introduces the broader debate, specifically the tension between the claim that the military has unique personnel needs and the demand of gays and lesbians that they be treated equally under the law. In addition, this chapter provides a brief overview of earlier policies concerning homosexuality in the military. Has the military always banned gays and lesbians from military service? If so, how were such regulations implemented and, if not, when did this practice begin? What happened during 1992 and 1993 that led to "Don't Ask, Don't Tell?" Why did Bill Clinton make the promise to end the ban and how was he held accountable? What happened once he announced the six-month period of study? This chapter takes the reader through the Congressional hearings, paying particular attention to the arguments made both for and against limiting the service of gays and lesbians. Chapter 2 describes how the military has implemented and enforced the law via its own regulations, training, etc. Once the federal law was passed, how did the Department of Defense respond? How does the military enforce the current policy? Chapter 3 addresses the way the policy has been argued to impact the military. The impact of such a personnel policy ranges from the less easily quantified (e.g., morale) to the more easily quantified (e.g., discharges). This chapter focuses primarily, though not exclusively, on the latter. Regardless of what one thinks about the service of gays and lesbians, it is undeniable that the policy has had an impact of the military. Be it in mission performance or dollars, what is the cost of the policy? Chapter 4, coauthored with noted scholar Aaron Belkin, turns to the international scene. While several of our NATO allies have had such policies, in recent years many have eliminated them. What have the results been? Has there been a measurable negative impact on recruitment, retention, or military effectiveness? With a focus on Canada, Australia, and Great Britain, the nations seen by many as most similar to the United States, this chapter explores the impact on those nations' militaries of rescinding their respective bans on gays and lesbians. Chapter 5 considers the "war on terror." Does the need to discharge gays and lesbians trump the need for Arabic linguists? Are gays and lesbians serving openly in Iraq? What might the service of gays and lesbians in time of war tell us about "Don't Ask, Don't Tell"? Finally, Chapter 6 discusses expectations for the future. Where do current efforts to repeal or overturn the law stand? Given the widespread deployment of U.S. forces, might we expect any changes in the near future?

Appendix I provides summaries of key legal decisions. By examining what the courts have said, or not said, regarding the policy, the reader is introduced to those aspects of the law most relevant to a consideration of the policy's future. Appendix II contains materials from the period during which the proposed policy was being studied, the language of the law itself, and excerpts from other documents that address the policy. This volume also includes a chronology of events, glossary of terms, and an annotated bibliography. The aim is to provide the reader with an accessible, yet comprehensive, overview of the policy. Although there is little doubt that the future will bring about change, this book reflects the history of "Don't Ask, Don't Tell" as well as its status as we approach the fifteenth year of the policy.

I cannot overstate the degree to which this book could not have been written without the assistance of others. To those I may have neglected to name, know that I very much appreciate your kindness and generosity. I must acknowledge the tremendous work of the Center for the Study of Sexual Minorities in the Military (CSSMM), now the Michael D. Palm Center at the University of California at Santa Barbara, and the Servicemembers Legal Defense Network (SLDN), located in Washington, DC. The extensive archival record available from both organizations was beyond invaluable. In particular, I must acknowledge the awe-inspiring work of Dr. Aaron Belkin at CSSMM/the Palm Center and C. Dixon Osburn at SLDN. They are beyond amazing. Thanks as well to Sharra Greer and Steve Ralls, both of SLDN. Their assistance, too, was critical. (Service member biographies are reprinted with the permission of SLDN, www.sldn.org.) Additionally, " 'Don't Ask, Don't Tell, Don't Pursue': A digital law project of the Robert Crown Law Library at Stanford Law Library" was of great benefit, particularly in identifying the relevant material from the Congressional hearings of 1993.

For their assistance in a variety of tasks ranging from library research to reading drafts, I must thank Nathaniel Frank, Joan Heggie, Connie Lenz, Sharon Preves, and Ann Verme. I must also acknowledge the gracious cooperation of those veterans who offered their stories and helped with clarification of the details. A 2006–2007 Hanna Grant from the College of Liberal Arts at Hamline University enabled me to hire a research assistant par excellence, Jenna Yauch. Jenna is one of the very best undergraduate students with whom I've had the privilege of working. For her hard work, which continued even when the money ran out, I am most appreciative. I would also like to acknowledge the support of F. Garvin Davenport. I am most grateful for the friendship and support he offered during particularly challenging times. Thanks as well to Adam Kane and Alicia Merritt at Greenwood/Praeger. Their patience and advice was most helpful in seeing this project to fruition. Finally, I would be terribly remiss if I did not acknowledge the support of my family, especially my partner, Elvira, and my son, Walker. Next summer is yours!

This volume is dedicated to gay, lesbian, and bisexual veterans everywhere, but especially to Sergeant Susan E. Miller, whose death at the hands of a fellow soldier was, I believe, largely attributable to the climate of sexism and homophobia that pervaded the military at the time of her service. Eliminating the federal law that contributes to that climate is one important step toward improving both the institution of the military and the lives of those who serve.

CHAPTER 1

Gay Men and Lesbians in the Military

Military leaders acknowledge that gay men and lesbians have always served in the U.S. military. Some gay men, lesbians, and bisexuals[1] have been very open with fellow service members. Others have completed thirty years of service, retiring with few, if any, of their peers aware of their secret. It is also true that the military, as an institution, has always struggled with how to control the presence of gay men and lesbians in the ranks. Typically, the answer has been some type of exclusionary policy. During the last century, the rules and regulations used to implement a doctrine of exclusion have existed in various forms and have undergone a variety of changes over time. The most serious change in this history took place in 1993 when, for the first time, the U.S. Congress passed legislation making the prohibition on the military service of openly gay men and lesbians federal law.

Though Congress created the law, it was up to military leadership to implement it. Some argued that this would be easy in an organization built upon hierarchy and chain-of-command. Others argued that the unique nature of the military makes any change challenging. The Department of Defense describes itself as "America's oldest, largest, busiest, and most successful company."[2] Although the business analogy may work well as an illustration of the breadth and depth of the organization, the history and mission of the armed forces are, of course, worlds apart from that of any typical business. The Department of Defense describes its mission as "warfighting, humanitarian, peacekeeping, evacuation, and homeland security," but says, "We are warfighters first and as such have no peers." Their bottom line is "to provide the military forces needed to deter war and to protect the security of the United States."[3]

Military personnel operate under a chain of command where it is imperative, perhaps life saving, that they take orders from those to whom they report. Service members must place unquestionable trust in their peers. In civilian employment, where workers do, of course, take orders, those orders rarely require one to perform tasks that are as onerous and unpleasant as they can be in the military. And, far less frequently do they involve situations of life and death. Additionally, unlike the majority of civilian employment where workers go home at the end of their day, in the military one might be called upon to sleep in a hole dug in the earth, spend hours in a small space with several other soldiers, live on a ship—likely "hot bunking"[4]—for months at a time, go for weeks without a shower, and so on. These are only two examples of the way the military, as a work environment, is distinct from most civilian occupations. And, these realities—typically described as issues of unit cohesion and privacy—are just two of the reasons, some have argued, it is critical that military personnel be comfortable with those with whom they serve.

Unit cohesion is, at its simplest, the ability of a unit—whether a company of Army engineers or a squad of Navy divers—to work together as one. Consideration of unit cohesion in the military typically centers on two types of cohesion: social cohesion and task cohesion. Social cohesion refers to the friendships, the caring for each other, and the positive relationships among group members. If a group exhibits high social cohesion, the argument goes, they are likely to engage in recreational activities together, work well together, and, generally, do better if they like each other. It was long believed that social cohesion was critical to group success and that social cohesion could only really be achieved in groups where members were either very similar to one another or, at the very least, members had no reason to feel dislike or hostility toward another member or members of the group. Thus, if a group contained a member, or members, with whom others in the group would not work well, the ability of that group to achieve their goals, to be successful, would be compromised.

Task cohesion, on the other hand, refers to a shared commitment to achieve a goal that is best, or only, achieved if everyone in the group cooperates. The members share a common goal and are motivated, it is argued, to work together to achieve that goal. Recent studies suggest that task cohesion may be far more important to group success than is social cohesion. And, it is unclear whether cohesion has a greater impact on success or success has a greater impact on cohesion. Regardless, the recent emphasis on task cohesion suggests that similarity of group members may be far less important than the group's desire to reach their goal. Thus, arguments about exclusion that rest on the importance of unit cohesion are not entirely wrong. They are, however, potentially misguided when they emphasize a need for homogeneity.

The second argument for excluding those who are different is the need to protect the privacy of the dominant group. That means, historically speaking, the privacy of whites may be compromised by the presence of nonwhites, particularly African-Americans, and the privacy of men may be compromised by the presence of women. Not surprising to anyone who has ever seen a movie featuring a submarine or military barracks, watched video footage shot from inside a tank, or heard a soldier talk about being "in the field," privacy is at a premium in the military. It is true that service members often use "gang" showers, makeshift field latrines, and have shared quarters, whether permanent or temporary. In addition, soldiers, sailors, airmen,[5] and marines must often change clothing and deal with various issues of personal and medical hygiene in close company. As with unit cohesion, the argument is that people are more comfortable if they are with others more similar to themselves. And, again, the argument is not completely lacking in merit. A great deal of social psychology illustrates the way in which people both benefit from and provide benefits to those they see as being more similar to than dissimilar from themselves. The question, of course, is whether such a finding is an acceptable justification for exclusion. Should African-Americans be excluded if a white person is more comfortable serving only with whites? Should women be excluded if men are more comfortable serving only with men? And, most pertinent to this volume, should gays and lesbians be excluded if heterosexuals are more comfortable serving only with heterosexuals? For better or worse, these questions have a long history within debates about military service. And, it is a complicated set of questions. At the core is this question: If the presence of a given minority group will negatively affect unit performance, even if the disruption is due to the prejudice of the majority group, is discrimination acceptable for the sake of the mission?

In the 1940s, when the military service of African-Americans was being debated, the General Board to the Secretary of the Navy concluded that the enlistment of African-Americans without restrictions on their service was unadvisable. The report stated:

> Enlistment for general service implies that the individual may be sent anywhere—to any ship or station where he is needed. Men on board ship live in particularly close association; in their messes, one man sits beside another; their hammocks or bunks are close together; in their common tasks they work side by side; and in particular tasks such as those of a gun's crew, they form a closely knit, highly coordinated team. How many white men would choose, of their own accord, that their closest associates in sleeping quarters, at mess, and in a gun's crew should be of another race? How many would accept such conditions, if required to do so, without resentment and just as a matter of course? The General Board believes that the answer is "Few, if any," and further believes that if the issue were forced, there would be a lowering of contentment, teamwork and discipline in the service.[6]

It was reasoned that African-Americans experienced a greater incidence of disease, particularly venereal disease; that the increased enlistment of African-Americans would cause a decrease in the enlistment of whites, particularly Southerners; that whites would refuse to obey the orders of African-American officers; and that, according to the Navy General Board, greater racial integration would lead to marriage between whites and blacks, something that even those who might otherwise support integration would not accept. All of these characterizations were linked directly to concerns of unit cohesion and privacy—for the white service members.

Just a few decades later, similar arguments were made against increasing the number of women in the military and opening more roles, particularly leadership roles, to women. While many of the arguments against expanding opportunities for women rested on the purported weakness, both physical and emotional, of women, many arguments were based on the presumed impact the presence of women would have on men. For example, it was argued that men would be distracted from their work by the presence of women, men wouldn't be able to "be themselves" (e.g., swear) around women, relationships between men would be compromised by the presence of women, and, surely men wouldn't take orders from women.

Although, in the instances of both race and gender, there have been difficulties to be sure, people of color and women have entered the military in significant numbers and have served admirably. Consider, as just one example, the military service of General Colin Powell. Having served in Vietnam as a young lieutenant, Powell ended his military career by serving as the 12th Chair of the Joint Chiefs of Staff from October 1989 until September 1993. Consider as well the military service of Colonel Rhonda Cornum. As a flight surgeon during the Persian Gulf War, Colonel Cornum was captured and held as a prisoner after her helicopter was shot down while on a search and rescue mission. Her service awards include, among others, the Distinguished Flying Cross, Bronze Star, Meritorious Service Medal, and Purple Heart. Both individuals, an African-American man and a white woman, rose through the ranks to serve with distinction. It is true that the military is a unique environment in which people are called upon to act and live in ways often unimaginable to their civilian counterparts. But, the military is also part of a nation whose founding documents assert that all are created equal and that none shall be denied equal protection under the law.

A History of Exclusion

While this volume deals with the current military policy, "Don't Ask, Don't Tell," this is not the first military policy to address the service of gay men and lesbians.[7] Neither has the military always had a policy that excluded gays and lesbians. In the early twentieth century, some of the first major investigations into homosexual activity took place in Newport, Rhode Island. Several sailors were imprisoned, others were discharged, and some of those implicated managed to escape conviction or discharge. Some have indicated that it may well be this early, and widely publicized, case that led to a more formal policy concerning the military service of gays and lesbians.

An important distinction worth noting is that, as has always been the case, sodomy and homosexuality are not synonymous. A person who did not identify as "gay" could be punished for engaging in sodomy. A person who identified as gay could be punished for being gay, but not necessarily be guilty of sodomy. That is, the regulations concerning homosexuality were distinct from the criminal code's treatment of sodomy. It is also worth noting that these early policies addressed only gay men. It wasn't until the increasing role of women occurred during the latter part of World War II that the issue of lesbian behavior was explicitly addressed.

During World War I it was only through the Articles of War of 1916 that homosexuality was addressed and only in the context of assault with intent to commit sodomy. Just after the war, in 1920, consensual sodomy was included as criminal behavior and was punishable by incarceration. After World War I it was the role of the medical community that led to a broader set of guidelines for dealing with homosexuality, or "sexual perversion," as it was known. But, there was little implementation of the new categorizations. While some service members were convicted of sodomy and some were discharged as homosexuals, there was no widespread movement to identify and eliminate those who fit the profiles that the psychiatrists had established.

During World War II, when it was critical to enlist all eligible men, while screening out those who were not seen as fit for service, the regulations concerning homosexuality drew a great deal of attention. In fact, the RAND Corporation has documented that the Army alone revised its policy on homosexuality twenty-four times between 1941 and 1945. Looking back from the era of "Don't Ask, Don't Tell," this period is historically important because of the increased emphasis on homosexual "proclivities" or "tendencies," as opposed to sodomy and confirmed homosexual relationships. Given the typically private pursuit of sexual activity, it was public behaviors that were more likely to cause concern. And, as has long been the case, violations of gender norms were those behaviors most likely to signal a "proclivity" or "tendency" toward homosexuality. The discourse on "conduct v. status" has its roots in the records of this time. By the end of World War II the dominant paradigm regarding the military service of gays and lesbians was that the focus should be on service members who could be labeled "gay," not those who were known to have engaged in the criminal activity of sodomy. "Even if no sexual activity had occurred, a growing body of policy supported the conceptualization of a homosexual personality who was to be barred from military service at induction or separated from the service upon his discovery."[8]

During the Cold War, policies—both military and governmental—focused on the alleged security risks posed by gays and lesbians. One of the most commonly cited was the presumed risk for blackmail. If a gay service member or gay employee of the federal government had such a secret, he or she was assumed to be vulnerable to Communist spies and other undesirables. This was one characterization that helped to continue the move away from same-sex sexual behaviors, and toward "gay identity." It was the mere state of being gay that posed the threat, not the private, consensual behaviors that had earlier been the center of concern. During the war it had been possible for someone identified as homosexual to be retained for the good of the service. And, lesbians had been largely "below the radar." After the war both of these issues were addressed when the Department of Defense released a memo mandating the separation of all homosexual personnel, regardless of sex.

In 1949 the Department of Defense stated that gay men and lesbians were security risks and were unfit for military service. Thus, a policy that reached across all military branches was more clearly established. Yet, each branch of service was to create and implement its own branch-specific regulation for dealing with the separation of gays and lesbians. And, both the position of the Department of Defense and the branch regulations were just that—policies and/or regulations that the military could have eliminated any time they chose. This would remain the case until the passage of "Don't Ask, Don't Tell," which is not merely Pentagon or branch regulation, but federal law.

In 1956 the Department of the Navy commissioned a review of the different policies concerning homosexuality and military service. This report became known as the Crittenden Report, named for the head of the board, a Captain Crittenden. What is surprising about the report is not so much that it was undertaken, but the controversial nature of its findings. The report was fairly critical of the policies that virtually mandated the dismissal of gay and lesbian service members, as well as of the investigative techniques that often led to such dismissals. Not surprisingly, few of the conclusions outlined in the report led to changes in the policy.

From this period through the later 1960s, widespread social change concerning perceptions of gays and lesbians was occurring. Gay and lesbian organizations were forming, protests were being held, people—including military veterans— were publicly and proudly identifying as gay or lesbian. In the face of research showing, for example, that most gay and lesbian service members completed their service honorably, it was becoming more difficult to argue that gays and lesbians were, somehow, inherently unfit for such service. And, while perceptions concerning the security risk posed by their service did not disappear, they were far less central to the debate than they had been in earlier years. Thus, new justifications for exclusion were necessary. The result was a broader characterization of gays and lesbians as morally questionable and as a potential liability because of their antisocial nature. By 1970 this approach had expanded to the point that one's "tendencies, desires, or interests"[9] could be used to render them suspect. The paradigm that had begun during World War II was, in fact, becoming even broader, making more service members vulnerable, especially those who, in light of the times, were more comfortable publicly challenging gender norms and expectations. At the same time, however, there was a loophole that permitted the retention of service members whose record was so outstanding as to overshadow the issue. During this period, it was possible for a gay or lesbian service member to go before an administrative board, openly acknowledge his or her homosexuality, and be retained. While not the norm, this loophole proved critical to the decisions in several prominent court cases.

While there have been many cases challenging the various military policies on gays and lesbians, two that stand out as illustrative of the above are those of Air Force Technical Sergeant Leonard Matlovich and Ensign Vernon E. (Copy) Berg III. In 1975, after twelve years of service including service in Vietnam and numerous commendations, Matlovich decided to challenge the policy. Berg was the son of a career naval officer and an honor graduate of the U.S. Naval Academy who, under investigation, acknowledged that he had been having an intimate relationship with a man. Although both men were initially discharged and had lost in the trial court, they won when the District of Columbia Court of Appeals ruled in their favor. The court ruled that if the policy permitted exceptions to be made, they must be made with consistency. In the case of each man it was not clear why he should not be granted an exception. The court sent the case back to the Air Force and Navy, respectively, with instructions for the military to explain why Matlovich and Berg did not warrant exceptions. After two years of silence from the Air Force and the Navy, the judge ordered Matlovich and Berg to be reinstated. Ultimately, the military offered cash settlements if the men would resign. Because the military could have appealed the case to the U.S. Supreme Court, and Matlovich and Berg would likely have lost, they accepted the settlements. The case, however, was significant because it served to highlight the arbitrary and capricious way in which the policy was administered.

In January 1982, quite likely in response to the Matlovich and Berg cases, a new policy, Department of Defense directive 1332.14, was implemented. This policy virtually eliminated the loopholes by which gays and lesbians could be retained. The policy stated:

> Homosexuality is incompatible with military service. The presence in the military environment of persons who engage in homosexual conduct or who, by their statements, demonstrate a propensity to engage in homosexual conduct seriously impairs the accomplishment of the military mission. The presence of such members adversely affects the ability of the armed forces to maintain discipline, good order and morale; to foster mutual trust and confidence among service members; to insure the integrity of the system of rank and command; to facilitate assignment and worldwide deployment of service members who frequently must live and work in close conditions affording minimal privacy; to recruit and retain members of the armed forces; to maintain the public acceptability of military service; and to prevent breaches of security.[10]

This change presented a unique challenge in the case of Miriam Ben-Shalom. Ben-Shalom was an Army reservist who had filed suit alleging the previous policy violated her rights under the First Amendment. As a soldier who had been "out" in her unit and had spoken to the press, she asserted that while she had acknowledged being a lesbian, she had not acknowledged same-sex sexual conduct or any likelihood of such conduct in the future. In 1980, the federal district court in Wisconsin held that the regulations did, in fact, create an infringement upon her rights. She was reinstated. However, when she sought to reenlist, she was denied under the new regulations that included a provision for discharge of those who made statements about their homosexuality. The Court of Appeals for the Seventh Circuit held for the government, asserting that her statement was not simply a statement of identity but served as a proxy for her intention to engage in same-sex sexual conduct, behavior that the regulations clearly prohibited. Thus, while Ben-Shalom prevailed in a case regarding the old regulations, she lost when challenging the new regulations.

This new policy appeared to be based largely on the perceived fears held by society and heterosexual service members, not, as had been the case in the past, on the perceived ability of gays and lesbians to perform their jobs. That is, nothing in the above language focuses on the fitness of the homosexual service members. Rather, it focuses on the alleged impact of their presence because of the reactions of others. This was the policy under which the military was operating when Bill Clinton was asked about what he would do about the "ban" on gays and lesbians in the military.

Clinton's Pledge to Lift the Ban

In October 1991, then-presidential candidate Bill Clinton found himself answering questions at Harvard University's Kennedy School of Government. Asked whether he would issue an executive order to rescind the ban on gays and lesbians in the military, Clinton responded, "Yes," adding, "I think people who are gay . . . should be given the opportunity to serve their country."[11] This issue surfaced throughout his campaign and, on November 11, 1992, eight days after winning the election, president-elect Clinton indicated that he would honor his pledge to end the ban in the U.S. armed forces. But, Clinton conceded that he would have to move slowly, taking into consideration the opinions of Congress and military leadership.

Many senior military officials, including the Chair of the Joint Chiefs of Staff, General Colin Powell, had already expressed their opposition to any move permitting gays and lesbians to serve openly in the military. Although many conceded that gays and lesbians had served honorably, the notion of gays and lesbians serving openly was, to them, completely unacceptable. They argued that such a move would lead to the complete undermining of morale and discipline and, potentially, downward trends in recruitment. Some also indicated that, in addition to a negative impact on the ability of the military to attract new recruits, they feared widespread resignations of current service members. And, not surprising for the times, AIDS and fear of an increased risk of contracting HIV also entered the debate.

There was a fierce tension between Clinton's desire to uphold his pledge and satisfy many of his gay and lesbian supporters and the undeniable hostility of both military and Congressional leadership. *The New York Times* had even referred to the response of the Joint Chiefs of Staff as "uncharacteristically aggressive."

However, after several weeks of public debate, primarily via the press, it appeared as though senior military leaders might be prepared to soften their position. Both General Powell and General Gordon Sullivan, the Army Chief of Staff, stated publicly that they were pleased to know that Clinton would be seeking their input. Powell even acknowledged that, were the ban to be lifted, the military would not fall apart. But, the more conciliatory approach did not obscure the fact that they were not pleased at the prospect of gays and lesbians serving openly. Similarly, Clinton appeared to have backed away from the notion of simply signing an executive order lifting the ban. Members of Congress had made clear that they would respond swiftly to such a move, perhaps passing legislation with such overwhelming support that it would not be vulnerable to Clinton's political authority.

Soon after his inauguration in January 1993, the country, not just military and political leaders, became engaged in a protracted debate over whether or not gays and lesbians were fit for military service. On January 21, the day after his inauguration, it was reported that the president had agreed to delay lifting the ban for a six-month period during which the impact of such a change could be studied and the Department of Defense could also play a role in drafting the policy. During this time the armed forces were to stop asking recruits about their sexual orientation and stop discharging military personnel for being gay or lesbian. In addition, this would give the president time to consult with senior military officials and members of Congress. Taking such steps was believed to be critical in the prevention of Congressional action that would have thwarted the president's desire to eliminate the ban. Secretary of Defense Les Aspin had told the president that the opposition was tremendous. In a confidential memo, Aspin had outlined a plan, indicating that it was clear that many in Congress were prepared to overturn an executive order they found unacceptable.

On January 25, 1993, the president met with the Joint Chiefs of Staff, affirming the essence of his pledge, that discrimination would not be tolerated. This group told the president that such a move would "seriously undermine morale and discipline, disrupt military readiness and threaten recruiting."[12] Nonetheless, on January 29, President Clinton directed Secretary Aspin to draft an executive order ending discrimination on the basis of sexual orientation with regard to military service. Clinton indicated that he wished to sign it by July 15. This window of time allowed for a period of study and would permit an interim policy to be established.

A variety of changes were to become effective immediately. For example, questions about sexual orientation were to be removed from military induction forms and military recruits would begin receiving training on appropriate sexual conduct. But, service members who were openly gay or lesbian, or against whom such charges were successfully made, could still be removed from active duty. Such individuals would be transferred to an inactive reserve status, "serving" in an unpaid, "on hold," status. Only if the ban were completely lifted would such personnel be able to petition for readmission to active duty.

Battle lines had been drawn. The president, members of Congress, the Department of Defense, gay rights advocates, military personnel, and civilians across the country were now engaged in a very public debate. During the next six months there were town hall meetings, protests and marches, the establishment of new social movement organizations, and hours upon hours of hearings in the U.S. Congress. Given the pages and pages of transcripts, it is not possible, nor desirable, to provide a real "blow-by-blow" account of Congressional hearings.[13] What follows is a chronological overview of the hearings, with specific attention to the themes that dominated the testimony.

House Hearings

On February 4, 1993, the Republican Research Committee's Task Force on Military Personnel convened a hearing on the subject of the proposal to end the ban on gays in the military. The hearing was cochaired by Representatives Jon Kyl of Arizona and Cliff Stearns of Florida. The hearings consisted of testimony by the representatives themselves, many of them veterans, and retired senior military officers. Representative Duncan Hunter of California asked whether, with no ban on the service of gay men and lesbians, young people might no longer see the military as a wholesome environment and what impact that would have on the ability of the military to do its job. Representative John Doolittle of California expressed concern about housing. Would the academies, he wondered, force a heterosexual cadet to share a room with a homosexual cadet?

Admiral Thomas Moorer (U.S. Navy, retired) testified:

> I must say that this issue, to me, is the most important, the most disturbing that I've ever encountered in war or peace because what is going on here is an effort in effect to downgrade and demean and break down the whole structure of our military forces . . . You might ask the question will the troops respect a platoon [leader] if it's well-known in their unit that he's a homosexual? And I can guarantee you that these young people . . . will spot a homosexual a mile away as soon as he comes in, and they'll have to name him Tessie or Agnes, or whatever, and then subsequently he'll get caught in some kind of sexual activity and then he's discharged.[14]

Moorer also wondered whether gays would dance together at the officers' club, what would happen to the children who were exposed to them on base, and whether AIDS would lead to a greater burden on the military budget.

General Frederick Kroesen (U.S. Army, retired) testified that morale, unit cohesion, and the overall ability of the military to accomplish its mission would be compromised. He suggested that a significant number of service members would not reenlist and that recruitment would be hurt. Kroesen also speculated that there would be an increase in charges of sexual harassment and discrimination.

Toward the end of the hearing, Representative Robert Dornan of California spoke concerning a variety of issues, including referring to the debate as a "blessing in disguise." Dornan, imploring his peers to use the term "homosexual" rather than gay and himself using the term "sodomites," stated that he was thankful for the opportunity to engage in a public debate over the issue, especially with a "flower child" in the White House. The hearing was by no account any kind of serious attempt to engage in honest debate about the issues. Rather, as reflected in the transcript, it was an opportunity for the committee members to garner support for their position in the hope of having some impact on the outcome of the debate.

The House again visited the issue on May 4 and 5. This time the venue was the House Committee on Armed Services, chaired by Representative Ronald Dellums of California. In his opening statement, Dellums made clear that he was supportive of eliminating the ban, but emphasized that a fair and balanced hearing would be undertaken. In addition to the members of Congress who might speak, twenty-five principal witnesses would be heard or would submit written statements. The American Veterans Committee and the Association of the United States Army also submitted prepared statements.

The ranking minority member, Representative Floyd Spence of South Carolina, provided opening remarks in which he asserted that the question should not be one of civil rights and that lifting the ban would hurt readiness, cohesion, and morale. Spence asked, "What are the implications for military readiness if the broader gay agenda in this country is introduced to the day-to-day military life?"[15] Those advocating for retaining the ban on service focused their arguments on the alleged negative impact that "openly" gay and lesbian personnel would have on military readiness. Those in favor of removing the ban focused on civil rights and the lack of negative impact that they believed would occur.

On May 4 testimony was provided primarily, though not exclusively, by retired military personnel. It is important to emphasize that not all such witnesses were testifying for maintenance of the ban and not all who spoke against the ban were themselves gay or lesbian. Military personnel, retired and active duty, were, in fact, speaking for both sides. Arguments against the open military service of gays and lesbians included the belief that to permit such service would violate the civil rights and privacy of heterosexuals, that violence would increase, and that the morale of heterosexuals would suffer leading to problems in recruitment and retention. Members were concerned with the distinction between closeted and open gays and lesbians. Representative Kyl stated, for example, "We agree that homosexuals have served and continue to serve, but ... what happens when homosexuals serve openly and what effect do openly serving homosexuals have on the discipline and the general well being of the military."[16]

Of particular interest is the discussion about values and prejudice. Representative Hunter described the "rejection of homosexuality" as a value. In response to testimony likening such a position to prejudice, Hunter stated, "Nobody has acknowledged in the least that that person might have the right to keep that value and consider it a legitimate value as opposed to the prejudices that were held in the past against people of different skin colors."[17] Again and again, those opposed to lifting the ban testified that forcing heterosexual service members to knowingly serve with those whose "lifestyle" was contrary to their own values. Brigadier General James M. Hutchens, a chaplain, asserted that such a policy change was tantamount to "trying to change people's religion."

The rhetoric often took extreme, and sometimes ugly, turns. For example, Colonel John Ripley (U.S. Marine Corps, retired), testifying that permitting gays and lesbians to serve openly would destroy the Marine Corps, referred to homosexuals as "walking depositories of disease."[18] He also described the "Queers, Cowards, and Thieves Rule" where if a service member was determined to be any of the three he [sic] would be isolated from the rest of the unit so that he might be protected from the hostilities of other personnel. Colonel Ripley recounted one episode in which it was determined that a fellow service member was "a well-known homosexual, and he went over the side," meaning over the side of the ship.[19]

A recurrent theme was the fear of increased violence. It was suggested by both Hutchens and Ripley that eliminating the ban on gay and lesbian service members would lead not only to violence but, potentially, to the destruction of the military. Hutchens used the term mutiny to describe what he thought would happen. Ripley stated, "Right now the military is so supercharged and electrified over this that they are prepared to take matters into their own hands." Representative Dellums commented, in his closing remarks, that he found the discussion of mutiny "shocking" and "potentially frightening."[20]

On May 5 testimony continued to come not only from retired military personnel, but also from members of the law enforcement and academic communities. The same arguments against lifting the ban continued to be made. But, as was the case during the previous day, testimony was not exclusively in opposition to lifting the ban. One witness, Professor David Segal, a sociologist at the University of Maryland, suggested that, while there might be a negative impact if a new soldier came out immediately upon joining a unit, "if, however somebody has been serving in the unit for a while, has proven himself as a soldier, and then comes out, his sexual orientation essentially becomes irrelevant."[21] Dr. Gregory Herek, a psychologist at the University of California at Davis, responding to claims that heterosexuals would respond with violence and that homosexuals were unfit for military service, testified that neither group was inherently incapable of adjusting to a policy under which gays and lesbians would serve openly. In his written statement Herek offered a number of recommendations for implementing such a policy. These included establishing clear norms that sexual orientation is irrelevant to performing one's duty and that everyone should be judged on her or his own merits; eliminating false stereotypes through education and sensitivity training for all personnel; setting uniform standards for public conduct that are applied equally to all personnel; dealing with sexual harassment as a form of conduct rather than as a characteristic of a class of people and establishing that all sexual harassment is unacceptable; and taking a firm and highly publicized stand that violence against gay personnel is unacceptable and will be punished quickly and severely.[22] Thus, while it was often overshadowed by the inflammatory and sensational rhetoric of those supporting the ban, some of the testimony heard in the House did advocate a more relaxed policy toward the military service of gays and lesbians.

On July 19, 1993, at the National Defense University in Washington, DC, President Clinton announced the new policy. He characterized the policy as "a real step forward," and emphasized what he believed was an emphasis on conduct, not status. In a carefully worded speech, Clinton stated: (1) gay men and lesbians have served with distinction, (2) there is no evidence that gay and lesbian service members are less able or more likely to engage in misconduct, (3) any misconduct is already covered by existing regulations, (4) the lifting of similar bans in other militaries or domestic police and fire departments had not had any measurable negative effect, and (5) even if the ban were lifted entirely, most gay men and lesbians will refrain from making open declarations as to their sexual orientation. Clinton conceded that not everyone would be happy with the policy, but described it as "an honorable compromise." He concluded by asking for the support of military leaders in implementing the "new" policy.

At various points during the next four days, both the House and the Senate heard testimony and had the opportunity to ask questions about the proposed policy. On July 21, 22, and 23, the Military Forces and Personnel Subcommittee of the Committee on Armed Services of the House of Representatives, chaired by Representative Ike Skelton of Missouri, held hearings titled "Assessment of the Plan to Lift the Ban on Homosexuals in the Military." The twelve principal witnesses who appeared or submitted written statements to the committee included Secretary of Defense Les Aspin, current and retired military personnel, and legal scholars. Representative Skelton opened the hearings by stating, "We must, in our subcommittee and hence the committee, write it [the law] to be fair to all uniformed personnel, write it to ensure unit cohesion, to keep our fighting forces the best because second place doesn't count in the battlefield, and write it to meet the constitutional standards. All of this we must do within five days."[23]

On the first day of hearings, the focus of the subcommittee was on the proposed policy itself. The subcommittee wanted to assess Department of Defense support for the policy and determine whether the policy seemed at all feasible. On the second day, the subcommittee sought to focus on the legal issues, specifically its constitutionality. They also tried to garner a greater understanding of the details of the policy, such as the notion of a "rebuttable presumption." Ultimately, their goal was to provide a final solution that would codify the issue and end the debate. Of course, we now know that Congressional action actually stimulated, rather than diminished, debate, a debate that continues today.

Those arguing against lifting the ban again testified that the military would be harmed, that it was an issue of values, and that it was acceptable to cater to the prejudices of the majority. Charles Johnson, a former major in the Marine Corps, said, "The point is not that middle America will not accept this, but that really a superior power, God, will not accept this."[24] Conversation among the representatives and witnesses included discussion of hypothetical situations such as "Joe" who loses his wallet containing a naked picture of his boyfriend and personnel who might be wearing t-shirts stating, "I am queer, I am here." Participants discussed the purported difficulty in having a soldier take orders from an openly gay or lesbian officer and, again, that the problem was really that of acknowledged homosexuality, not homosexuality per se. Representative Dornan, admittedly one of the most rabidly antigay members of Congress, stated, "And you gentlemen all know that the best of your troops can never respect and thereby follow orders totally from someone who likes taking it up the bum, no matter how secret he keeps it. Once it leaks out, they think this person is abnormal, perverted, and a deviant from the norm."[25]

In focusing on the constitutionality of a law that, by prohibiting statements (e.g., "I am gay"), essentially punishes someone's speech, Cass Sunstein, a law professor at the University of Chicago, testified that it would likely be very difficult to win a constitutional challenge to the proposed law, particularly given the Supreme Court's demonstrated deference to the military. Other constitutional questions included those of equal protection and due process. Charles Dale noted that none of these have been successful avenues for challenging previous restrictions on the service of gays and lesbians.

One very significant piece of testimony focused on the distinction between status and conduct. Status was, allegedly, not punishable. That is, one's identity as a gay man or lesbian was not, in and of itself, to be cause for dismissal. The prohibition was, allegedly, homosexual conduct. Representative Skelton asked Jamie Gorelick, general counsel from the Defense Department, "A statement to the effect that if someone is gay, that is considered conduct; is that not correct?" Gorelick replied, "That is correct."[26] Skelton went on to present a number of scenarios in which someone states he [sic] is gay and pressed Gorelick on the likely outcome, legally and practically, to each scenario. The bottom line is that making a statement that one is gay is seen as a proxy for conduct and would, therefore, be a punishable action.

Further testimony was focused on constitutional law and standards of judicial review.[27] Gorelick, citing the rational basis standard of review, the lowest standard, testified that the court would likely uphold the law. Representative Hunter asked Gorelick, "So you think there is a rational basis for excluding, from the military, a person who acts out his orientation in the privacy of his own home and is reported by his commander to a service investigative agency or to a commander?" She replied, "Yes."[28]

On the final day of the hearings, Representative Skelton noted that the policy was "not that different from the old policy." Although a minor point in the transcripts of the hearings, this was an important statement coming from someone who, by all accounts, was opposed to the open service of gay and lesbian military personnel. In that characterization of the proposed policy, Skelton actually shared the view of many of those advocating for elimination of the ban. The new policy was, at its core, remarkably similar to the one it was to replace. The hearings in the House ended, with congratulations all around, at 11:00 AM on Friday, July 23, 1993.

Senate Hearings

It has been noted that the Senate Committee on Armed Services hearings were the most influential because they provide the most detailed legislative history and that this committee wrote the legislation that the House would adopt without major changes.[29] As soon as the senators returned from recess the issue was being addressed on the floor. On January 27, 1993, one week after President Clinton's inauguration, Senator John Kerry spoke in support of gay and lesbian service members, asking that everyone think carefully, quietly, and sensibly about the issue. Senator J. James Exon of Nebraska said that he thought that the President was making a mistake. His colleague, Senator Bob Kerrey of Nebraska, said he thought that such a policy change was a good thing. Senator Sam Nunn of Georgia, Chair of the Senate Committee on Armed Services, outlined the various issues raised by the conversation. These ranged from sodomy to whether partner benefits would apply to same-sex partners to the use of bathrooms. Everyone had an opinion and much of the record reflects the wide-ranging concerns expressed by members of the Senate.

For reasons whose explanations go far beyond the parameters of this volume, on February 4, Senate debate regarding the Family and Medical Leave Act of 1994 addressed the issue of gays and lesbians in the military.[30] This was, in a sense, the first real discussion of the issue to occur on the floor of the Senate. But, while senators continued to read material into the record, cite letters from constituents, etc., most of the discussion would take place in the hearings of the Committee on Armed Services.[31] These hearings took place on March 29 and 31, April 29, May 7, 10, and 11, and July 20–22. On September 9 the issue again came up in the context of the National Defense Reauthorization Act of 1994 and in remarks made by Senator Edward Kennedy. It is impractical, if not impossible, to summarize every piece of testimony, every argument, every opinion that the Senate heard on the issue. The remainder of this chapter characterizes the testimony that was presented and provides specific examples of some of the arguments that were made.

On March 29, Senator Sam Nunn opened the Senate hearings. He provided a snapshot of the recent debate, emphasizing the need to focus on military readiness. Nunn stated, "When the interests of some individuals bear upon the cohesion and effectiveness of an institution upon which our national security depends, we must, in my view, move very cautiously. This caution, in my view, is not prejudice; it is prudence."[32] Senator Strom Thurmond, the ranking minority member of the committee, offered his opening remarks as well. He said, "This is not an issue of being for or against homosexuals as a group or homosexuality as a lifestyle .... The record is replete with instances of dedicated and heroic service by many gays in the ranks of our armed services. The difference is that they served then and serve now as soldiers, sailors, airmen and marines and not as gays in the military."[33] As with the other hearings and statements, Thurmond emphasized the issues of military readiness and national security.

Four individuals testified to the historical and legal background of the issue of gays and lesbians in the military. The prepared statements were careful, reasoned presentations, regardless of the witnesses' viewpoints. Dr. David F. Burrelli, a defense analyst, and Stephen Saltzburg, a professor of law at the George Washington University, both testified that it was true that many homosexuals had served in the military, but noted that in most instances their peers were unaware of their sexual orientation. David Schleuter, a professor of law at Saint Mary's University, stated that a key question was whether the military should have to accept conduct that some find unacceptable. Testimony was also presented by legislative attorney Charles Dale.

The question and answer period, even when discussing history and law, illustrated the sensationalized nature of the debate. Senator Lauch Faircloth of North Carolina asked, "What if—and how would you feel if—your 17- or 18-year-old son—and that is a pretty young boy—became under the influence of an aggressive 40-year-old homosexual who was his drill sergeant, or 35 pick an age?" And, again, as was true in the House, the question of whether the open service of gays and lesbians would infringe upon the privacy rights of heterosexuals was raised. Rarely, if ever, was the question of whether the ban infringed upon the privacy rights of gay and lesbian service members raised.

On March 31 the subject of the hearings was "The Role of Unit Cohesion in Developing Combat Effectiveness." Unit cohesion would prove to be the catch phrase of the debate. Witnesses were William Henderson, the former commander of the Army Research Institute, David Marlowe, the chief of the Department of Military Psychiatry at Walter Reed Army Institute of Research, and Lawrence Korb of the Brookings Institution. Under President Ronald Reagan, Korb had served as Assistant Secretary of Defense (Manpower, Reserve Affairs, Installations and Logistics). In that capacity he authored Department of Defense Directive 1332.14, the regulation that, from 1982 until the implementation of "Don't Ask, Don't Tell" in 1993, provided the guidelines for discharging gay and lesbian enlisted personnel.[34]

Later the next month, on April 29, the Senate resumed hearings, focusing on testimony regarding the experiences of foreign militaries. Witnesses included Dr. Charles C. Moskos, professor of sociology at Northwestern University, Dr. David R. Segal, professor of sociology at the University of Maryland, Dr. Judith H. Stiehm, professor of political science at Florida International University, and lieutenant general Calvin Waller (U.S. Army, retired). Witnesses provided testimony concerning the policies of other nations, many of which had more relaxed policies than the United States, and the general issue of the exclusion of gays and lesbians from military service. Dr. Moskos echoed the frequent refrain of many who dismiss cross-national comparisons when he asserted that the status of the United States as a military power places it in a somewhat unique position. General Waller recommended that the ban not be lifted, asserting that doing so would result in a second-rate military.

In early May, the Senate turned to testimony from its own members. Senators Howard Metzenbaum (New Jersey), Frank Murkowski (Alaska), John Kerry (Massachusetts), Barbara Boxer (California), Conrad Burns (Montana), and Dianne Feinstein (California) all spoke concerning the proposed legislation. Regarding the issue of being "openly gay" in the military, one member of the committee, Senator John Warner (Virginia), said, "... the transition from the quiet manner in which they perform their duties to an open advocacy of their sexual preferences is the difficulty that this Senator, and I think many others, have."[35] Senator Kerry testified, "Some folks say they do not mind living or showering with someone who is gay as long as the fact is not explicit. Only once it becomes explicit, somehow the world is going to end. Now, I do not know exactly what those who express those kinds of fears are thinking. I mean, are they that irresistible?"[36]

The following week, on May 10, seventeen persons from the U.S. Navy and U.S. Marine Corps provided their input.[37] This hearing was held in conjunction with the committee's field visit to the Norfolk Naval Complex. In the morning, members of the committee visited the attack submarine, the Montpelier. Opinions expressed by the crew ranged from "I couldn't care less. There are already gays on board ship ... " to "I am definitely against lifting the ban," with Senator Nunn conceding that he heard more support for eliminating the ban than he had expected. But, perhaps the greatest impact of the visit on the debate was the result of a carefully staged photograph showing Senators Nunn and Warner talking with three sailors wedged in the tight confines of a submarine bunk. Appearing in newspapers across the country, the image of sailors sharing such tight quarters spoke volumes for those already concerned with unit cohesion and privacy.

During the afternoon hearing, Sgt. Brian Jenisch (U.S. Marine Corps) testified that "... as a heterosexual we do not have the physical opportunity to have sexual urges while we are in the field. On the other hand, homosexuals, they could probably have urges more because if one of them is on a security mission, he lets down his guard, he has an urge, he says, okay, my buddy is over here, let me go over here, whatever, that is letting down their guard ... "[38] The sergeant went on to describe how deleterious the presence of a gay marine would be to the ability of the group to do its job. Lieutenants (JG) Tracy Thorne and Richard "Dirk" Selland testified that, as gay sailors, they knew the opposite to be the case.

The following day, more testimony was provided by current and former members of the U.S. military. This testimony focused on the proposed policy concerning gays and lesbians in the U.S. military. Witnesses included General Norman H. Schwarzkopf (U.S. Army, retired) and Margarethe Cammermeyer, a former colonel in the Washington Army National Guard who had been discharged for stating that she was a lesbian. Prefacing his remarks with his support for individual rights, Schwarzkopf testified that his opposition to lifting the ban was situated in his concern for the military and a reduced ability of the military to protect the nation. He emphasized the need for unit cohesion and the polarization that would result from the presence of an openly gay person in a small military unit. He also mentioned the negative impact on recruiting that accepting openly gay men and lesbians would have on the military and the likely loss that would be experienced by those choosing to leave rather than serve alongside openly gay men and lesbians.

The Senate began additional hearings on July 20, the day after President Clinton announced the new policy. As in the House, the purpose of these hearings was to get additional information that might be needed before approving or making changes to the proposed legislation. During the first day, a range of the most senior military personnel, such as General Colin Powell, Chair of the Joint Chiefs of Staff, and Secretary of Defense Les Aspin, spoke before the committee. Testimony was similar to that presented in earlier hearings. General Powell reiterated his position that homosexuality was incompatible with military service. Unit cohesion was, again, highlighted as a primary concern. The Joint Chiefs reiterated their opinions that while many gays and lesbians had had successful careers while remaining closeted, openly gay service members would have a profoundly negative effect on the armed forces.

On July 21, additional senior military personnel and Jamie Gorelick, general counsel at the Department of Defense, provided testimony. Senator John Glenn of Ohio wondered what would happen if a sergeant marched in a parade in drag and pink hair. His point was to consider whether or not such an action constituted "telling." Gorelick replied, "One can draw conclusions from activities that, if you will, speak louder than words." But, she also emphasized that it isn't possible to provide a list of activities that automatically serve as credible evidence. As an example, she mentioned that a service member might be able to advocate for gay rights without those actions serving as credible evidence of that person's homosexuality.

Gorelick continued her testimony on July 22, accompanied by other members of the military legal community. There seemed to be a reasonable amount of confusion over the distinction between the previous and current policies. There was even confusion over which policies the language of "previous" and "current" referred. Gorelick spoke using the language of "current policy" and "July 19 policy." Under the current policy, that in effect since 1981, a service member was, according to Gorelick, discharged for conduct, not homosexuality per se. The major distinction articulated by Gorelick was that under the current (i.e., pre-1993) policy recruits were asked whether or not they had engaged in homosexual activity. Under the proposed policy, as well as the interim policy, this was forbidden.

She explained that the previous policy suggested that anyone who stated he or she was homosexual was assumed to be homosexual. Gorelick stated, "We used to say, in the old policy, 'If you say you are a homosexual, we will presumptively conclude that you are.' What is a homosexual under our policy? Someone who engages in acts or has a propensity or intent to do so. So, we say now, 'If you say you are a homosexual, we presumptively conclude that you engage in acts or have a propensity or intent to do so.' We have simply taken out the intervening point of: What is a homosexual?"

Senator Nunn responded, "Another way of saying that is if someone identifies themselves by saying, 'I am a homosexual,' but when it gets down to asking them or them telling you what they mean by homosexual, they convince you that what they mean by homosexual is not the definition of homosexual, then they do not meet the definition of being homosexual." Ms. Gorelick responded, "That is correct."[39] She went on to explain that the accused bears the burden of the rebuttable presumption, or proving that while he or she may "be" a homosexual, he or she does not engage in or intend to engage in homosexual acts.

They also discussed the way in which marrying, or attempting to marry, someone of the same sex served as a proxy for conduct. A question which the committee did not appear to address is this: If the real problem for the military is the open homosexual, how is the military negatively impacted by the person who is openly homosexual, but successfully rebuts the presumption that he or she engages in homosexual acts. While the logical conclusion on the part of those supporting a ban is that having rebutted the presumption makes one "pure" and thus not divisive by his or her presence, this part of the debate appears absent from the discussion. At 9:33 A.M. on Thursday, July 22, 1993, hearings in the Senate came to an end.

In addition to the testimony and prepared statements submitted by witnesses, other documents were entered into the official record. For example, nineteen "model testimonials" were submitted by military personnel and veterans supportive of lifting the ban. Of these, seven were submitted anonymously. One was submitted by an openly lesbian lieutenant colonel in the Israeli Defense Forces. All others were submitted by U.S. personnel, some of whom identified as heterosexual.

An organization known as the Campaign for Military Service submitted several documents including their own proposal for lifting the ban. Dated May 20, 1993, this proposal outlined six issues that would need to be addressed: (1) The status of "being gay" should not serve as a basis for exclusion; (2) Private, consensual same-sex sexual activity should not serve as a basis for exclusion; (3) All prohibited sexual conduct, among all service members (e.g., sexual harassment) should be enforced; (4) Policies concerning public display of affection should be developed and enforced equally among all service members, heterosexual and homosexual; (5) Partnership benefits are not at issue since they are provided only through marriage and same-sex partners may not be legally married[40]; and (6) Those discharged under previous policies will have to be given the opportunity to have their discharges evaluated and, where applicable, upgraded. In her conclusion to this document, the final document in the Senate hearings materials, Georgetown law professor Chai Feldblum, serving as legal coordinator for the

Campaign for Military Service, wrote, "Gay men, lesbians, and bisexuals have been excellent members of the armed forces. They have been forced, however, to live a constant lie—a lie at odds with their military and human values of integrity and honesty. Lifting the ban will allow such individuals to finally serve their country with full dignity and honor."[41]

Public Law 103-160

After six months of debate, the hearings were over. The debate, both inside and outside of Congress, would, of course, continue. In September, both the Senate and the House debated the National Defense Authorization Act for Fiscal Year 1994, the legislation within which the new policy would be housed. In the Senate, Dan Coats (Indiana) stated, "The President's policy on homosexuals in the military would have undermined morale and prevented commanders from dealing with problems in their units. Make no mistake. The legislation before us does not codify the administration's flawed approach—it overturns it. In fact, this Defense bill is primarily a success because the President was forced to retreat on several key issues."[42]

Senator Barbara Boxer (California) sought to amend the bill, striking the language dealing with gays and lesbians in the military. Instead, she asked that the bill permit the president to resolve the matter in consultation with the Secretary of Defense and other military advisers. She provided several reasons for her opposition to the proposed legislation, including the fact that the study commissioned by the Department of Defense itself, the RAND report, found that sexual orientation was irrelevant to military service. Senator Paul Wellstone (Minnesota) responded in support of the Boxer amendment, stating, "We are today about to codify a policy based on fear and based on prejudice. It is a policy that does not look forward, it looks backward."[43] Her effort failed with 33 voting in favor of the amendment, 63 opposed.

As is typically the case, there was extensive Senate debate surrounding many aspects of the Act and a total of 107 amendments proposed, most of which had nothing to do with gays and lesbians. On September 14, 1993, the Act was passed in the Senate on a vote of 92–7. Senators Boxer and Wellstone were among the seven nay votes.

In the House, at 2:26 in the afternoon of September 28, Representative Martin Meehan (Massachusetts) offered an amendment analogous to the one proposed by Senator Boxer. It failed, 169–264. At 3:01 P.M., Representative Duncan Hunter (California) proposed an amendment that would have required the Defense Department to ask recruits whether they were homosexual or bisexual, and whether the recruit engaged in, or had a propensity to engage in, homosexual acts. This amendment would have restored the "asking" that the new policy eliminated. It failed by a vote of 144–291. At 3:37 P.M., Representative Ike Skelton (Missouri) offered an amendment that restated the language concerning gays and lesbians as it was originally proposed. After a procedural aside, the amendment passed.

On the following day, September 29, the Act passed in the House on a vote of 268–162.

Having worked its way through both chambers of Congress and subsequent committee action, on November 30, 1993, President Clinton signed the Act into law as Public Law 103-160. Section 571 of that law, codified at 10 United States Code 654, would become known as "Don't Ask, Don't Tell."

Notes

1. "Don't Ask, Don't Tell" also prohibits the open service of bisexual persons. Throughout most of this volume, I use the term "gays and lesbians." Though some will disagree with this decision, I do so to avoid the lengthier descriptor, but also to avoid the shorter and somewhat gender-specific term "gay." In the military context, it is particularly important to emphasize the presence of women. The term "homosexual" is used when quoting or referring to materials, etc. that use this term specifically.

2. DOD 101, An Introductory Overview of the Department of Defense, http://www.defenselink.mil/pubs/dod101/.

3. Ibid.

4. Hot bunking is the expression for having more than one person assigned to a bunk so that while one person is working, the other is sleeping. In an environment where someone is always on duty, this saves space in the allocation of sleeping quarters.

5. This is the Air Force term for both women and men.

6. Memo from the Chairman General Board to the Secretary of the Navy, dated February 3, 1942. http://www.trumanlibrary.org/whistlestop/study_collections/desegregation/large/documents/index.php?documentdate=1942-02-03&documentid=4&studycollectionid=deseg&pagenumber=1.

7. The policy was originally referred to as "Don't Ask, Don't Tell, Don't Pursue." In February 2000, "Don't Harass" was added. The policy is informally referred to as "Don't Ask, Don't Tell," the name that will be used in this volume.

8. Timothy Haggerty, 2003. "History Repeating Itself: A Historical Overview of Gay Men and Lesbians in the Military Before 'Don't Ask, Don't Tell.'" In Aaron Belkin and Geoffrey Bateman (Eds.), *Don't Ask, Don't Tell: Debating the Gay Ban in the Military*, Boulder, CO: Lynne Rienner Publishers, p. 17.

9. Ibid.

10. http://dont.stanford.edu/regulations/regulation41.pdf#search=%221332.14%201982%22.

11. LTC Kevin Connors, "Clinton's Policy Relating to Gays in the Military: Lessons in Politics at the National Level," National Defense University, National War College, unpublished paper, http://64.233.167.104/search?q=cache:uilUa2jLZDMJ:www.ndu.edu/library/n1/99-E-33.pdf+clinton+pledge+lift+ban&hl=en.

12. Eric Schmitt, "Joints Chiefs Hear Clinton Again Vow To Ease Gay Policy," *The New York Times* January 26, 1993, A1.

13. For an exhaustive account of Congressional comment on the issue, researchers are encouraged to visit http://www.thomas.gov and search the Congressional Record for the 103rd Congress. Many remarks which were presented on the floor of the House and Senate, but not in formal hearings, are available for review.

14. Hearing of the Republican Research Committee's Task Force on Military Personnel; subject: Proposal to End the Ban on Gays in the Military, February 4, 1993, Washington, DC. Accessed at http://dont.stanford.edu/hearings/hearings.htm on May 1, 2006.

15. Policy Implications of Lifting the Ban on Homosexuals in the Military, Hearings Before the Committee on Armed Services, House of Representatives, May 4 and 5, 1993, p. 2.

16. House Hearings, May 4, 1993, http://dont.stanford.edu/hearings/may41993.pdf.

17. Ibid.

18. Ibid.

19. Ibid.

20. Policy Implications of Lifting the Ban on Homosexuals in the Military, Hearings Before the Committee on Armed Services, House of Representatives, May 4 and 5, 1993, p. 196.

21. House Hearings, May 5, 1993, http://dont.stanford.edu/hearings/may51993.pdf.

22. Oral Statement of Gregory M. Herek, Ph.D., to the House Armed Services Committee, http://psychology.ucdavis.edu/rainbow/html/miltest2.html.

23. Assessment of the Plan to Lift the Ban on Homosexuals in the Military, Hearings Before the Military Forces and Personnel Subcommittee of the Committee on Armed Services, House of Representatives, p. 1.

24. Assessment of the Plan to Lift the Ban on Homosexuals in the Military, Hearings Before the Military Forces and Personnel Subcommittee of the Committee on Armed Services, House of Representatives, http://dont.stanford.edu/hearings/PlanAssessment.pdf.

25. Ibid.

26. Assessment of the Plan to Lift the Ban on Homosexuals in the Military, Hearings Before the Military Forces and Personnel Subcommittee of the Committee on Armed Services, House of Representatives, p. 171.

27. When considering a constitutional challenge, the court invokes a particular standard of review that is dependent upon the question raised or the class of persons alleging a violation of their rights. The claim that a "fundamental right" (e.g., right to vote) is violated demands a higher standard of review than does a right not held to be fundamental (e.g., right to work). And, a class of persons granted "suspect classification" (e.g., race) demands a higher standard of review than does a class not granted suspect classification (e.g., high school athletes). A higher standard of review means that it is more difficult for the government to show that it is justified in denying the right or discriminating against a class of persons.

28. Ibid.

29. "Memorandum from Steve Jackson to Professor Janet Halley, Stanford Law School, Presenting Legislative History Research On The Issues Of Intent To Censor Speech and Intent To Accommodate Troop Prejudices," http://dont.stanford.edu/hearings/memo.pdf.

30. Amendments to legislation are often introduced that have no obvious connection to the legislation to which they are being attached. Such a move enables members of Congress to speak or vote on an issue that otherwise wouldn't come to the floor. In this instance, members of Congress were not discussing the policy in relation to the Family Medical Leave Act. Rather, members of the Senate sought to confirm that no amendment, bill, or resolution relating to the issue of homosexuals in the military would be in order any earlier than (1) July 15, 1993, (2) the conclusion of the Senate hearings, (3) the receipt from the House of a measure dealing with the issue of homosexuals in the military, or (4) the issuance of a directive by the president prior to July 15, 1993.

31. Although a handful refer to other issues (e.g., the resignation of Surgeon General Jocelyn Elders), a search of Senate records for the 103rd Congress using the search term "homosexual" returned 116 hits on thomas.gov, many of these hits are senators offering their thoughts on the issue of gays and lesbians in the military.

32. Hearings before the Committee on Armed Services, U.S. Senate, p. 3.

33. Ibid., p. 5.

34. DoD Direction 1332.30, promulgated in 1986, provided guidelines for the separation of officers.

35. http://dont.stanford.edu/hearings/hearings5-7-93.pdf.

36. Ibid.

37. Names of these, and other, witnesses can be found in the official record, available at http://dont.stanford.edu/hearings/ToC.pdf.

38. Policy Concerning Homosexuality in the Armed Forces, Hearings Before the Committee on Armed Services, Senate, May 10, 1993, p. 581.

39. Policy Concerning Homosexuality in the Armed Forces, Hearings Before the Committee on Armed Services, U.S. Senate, July 22, 1993, p. 805.

40. This document was drafted in 1993, over ten years prior to the first legal same-sex marriages in the United States.

41. Ibid.

42. Excerpts from Senate Debate re: National Defense Authorization Act of 1994, http://dont.stanford.edu/regulations/SenateDebate.html.

43. Ibid.

CHAPTER 2

Implementing "Don't Ask, Don't Tell"

Before examining the implementation of the new policy, it is worth considering what the public opinion concerning gays and lesbians, and gay and lesbian service members in particular, was like in 1993. During the Congressional hearings, much was said about public opinion on the issues and the need to listen to public opinion. The fact that there was less than a majority of public support for the rights of gays and lesbians was provided as justification for a policy of exclusion. Separate from remarks about what members of the American public thought were those data indicating what members of the military themselves thought about gays and lesbians and, in particular, the military service of openly gay and lesbian persons.

In 1993 the General Social Survey asked respondents, "What about sexual relations between two adults of the same sex—do you think it is always wrong, almost always wrong, wrong only sometimes, or not wrong at all?" Seventy-eight percent responded that it was "always wrong, almost always wrong, or wrong only sometimes." The remaining 22 percent said "not wrong at all." Thus, generalizing to the American public, a little over three-quarters indicated that they believed homosexuality was, to some degree, wrong. As pointed out in *Sexual Orientation and U.S. Military Personnel Policy: Options and Assessment*, the RAND study published in 1993, when the wording of such questions was changed slightly, the level of nonacceptance was reduced. They cite as one example a poll showing that 54 percent of respondents agreed with the statement, "Homosexual relationships between consenting adults [are] morally wrong."[1] Although a majority, in either case, viewed homosexuality as wrong, many Americans seemed to make a distinction between morality, as above, and civil rights. For example, in a CBS/*New York Times* poll conducted in January 1993, 79 percent of respondents indicated that homosexuals should have equal rights in terms of job opportunities.[2] On the other hand, a Yankelovich poll conducted during the same month found that when the question focused on legal protections, support was considerably lower. Forty-eight percent of respondents agreed that "laws which protect the civil rights of racial or religious minorities should be used to protect the rights of homosexuals."[3] The interpretation of polling data must be done with great care and even the best polls are often subject to methodological challenge. But, there is little doubt that, across the range of polls conducted during that period, a majority of the American public was still demonstrating little support for the civil equality of gays and lesbian citizens.

In a Gallup poll conducted in January 1993, just as the debate over the public gays in the military was beginning, a slight majority of 53 percent said "should" to a question asking whether homosexuals should or should not be able to serve in the armed forces. However, a CBS/*New York Times* poll conducted that same month found only 42 percent saying that they favored permitting homosexuals to serve in the military. The *Los Angeles Times* conducted polls during January and February and found that the percentage of respondents who approved, either strongly or somewhat, with allowing "openly homosexual men and women to serve in the armed forces of the United States" actually dropped from 45 percent in January to 40 percent in February. During the summer of 1993, NBC and the *Wall Street Journal* conducted a poll in which they asked, "Do you favor or oppose allowing openly gay men and lesbian women to serve in the military?" Forty percent said "favor," 52 percent said "oppose," and 8 percent had no opinion. Again, much can be made of the particular phrasing of a question and sampling methodology, but, overall, it appeared that the country was just about split in its opinions toward permitting gays and lesbians to serve in the nation's military.

In addition to the work done by the RAND Corporation, two significant sources of information concerning what members of the military thought came from the *Los Angeles Times* and two sociologists, Charles Moskos and Laura Miller. These findings, while somewhat flawed methodologically, are valuable nonetheless. The *Times* relied on persons willing to stop and be interviewed, not a random sample. Moskos and Miller, too, were unable to do random sampling, relying on convenience samples in a limited number of areas. RAND conducted focus groups and obtained rich anecdotal data, but the overall sample was quite small. Nonetheless, each study did the best it could with what it had and each offers important insight into the thoughts of military personnel on the issue. In general, military personnel were opposed to lifting the ban on the military service of gays and lesbians. In the *Times* study, only 18 percent of respondents indicated that they supported ending the ban while 74 percent were opposed. Compared to the general public, where opinions were about split, military personnel were far more likely to oppose lifting the ban.

These data, both polling data and social science research, were widely cited during the six months of Congressional discussions and debates. Those opposed to a policy change cited the lack of public and military support for such a change.

They questioned the wisdom of making such a purportedly dramatic change in the face of resistance. Those advocating for change frequently cited the fact that fewer than ten years before the U.S. Supreme Court declared laws against interracial marriages unconstitutional (*Loving v. Virginia*, 1967), 94 percent of whites opposed interracial marriage.[4] Even more frequently noted was the widespread opposition to school desegregation both before and after the Court's decision in *Brown v. Board of Education* (1954).

While widespread support to lift the ban would have made it fairly easy to conclude that the time was right for such a change, the reverse isn't necessarily so. That is, societal or military opposition to lifting the ban doesn't mean such change is wrongheaded. As suggested in Chapter 1, when President Truman issued an executive order to desegregate the armed forces, it was in the face of great opposition that he did so. Data on what we think shouldn't necessarily drive policy, especially when the policy concerns civil rights. But, such data are important when considering how policy change will be implemented, whether within an organization or across society. For example, if the impact of such a policy is that large numbers of individuals really will refuse to serve in the military, it is, at the least, prudent to consider such a response. But, of course, part of such consideration must be the likelihood that threats such as, "I'll get out if I have to serve with them," will be carried out.

Implementation

An assertion is sometimes made that "Don't Ask, Don't Tell" is not a military policy at all, but, rather, a law that was passed by the Congress with which the military must comply. In a technical sense, this is true. But, as should be readily apparent from Chapter 1, there is no doubt that military leadership, at least during the 1993 debate, supported the exclusion of gay men and lesbians from military service. Nonetheless, when the law, with its minor changes from the previous regulation, was passed in November, it was the job of the Department of Defense, and its military branches, to see that it was implemented.

The policy provides that service members will be discharged if any one of the following three conditions is met: (1) that the member has engaged in, attempted to engage in, or solicited another to engage in a homosexual act or acts; (2) that the member has stated that he or she is a homosexual or bisexual; or (3) that the member has married or attempted to marry a person known to be of the same biological sex.[5] The first condition may be countered by findings that "(a) such conduct is a departure from the member's usual and customary behavior; (b) such conduct, under all the circumstances, is unlikely to recur; (c) such conduct was not accomplished by use of force, coercion, or intimidation; (d) under the particular circumstances of the case, the member's continued presence in the armed forces is consistent with the interests of the armed forces in proper discipline, good order, and morale; and (e) the member does not have a propensity or intent to engage in homosexual acts."[6]

The policy does not use the term "sexual orientation." Rather, it refers to homosexual(s), bisexual(s), and homosexual acts. These terms are defined as follow:

> (1) The term "homosexual" means a person, regardless of sex, who engages in, attempts to engage in, has a propensity to engage in, or intends to engage in homosexual acts, and includes the terms "gay" and "lesbian." (2) The term "bisexual" means a person who engages in, attempts to engage in, has a propensity to engage in, or intends to engage in homosexual and heterosexual acts. (3) The term "homosexual act" means—(a) any bodily contact, actively undertaken or passively permitted, between members of the same sex for the purpose of satisfying sexual desires; and (b) any bodily contact which a reasonable person would understand to demonstrate a propensity or intent to engage in an act described in subparagraph (a).[7]

The policy also requires that service members be briefed about the policy when they enter military service and periodically thereafter. In addition, the policy requires that if a service member is believed to have made a declaration of homosexuality as a way of avoiding or terminating military service, such a statement will not be a bar to service. Finally, the policy provides an exception such that if separation is viewed as contrary to the best interest of the armed forces, the service member will not be discharged.

On December 22, 1993, Secretary of Defense Les Aspin released the Department of Defense regulations that would implement the newly codified policy excluding openly gay and lesbian persons from military service. The regulations, as directed by the law, addressed five areas: accessions, separations, criminal investigations, personnel security, and military training. The policy changes were to be effective from February 5, 1994, with previous regulations remaining in place until that time, unless the Secretary of Defense determined that the new regulations should be applied in an existing case. Aspin noted that each service was expected to implement the policy within approximately forty-five days.

Accessions

Prior to the interim policy, recruits were routinely asked whether they had ever engaged in homosexual conduct. For example, in the late 1970s, item 5f on DD Form 1966/4 (August 1, 1975), along with items addressing the applicant's history with regard to issues such as narcotic use, glue sniffing, marijuana use, alcohol-related job loss or arrest, and hospitalization for mental illness, asked, "Have you ever engaged in homosexual activity (sexual relations with another person of the same sex)?" This practice continued until the interim policy was established in early 1993. The new policy directed that it be permanently eliminated.

Current regulations for the Military Entrance Processing Command (USMEP-COM) include an applicant briefing on the separation policy. The statement provides examples of unacceptable conduct that may be grounds for separation, including disciplinary infractions, parental responsibilities that interfere with deployment, not meeting weight standards, and homosexual conduct. In addition to providing the language of the law regarding homosexual acts, statements, and marriage, the briefing says, "Although we have not and will not ask you whether you are a heterosexual, homosexual, or a bisexual, you should be aware that homosexual acts, statements that demonstrate a propensity to or intent to engage in homosexual acts, and homosexual marriages or attempted marriages are grounds for discharge from the armed forces."

While the Department of Defense did direct, as above, that "no applicant will be asked about his or her sexual orientation as part of the accession process," this is not entirely the case. The enlistment form, DD Form 1966/1 (October 2005), "Record of Military Processing," asks about marital status and number of dependents. While marital status is, of course, not equivalent to sexual orientation, indicating that one is married is generally taken as a statement of one's heterosexuality.[8] Though the Department of Defense asserts that "sexual orientation is considered a personal and private matter," the military routinely requires that service members document their marital status and dependents, particularly for the provision of benefits. While these procedures are in no way tantamount to asking if one is gay or lesbian, they are contrary to the assertion that statements about one's sexual orientation are inappropriate in the military environment.

For example, the U.S. Army provides instruction to its leaders via the publication *Hot Topics: Current Issues for Army Leaders*. In winter 2000 the topic was "Don't Ask, Don't Tell." The publishers defined sexual orientation as "an abstract preference for persons of a particular sex" and stated that "[w]hile on active duty, soldiers will not be asked about their sexual orientations unless there is credible information of homosexual conduct." While one might understand the spirit of the statement, it is critical to acknowledge that (1) sexual orientation is not a substitute term for gay or lesbian, that is, everyone possesses a sexual orientation, and, as above, (2) to the degree that, in a military context particularly, indicating a marital status of "married" is akin to declaring one's heterosexuality, the military routinely asks about sexual orientation.

In 1997, three years after the implementation of the new policy, Servicemembers Legal Defense Network (SLDN) published *Conduct Unbecoming: Third Annual Report on "Don't Ask, Don't Tell, Don't Pursue."* One of their recommendations was that the military revise recruiting forms so that they no longer ask about homosexual conduct. A Department of Defense review of policy implementation found that such violations had, in fact, occurred. In 1994, as an effort to save money, rather than immediately print new forms, recruiters had simply been directed to strike through the unlawful questions. This procedure was not always followed. In August 1997, over three years after the policy was implemented, the

Department of Defense directed that all old forms be discarded. As late as 2001 some of the old forms were still in use.[9]

Separations

The regulations concerning separation were revised, in the view of Congress and the Department of Defense, to focus on conduct rather than identity, that is, on homosexual acts, not the status or identity of being gay, lesbian, or bisexual. Homosexual acts need not be proven as there exists a presumption that a statement of status or identity (e.g., "I am gay") means that the speaker has engaged and intends to engage in homosexual acts. The directive also provides that individuals under investigation have the opportunity to rebut the presumption of homosexual acts by proving that he or she did not engage in homosexual acts, nor possessed the propensity to do so. A number of directives were issued to assist the Department of Defense and branches to understand the changes that would have to take place.

Contained within Department of Defense Directive 1332.14 are guidelines concerning enlisted separations under "Don't Ask, Don't Tell." The conditions under which a person is considered to have engaged in homosexual conduct are outlined, that is, engaging in, attempting to engage in, or soliciting another to engage in a homosexual act or acts. There is, however, the provision that a service member may be retained if all of the following five facts are established: (1) Such acts are a departure from the member's usual and customary behavior; (2) Such acts under all the circumstances are unlikely to recur; (3) Such acts were not accomplished by use of force, coercion, or intimidation; (4) Under the particular circumstances of the case, the member's continued presence in the Armed Forces is consistent with the interest of the Armed Forces in proper discipline, good order, and morale; and (5) The member does not have a propensity or intent to engage in homosexual acts.[10]

Under this directive, propensity is defined as "more than an abstract preference or desire to engage in homosexual acts; it indicates a likelihood that a person engages in or will engage in homosexual acts." However, a service member may rebut the presumption by "presenting evidence demonstrating that he or she does not engage in, attempt to engage in, have a propensity to engage in, or intend to engage in homosexual acts."[11] One of the difficulties with this language is what is sometimes referred to as "proving the negative."

One may, in fact, be able to establish that one did not do something he or she is alleged to have done in the past. And, one can easily prove that he or she will do something that others predict you will do. You simply do it. That's the proof. It is far more difficult to prove beforehand that you won't, in the future, do something that others predict you will do.

In making a determination of whether the service member has rebutted the presumption, personnel may consider, among other things, (1) whether the person has engaged in homosexual acts in the past; (2) the credibility of the individual under review; (3) testimony from others about the person's past conduct, character, and credibility; (4) the nature and circumstances of the person's statement (e.g., "I am gay"); and (5) all available evidence concerning the likelihood that the person will engage in homosexual acts in the future.

The directive concerning homosexual conduct specifically provides exceptions to policy. One prominent exception is that nothing requires that a member be separated from service when the acts, statements, or marriage were carried out for the purpose of avoiding or terminating one's service obligation and when such separation would be contrary to the best interest of the military. Additionally, and of particular interest in current times, is that the directive states that "Nothing in these procedures... [p]recludes retention of a member for a limited period of time in the interests of national security..."[12]

Department of Defense Directive 1332.30 covers the separation of regular and reserve commissioned officers. Directive 1332.40 covers the procedures for such separation and is, in substance, virtually identical to the procedures regarding enlisted personnel.

When one leaves military service he or she receives a discharge characterization. If someone is separated within 180 days of joining the service, an uncharacterized discharge may be granted. Otherwise, a discharge under "Don't Ask, Don't Tell" normally results in the receipt of an Honorable Discharge or General (under honorable conditions) Discharge. The characterization is based on the service member's record. The description "Under Other Than Honorable Conditions" is given only when there is a finding that the homosexual act occurred under a variety of conditions such as with a subordinate, in public view, aboard a military vessel or aircraft, or when there is another charge or charges involved in the separation.

The characterization of one's discharge is very important because it is one of the key elements in determining benefits eligibility and can impact civilian employment. In some cases commanding officers have recommended lesser discharges than the service member's record would suggest is appropriate. The service member does have the right to contest the recommendation, but many times the person being discharged doesn't know his or her rights or is under pressure to simply "get it over with." Once the discharge has been issued, it is not impossible to secure an upgrade, but it is very difficult.

One interesting footnote to the issue of separation is the policy of the Army Reserve and Army National Guard during a time of heavy overseas deployments. Those opposed to the policy have long suspected that the military often looked the other way when it needed to retain service members. In September 2005, it was revealed that FORSCOM (Forces Command) Regulation 500-3-3, published in 1999, provided for exactly such a scenario.[13] If, prior to the receipt of alert notification, a Reserve or Guard unit has requested and received approval for the discharge of a service member under "Don't Ask, Don't Tell," the member will be discharged. If the discharge has been requested, but approval has not yet been received, the service member will be on hold pending a decision. However, if the unit receives alert notification prior to the request for discharge, regardless of whether or not they possess the information to support such a request, discharge is not authorized and the service member will be ordered to deployment on active duty with the unit.

Kim Waldron, a civilian spokesperson for FORSCOM, described this regulation as aimed at preventing Reserve and Guard members from feigning homosexuality to avoid combat. Waldron said, "The bottom line is some people are using sexual orientation to avoid deployment. So in this case, with the Reserve and Guard forces, if a soldier 'tells,' they still have to go to war and the homosexual issue is postponed until they return to the U.S. and the unit is demobilized."

Waldron described the regulation as consistent with "Don't Ask, Don't Tell" in that the policy permits the military to retain personnel in order to prevent service members from avoiding further military service.[14]

The irony to the FORSCOM regulation is that in its effort to prohibit the discharge of heterosexual service members, the military is choosing to retain gay, lesbian, and bisexual service members. That this occurs during war is particularly striking in that the centerpiece of early justification for the policy was the negative impact that the presence of gay, lesbian, and bisexual service members was alleged to have on unit cohesion, especially during times of war.

Criminal Investigations

Under previous regulations, military authorities routinely conducted investigations to determine the sexual orientation of military personnel. Investigations were often initiated on the basis of rumor and speculation. Activities ranging from copying down license plates of cars outside bars that catered to the gay and lesbian community to coercive interrogation of suspects and their friends and coworkers were commonplace. Under the new policy, such investigations are prohibited.

The policy does, however, establish guidelines for "fact-finding inquiries into homosexual conduct." Under these guidelines only a servicemember's commander is authorized to initiate such an inquiry and it must be undertaken only when the commander has received "credible information" that there is a basis for discharging the member. The basis for discharge consists of the three factors outlined in "Don't Ask, Don't Tell": an act, a statement, or marriage.

The determination that credible information exists must be based on "articulable facts, not just a belief or suspicion."[15] Examples of situations that do not constitute credible information include, but are not limited to, information based on or consisting of suspicion regarding conduct; opinions, rumor, or suspicion regarding one's sexual orientation; and "associational activity such as going to a gay bar, possessing or reading homosexual publications, association with known homosexuals, or marching in a gay rights rally in civilian clothes."[16] Situations that do constitute credible information include a reliable person stating "that he or she observed or heard a service member engaging in homosexual acts, or saying that he or she is a homosexual or bisexual or is married to a member of the same sex."[17] Additionally, a reliable person stating "that he or she heard, observed, or discovered a member make a spoken or written statement that a reasonable person would believe was intended to convey the fact that he or she engages in, attempts to engage in, or has a propensity to engage in homosexual acts" is considered a source of credible information.[18] And, if a reliable person observes nonverbal behavior that a reasonable person would believe provides this information, this, too, constitutes credible information.

Ultimately, it is the commander who determines what constitutes credible information, who is considered a reliable person, and whether or not an inquiry will be initiated. The directive specifically states that informal fact-finding inquiries and administrative separation procedures are the preferred means by which cases of homosexual conduct should be handled.

Although the policy concerning homosexual conduct is informally known as "Don't Ask, Don't Tell," the guidelines do permit commanders who have received what they deem to be credible information to ask if a service member is heterosexual, homosexual, or bisexual. They are, however, instructed to advise the service member of the policy concerning homosexual conduct. If a service member declines to answer, commanders are encouraged to "consider other available information."[19] Unlike a court of criminal law where the burden of proof typically lies with the prosecution, under "Don't Ask, Don't Tell" the service member bears the burden of proving that he or she has not and will not engage in homosexual conduct.

It should be noted that the guidelines under 1332.14 and 1332.40 do not apply to sexual misconduct investigations conducted by Department of Defense criminal investigative and law enforcement organizations in accordance with Department of Defense Instruction 5505.8. Defense criminal investigative organizations and other Defense law enforcement organizations are prohibited from conducting investigations solely to determine a service member's sexual orientation. This means, in short, that the guidelines for ensuring that inquiries regarding homosexual conduct are conducted with great care do not apply if the investigation is initiated because of an alleged incident of sexual misconduct (e.g., sexual assault).

Personnel Security

The new policy also requires that investigations conducted for security purposes are not to be used solely to determine a service member's sexual orientation. Additionally, the questionnaires used in the conduct of a security clearance investigation are not to ask about an applicant's sexual orientation. Should such an investigation reveal that a person is gay or lesbian, the information is to be considered only in evaluating eligibility for the security clearance, not suitability for military service.

The personnel security program under the Department of Defense constitutes the regulation for conducting security clearance investigations. Interestingly, the regulation specifies that while allegations of criminal conduct should be referred to the appropriate Department of Defense investigative agency, "allegations about private consensual sexual acts with adults shall not be referred or reported to law enforcement agencies or to Military Departments for any purpose."[20] This exception does not apply when the alleged offense occurred under those conditions that warrant, as above, a discharge of Under Other Than Honorable Conditions. These include, for example, an act that takes place in the barracks on a military installation.

In addition, the regulation states, "Information about a person's sexual orientation or statements by a person that he or she is a homosexual or bisexual, or words to that effect, shall not be referred or reported to law enforcement agencies or to Military Departments (other than consolidated adjudication facilities for any purpose. If investigative reports containing such information are referred to law enforcement agencies or Military Departments for other reasons, such information will be removed."[21] The regulation is, on its face, very clear about the fact that a security investigation is, under no circumstances, to be used as a mechanism for finding and expelling gay and lesbian service members.

The difficulty arises when one considers that sexual conduct that is believed to make the applicant susceptible to coercion or sexual conduct that indicates poor judgment may be considered in the course of the investigation. This leaves a fair amount of gray area in that what one investigator considers indicative of poor judgment may not be true for the next. Another difficulty is that not all persons being investigated are aware of what they must reveal and what they may refrain from revealing. For example, if an applicant, not knowing or understanding the limitations described above, denies that a roommate is in fact a same-sex romantic partner and later concedes that fact, he or she now risks denial of the clearance due to the lack of honesty. The two policies, misunderstood by many, become a double-edged sword of sorts.

According to SLDN, "Most security investigators seem to be complying with current policy and not asking about sexual orientation or activities. Some investigators, however, ignore the rules and ask inappropriate questions concerning sexual orientation or activities."[22]

One unfortunate way in which "Don't Ask, Don't Tell" and the issue of security clearances intersect is for military veterans who may have, at one time, lied about being gay or lesbian or who may have past criminal offenses as a result of being gay or lesbian. If it is discovered that someone lied and later recanted, an investigator could use that as an indication that the applicant is less than trustworthy. If someone was arrested for criminal sexual activity, specifically activities that would have been ignored had the participants been heterosexual (e.g., "public" sex), that arrest would likely preclude the granting of a clearance. In some cases the two situations have occurred together. One military veteran, while on active duty, was charged with indecent sexual assault and, while denying the assault, conceded that he was, in fact, a homosexual. Several years after his discharge he was undergoing a routine review of his security clearance in his capacity as a civilian employee of a government contractor. As the investigation went on, the applicant found himself caught up in a series of lies and was ultimately denied the clearance. Although the applicant was, in fact, guilty of the original offense of indecent sexual assault, there is a very good chance, for reasons beyond the purview of this chapter, that had he not had to hide his homosexuality, the offense and subsequent lies may never have occurred.[23]

Military Training

The armed forces were also directed to brief service members regarding the law and applicable branch regulations. Each branch would, therefore, be required to devise a plan to insure that those entering service and those continuing in service would receive periodic training on the subject of homosexual conduct in the military. Because it is not reasonable to describe the way each branch of service has responded, materials from the U.S. Army, the largest branch, will be used herein.

In the initial months, and even years, following the official implementation of the policy, few seemed to understand the policy and exactly what it obligated service members to do and not to do. Especially critical was the understanding by commanders of their role. In early 1997, three years after the policy was to be implemented, the annual report of SLDN stated, "... many military members continue to ask, pursue and harass service members in direct violation of 'Don't Ask, Don't Tell, Don't Pursue.' The violations result from a lack of leadership, training and recourse to stop illegal investigations. Some commanders, criminal investigators and inquiry officers blatantly disregard the clear limits on gay investigations. Others simply do not know any better, as the services have failed to implement adequate, ongoing training in the field."[24]

In 2004, the tenth anniversary of the policy, SLDN described the early confusion. They cited, as examples from 1994, a Navy memorandum "suggesting that public displays of support for gay activities by Navy members may be 'inconsistent with good military character,'" and an Air Force memo "instructing investigators to question parents, siblings, school counselors, roommates, and close friends of suspected gay service members."[25] Both actions were blatant violations of the policy.

One result of their findings was the conduct of a *Review of the Effectiveness of the Application and Enforcement of the Department's Policy on Homosexual Conduct in the Military,* by the office of the Under Secretary of Defense (Personnel and Readiness). The report, published in April 1998, found that there were "only isolated instances in which inquiries were made without the requisite factual basis, or in which the scope of an investigation was expanded in a way that was inconsistent either with the express terms of the policy or its spirit."[26] The report concluded that assertions of numerous "witch hunts" and other abuses were unfounded. The authors did note that while they found the policy "generally being implemented properly," there were "a number of areas . . . in which the policy could be usefully clarified or implementation could be otherwise enhanced."[27]

The report also noted that, despite widespread requirements and efforts at providing adequate training, "...some commanders, attorneys and investigators report that they have not received training on the homosexual conduct policy." They further noted that "a lack of familiarity with the policy has likely been a contributing factor in those cases in which the policy has not been fully followed."[28] Their final recommendation was that the Inspectors General make training regarding this policy a specific item in their inspection routine. There is little debate over the assertion that, during the first few years, training on the new policy was inadequate, sometimes leading to discharges that might not otherwise have occurred.

Although violations persist, especially those related to harassment and command response to assertions of harassment, training efforts appear to have improved dramatically. In early 2000, then Secretary of Defense William Cohen announced that he had received and granted approval to each branch's training plans. In his announcement, harassment was a key issue with Cohen stating that harassment and/or threats would not be tolerated.

In the winter of 2000, the magazine *Hot Topics: Current Issues of Army Leaders* published an entire issue on "Don't Ask, Don't Tell," aimed at helping commanders implement the policy appropriately. Major General John G. Meyer, Jr., Chief of Public Affairs, wrote in his opening message, "...we are determined to continue to implement the 'Don't Ask, Don't Tell' policy with equity and fairness to all of our soldiers."[29] The question, of course, remains—how does one implement a policy of discrimination fairly?

Nonetheless, this document carefully provides a brief history of the policy, a series of definitions, and detailed information on what commanders must and must not do in the course of enforcing the policy. This document is, however, flawed in several ways. One is that it states, echoing only other Department of Defense documents, that applicants to the Army may not be asked to reveal their sexual orientation. As discussed earlier in this chapter, enlistment forms ask very clearly about marital status. This document states that soldiers will not be asked about their sexual orientation except in cases where credible information concerning homosexual conduct has been received. Yet, soldiers are routinely asked about their married partners and benefits are provided accordingly. Although not their intent, the Department of Defense conflates sexual orientation with homosexuality thereby creating a double standard of what may and may not be discussed. Such oversights only add to the confusion, even when efforts at training are admirable. One of the areas most confusing to commanders is that of credible information. The *Hot Topics* issue attempts to describe when credible information exists. Yet, in doing so it relies on a "reliable person" standard while failing to provide guidelines for what constitutes a "reliable" person. This issue also notes the inclusion of the policy as a point of inspection, pointing out that, in prior years, while commanders and attorneys had received training, law enforcement personnel did not.

In July 2001, the Army published its first training guide on the policy, the first of its kind in any of the military branches. Unlike directives and publications aimed at Army leadership, *Dignity & Respect: A Training Guide On Homosexual Conduct Policy* was for the troops. And, like many training manuals over the years the format was that of a comic book. The booklet, no longer being issued, described the policy and addressed conduct, admission, and harassment. In the section on conduct, one soldier asks for an explanation of "don't ask." In response, Major Rivers, the character providing the instruction, says, "Soldiers shouldn't go around asking each other about their sexual preference [sic]."[30] Yet, in the section on harassment the scenario provided begins as follows:

Female soldier: "I am looking forward to a great weekend."

Male Soldier 1: "Oh, yeah? What are you doing?"

Female Soldier: "I have a date."

Male Soldier 2: "You? A date? I would believe that Gates over there had a date with another man before I'd ever believe that you have a hot date."

Male Soldier 1: Hey, Gates, would you enjoy a date with a good looking man, too?"

Although the soldiers are, of course, not explicitly asking about sexual orientation, it is implicit in their conversation. The male soldiers, not surprisingly, assume that the female soldier's date is with a man. Neither the discussion about dating nor the implied "asking" in their chatter with their female colleague is addressed as inappropriate. Rather, the supervisor's response is limited to the teasing of another soldier about his liking men. Given the focus of the booklet, this is understandable. Yet, it adds to the confusion when, earlier in the same booklet, the reader is instructed that discussing sexual orientation is inappropriate.[31]

Soldiers, living and working together, often "24/7," are asked, and do tell, that they are heterosexual. It would be foolish to think otherwise. The point is that training materials that provide guidance that says "Don't discuss sexual orientation," but use a scenario about talking about dating, increase the potential for misunderstanding. While the guide may have been an effective way of providing factual information about the actual words of the policy, ultimately it was a confusing, and saccharine, account of what the policy involves.

One piece of information provided in this training guide that is not always provided elsewhere (e.g., *Hot Topics*) is what constitutes a "reliable person." A commander, it suggests, must ask whether the person is known to have provided inaccurate information in the past, whether he or she is trusted by the chain of command to provide accurate information, and perhaps most importantly, whether there is any reason to suspect that this person would submit a false report. The key to a commander deeming information to be credible is whether or not the person providing the information is deemed reliable. Thus, while this training guide attempts to make clear what constitutes reliability, it is also clear that discretion lies with the commander. While the words themselves may be clear, the subjective position of the commander has great impact on how those words are carried out.

In February 2003, the U.S. Army Training and Doctrine Command (TRADOC) published Pamphlet 600-26, a document aimed at its own leadership and one example of the kind of materials that various commands are making available. As has been true in recent years, the emphasis appears to be training around the issue of harassment. In specific, rather than explanations of the broad meaning of the policy, many recent directives have focused on the need to prevent the harassment of those perceived to be gay or lesbian and the need to prevent the harassment of those who bring harassment on the basis of that perception to the attention of the chain of command.

The pamphlet includes memoranda from various military leaders in which they affirm their support for the policy and the need for recurrent training. In a message dated January 2000, the Deputy Chief of Staff for Personnel, Headquarters Department of the Army, provided the additional guidance regarding training: (1) "All soldiers will receive refresher training on homosexual conduct policy within 90 days of the date of this message. The Deputy Chief of Staff for Personnel will establish a world-wide-web page with resource material and publish training materials to be used in this training," and (2) "TRADOC has been directed to incorporate institutional training on homosexual conduct policies into all states of the Professional Military Education (PME) system within 90 days of the date of this message."[32] Three years later the Web address provided was not functional.

A search for the Web page of the office of the Deputy Chief of Staff for Personnel revealed what appeared to be an up-to-date page with an A–Z index containing a link to "Homosexual Conduct Policy Training Materials (Human Resources)." That page contained, at the time it was reviewed in 2007, three PowerPoint presentations on the policy as well as a trifold brochure with instruction for how to obtain copies of the brochure. One of the PowerPoint presentations was from 2001; the others appeared to be older. The brochure contained no date, but appeared to accurately reflect current policy and directives. The page also contained links to the relevant part of the U.S. Code, a Department of Defense press release from 1999, and messages from superior authorities in the chain of command.

The TRADOC pamphlet includes "Homosexual Conduct Policy Talking Points." The second of four points is that extensive and recurrent training is to be conducted with the aim of eliminating all types of harassment. It states, "While even one case of harassment is one too many, we believe that the policy is well understood, that commanders implement it in a manner that is fair and consistent, and that abuses are the exception rather than the rule."[33] Interestingly, this official document also cites the work of SLDN stating, "While one case is too many, the anecdotal evidence collected by the Servicemembers Legal Defense Network is not representative of the prevailing climate in the Army."[34]

In January 2006, the Department of the Army published the most recent version of Army Regulation 350-1, Army Training and Leader Development, the primary publication for Army training and leader development. In this document the homosexual conduct policy is mentioned six times. A section on command climate training states that harassment on the basis of sexual orientation, among other things, will not be tolerated and specifies that both initial and annual awareness training will be provided to all soldiers. The section regarding the Deputy Chief of Staff for Personnel states that training information and materials are to be made available on-line. Reserve commands are directed to conduct training each year during the two-week AT (annual training) period. TRADOC is directed to manage all training programs, including those regarding the homosexual conduct policy. Commandants and commanders of major command schools are required to provide such training in all professional military education courses. Finally, a table listing all common military training units includes training on the policy under the subject "command climate."

If the Army is any example, the military has gone to great lengths to make certain that its commands understand and implement the policy of "Don't Ask, Don't Tell" in the appropriate manner. But, as with any law, there is the "de jure" application, that is, based on the law. And, then, there is the "de facto" application, that is, in practice.

Harassment

As suggested above, while training and, relatedly, understanding of the policy itself have improved dramatically, harassment continues to plague the services. In December 1999 the office of the Inspector General of the Department of Defense was asked to assess the environment, specifically with regard to the homosexual conduct policy. The Inspector General surveyed 71,570 active duty service members. Eighty percent of those responding indicated that they had heard "offensive speech, derogatory names, jokes, or remarks about homosexuals in the last 12 months."[35] Thirty-seven percent indicated that they had witnessed or experienced an incident that they believe constituted harassment. About 5 percent felt that such harassment was tolerated by the chain of command. Interestingly, while 57 percent stated they had had no training on the homosexual conduct policy, 97 percent believed that they had "at least some understanding" of the policy. While half of those responding felt that the policy was "moderately or very effective at preventing or reducing harassment," 46 percent felt it was slightly effective or not effective.[36]

One striking finding in the report is that "73 percent of the respondents who said that a senior person had witnessed the harassment reported that the senior person did nothing to immediately stop the harassment."[37] SLDN has described harassment in the armed forces as a "growing epidemic."[38] Though harassment itself is not addressed in the underlying policy of "Don't Ask, Don't

Tell," it has become a critical part of the regulations that the various branches have developed for implementation of the policy.

In 2000, the Department of Defense, under then Secretary William Cohen, adopted an Anti-Harassment Action Plan containing thirteen points intended to reduce harassment and improve the way situations of harassment were addressed. The plan included two general recommendations. The first was that the Department of Defense should adopt a broad principle concerning harassment, including harassment based on sexual orientation. Secondly, the Department of Defense should issue a directive to the entire department making clear that harassment based on sexual orientation is unacceptable and that commanders would be held accountable for failure to enforce the directive.

There were three recommendations concerning training, including that training be tailored to its audience and reviewed annually. Three recommendations addressed reporting. For example, service members must know that they need not make a statement of sexual orientation in order to file a harassment complaint. Three recommendations concerned enforcement and the need for commanders and military leadership to take action against those who would disregard policies concerning harassment. Finally, two recommendations addressed measurement. In these last two recommendations, the military is to evaluate the effectiveness of the plan itself in addressing mistreatment and harassment.

In 2003, twenty-two members of Congress sent a letter to Secretary of Defense Donald Rumsfeld asking that the Department of Defense examine its implementation of the plan and report back to Congress. That September, Congress was told that the Department of Defense would do so. According to SLDN, they have done nothing.

In an environment already suffering for lack of resources, it should not be surprising to see commanders put their energies elsewhere. Yet, the Inspector General's finding that 80 percent of service members acknowledge having heard derogatory antigay remarks and 37 percent saying that they witnessed antigay harassment should give the leadership pause. Faced with the undeniable fact that harassment is pervasive, there is little question that military leaders have failed to execute the action plan adopted by the Department of Defense in 2000.

On its face, "Don't Ask, Don't Tell" is meant to permit gay and lesbian service members to serve, provided they remain silent about their sexual orientation. This is exceedingly difficult in an environment where harassment on the basis of sexual orientation persists and can, at the extreme, be life-threatening. It may well be, as will be discussed in the next chapter, that a "ban" on gay and lesbian service members is now enforced not by policy, per se, but by the failure to address widespread harassment. That is, while gay and lesbian service members may be less likely to be discharged because of witch hunts and improper investigations, they may more often feel forced to "tell," seeking discharge because of harassment that puts their safety in question. If that is the case, it seems incontrovertible that the policy, broadly stated, is not working.

Conclusion

"Don't Ask, Don't Tell" was implemented during a time when a majority of the American public did not support the military service of openly gay and lesbian citizens. Within the military, there was also a lack of support. The latter made implementation of the policy particularly challenging. There is no doubt that the size of the bureaucracy also created challenges. Creating and successfully providing adequate training to an organization—in fact, an institution—comprised of hundreds of thousands of personnel was no small task. It is clear that there were failures. Yet, it also appears that the situation is improving. Faced with a policy that is inherently flawed and individuals who resist adhering to the spirit of the policy, the military—as an organization—does appear to be making a genuine effort toward what Congress would view as successful implementation of the law that they created. The problem is that the policy itself is confusing. Thus, training on the policy is confusing as well.

Notes

1. RAND Report, p. 193.
2. Ibid., p. 442.
3. Ibid., p. 446.
4. http://www.usatoday.com/educate/college/casestudies/Multicultural.pdf.
5. U.S. Code, Title 10, Section 654, Policy concerning homosexuality in the armed forces.
6. Ibid.
7. Ibid.
8. While it is true that, as of May 2004, same-sex marriage is legal in the state of Massachusetts, it is fair to say that, across society, when one says that s/he is married, the assumption is generally that the speaker is married to someone of the opposite sex.
9. Servicemembers Legal Defense Network (SLDN) received calls as late as 2001 from recruits who were completing forms containing the question about homosexuality and unsure whether they were obligated to answer the question.
10. Department of Defense Directive 1332.14, page 27, paragraph E3.A1.1.8.1.2.1.
11. Ibid., paragraph E3.A1.1.8.1.2.2.
12. Ibid., page 31, paragraph E3.A1.1.8.4.7, E3.A1.1.8.4.7.3.
13. "Researchers Locate Army Document Ordering Commanders Not to Fire Gays," September 13, 2005, http://www.palmcenter.org/press/dadt/releases/researchers_locate_army_document_ordering_commanders_not_to_fire_gays.
14. Lou Chibbaro, Jr., "Out Gay Soldiers Sent to Iraq," Washington Blade, September 23, 2005.
15. Department of Defense Directive 1332.14, page 69, paragraph E3.A4.3.1.
16. Ibid., paragraph E3.A4.3.3.4.
17. Ibid., paragraph E3.A4.3.4.1.
18. Ibid., pages 69–70, paragraph E3.A4.3.4.2.

19. Ibid., page 70, paragraph E3.A4.4.3.

20. Department of Defense Personnel Security Program, DoD 5200.2-R, June 2002 (Draft), p. 25.

21. Ibid., p. 26.

22. SLDN, "Survival Guide: Security Clearances."

23. Decision of Administrative Judge Joan Caton Anthony, ISCR Case No. 03-00108, January 12, 2004.

24. *Conduct Unbecoming: Third Annual Report on "Don't Ask, Don't Tell, Don't Pursue,"* 1997, http://www.sldn.org/binary-data/SLDN_ARTICLES/pdf_file/166.pdf.

25. *Conduct Unbecoming: The Tenth Annual Report on "Don't Ask, Don't Tell, Don't Pursue, Don't Harass,"* 2004, p. 16, http://www.sldn.org/binary-data/SLDN_ARTICLES/pdf_file/ 1411.pdf.

26. Report to the Secretary of Defense, Review of the Effectiveness of the Application and Enforcement of the Department's Military Policy on Homosexual Conduct in the Military, Office of the Under Secretary of Defense (Personnel and Readiness), April 1998, http://www.defenselink.mil/pubs/rpt040798.html.

27. Ibid.

28. Ibid.

29. *Hot Topics: Current Issues for Army Leaders*, Winter 2000, Office of the Chief of Public Affairs.

30. Misc Pub 600-5, *Dignity & Respect: A Training Guide On Homosexual Conduct Policy*, 1 May 2001, p. 4.

31. This is a fine point. Heterosexuals fail to recognize the multitude of times that, in simply discussing their lives, they are talking about their sexual orientation. This booklet reflects that lack of awareness as well as the conflation of "sexual orientation" with only gay, lesbian, and bisexual identity.

32. TRADOC (Training and Doctrine Command) Pamphlet 600-26, Guide for Implementation of the Homosexual Conduct Policy (HCP), 13 February 2003, p. 5, https:// 134.11.61.26/CD8/Publications/TRADOC/TRADOC%20Pam/TRADOC%20Pam%20600- 26%2020030213.pdf.

33. Ibid., p. 7.

34. Ibid.

35. Military Environment with Respect to the Homosexual Conduct Policy, March 16, 2000, Report No. D-2000-101, http://dont.stanford.edu/commentary/evaluation101. pdf#search=%22D-2000-101%22, p. 4.

36. Ibid.

37. Ibid.

38. *Conduct Unbecoming: The Tenth Annual Report on "Don't Ask, Don't Tell, Don't Pursue, Don't Harass,"* 2004, p. 6, http://www.sldn.org/templates/law/record.html?section=22& record=1411.

CHAPTER 3

Institutional and Individual Impact

The impact of any personnel policy ranges from the less easily quantified (e.g., unit cohesion) to the more easily quantified (e.g., discharges). Such policies have, at a minimum, an impact on both the institution and the individual. While there is arguably an even more widespread impact (e.g., communities, social movement organizations, the law, and families), this chapter focuses on the impact that "Don't Ask, Don't Tell" has had on the military and on those individuals who have had their careers cut short as a result of the policy.

Between 1994 and 2006, inclusive, 11,704 people were discharged under "Don't Ask, Don't Tell." The numbers increased steadily between 1994 and 1998, taking a slight dip in 1999 and rising again in 2000. The peak year was 2001, when 1,273 service members were separated from service. The figures declined each of the following three years (906, 787, 668 discharges, respectively) and experienced a slight rise in 2005 when 742 discharges were processed. The numbers, while informative, don't really capture the impact, either on the institution or on the individual. To try to understand the impact of the policy on the nation's armed forces, we begin by looking at aggregate figures for who was discharged, the projected financial cost of the discharges, and the unique impact on women. We then turn to the stories of some of the individuals who were discharged under the policy.

Discharges under "Don't Ask, Don't Tell"

As mentioned above, as of the end of 2006, over 11,000 service members have joined the military only to be discharged under "Don't Ask, Don't Tell." What led to their discharges? How do discharges compare across branch, by race, by gender? To try to understand who is being discharged, at the aggregate level, we rely on the work of the Servicemembers Legal Defense Network (SLDN) and research conducted by the U.S. government itself.

In February 2005, the U.S. Government Accountability Office (GAO) published a report titled *Military Personnel: Financial Costs and Loss of Critical Skills Due to DOD's Homosexual Conduct Policy Cannot Be Completely Estimated*. This statement is true because the Department of Defense does not maintain data on what it costs to conduct investigations and inquiries, provide counseling and pastoral care associated with the policy, process separations under the policy, or conduct reviews of discharges under the policy. But, the report is useful both for the financial projections and the descriptive data.

Between the years 1994 and 2003, inclusive, 1 percent of those separated under the policy were discharged because they married or attempted to marry someone of the same sex. Sixteen percent were separated for engaging in, attempting to engage in, or soliciting another to engage in a homosexual act or acts. And, 83 percent were separated for stating that he or she was homosexual or bisexual, or for saying something taken to have the same meaning. Thus, the vast majority of personnel were discharged for statements that serve as proxies for conduct, not the conduct itself.

Of the 5,763 discharges that were characterized, 82 percent were characterized as "Honorable," 13 percent as "General (under honorable conditions)," and 5 percent were given "Under Other Than Honorable Conditions." Uncharacterized, or entry-level separations, were granted to 3,304 individuals. These separations are typically granted to a service member who is separated within 180 days of entry.[1] Thirty-five percent of those discharged were in the Army, 31 percent in the Navy, 25 percent in the Air Force, and 8 percent in the Marines. Seventy-one percent of those discharged were white, 12 percent were black, 16 percent had a racial and/or ethnic identity that was unknown, and 1 percent were characterized as "other." Of those discharged during this period, 73 percent were male and 27 percent female.

According to the GAO, 757 of those discharged held occupations that the Department of Defense deemed critical. Most of those individuals were in their first term of service. Three hundred and twenty-two of those discharged had important foreign language skills (e.g., Korean, Farsi, or Arabic) with ninety-eight having completed training at the Department of Defense Language Institute. The GAO reports that 63 percent of those ninety-eight service members "had proficiency scores at or below the midpoint on DOD's language proficiency scales for listening, reading, or speaking."[2] The midpoint is described by the Department of Defense as "limited working proficiency, plus."[3] The choice to frame the findings around "at or below midpoint" versus "at or above midpoint" seems questionable when one realizes that, according to the Department of Defense's own guidelines, students may graduate with proficiency scores below the midpoint in all three areas of assessment. Analysis of whether the military lost one highly proficient Arabic linguist or a dozen with questionable proficiency seems to miss the point. No matter the number, the military is losing individuals who have voluntarily agreed to serve and who have valuable skills the nation needs.

The Financial Cost

In 1994, in their first annual report on "Don't Ask, Don't Tell," SLDN estimated that $17.5 million had been spent training replacements for the service members discharged during the first year of the policy. This figure does not include the cost of investigations, discharge proceedings, or other costs associated with implementation of the policy (e.g., training). In 1995 this figure rose to an estimated $21 million and in 1996 to $25 million.

Just over ten years after the policy became law, the GAO was tasked with determining the annual financial cost of administering the policy and the extent to which the policy has led to the separation of those in critical occupations, including foreign language skills. Methodologically, those conducting the inquiry had to rely on a variety of resources from across the branches. Not all branches were able to provide the same data. And, since the researchers did not review each individual file, there was no way of calculating the actual cost. That is, they were unable to distinguish between, for example, a case that took several months and, therefore, "cost more" and the case in which a service member was processed and separated within the week.

Ultimately, using primarily recruitment and training cost data for the Department of Defense overall, the GAO concluded that "it would have cost DOD about $95 million in constant fiscal year 2004 dollars from fiscal year 1994 through fiscal year 2003 to recruit replacements for enlisted service members separated for homosexual conduct."[4] Additionally, the GAO obtained estimates, provided by the Air Force, Army, and Navy, for the cost to train those recruited to replace discharged service members. These figures were $16.6 million, $29.7 million, and $48.8 million, respectively. Combining the costs to recruit and train replacements, GAO estimates that it cost about $190 million to replace those discharged under "Don't Ask, Don't Tell." Given the constraints on available cost data, there is little doubt that this figure serves as a very conservative estimate of the financial cost of the policy to the military and, in reality, the taxpayer. This is certainly the argument made in a Blue Ribbon Commission Report published at the University of California in February 2006.

Concerned with the methodology employed by the GAO, the commission sought to replicate the research. The commission, composed of scholars, military personnel, and former members of the Department of Defense, was chaired by Dr. Aaron Belkin at the University of California–Santa Barbara. Because of their concerns with methodology, however, the commission did not, of course, replicate the research by following GAO's procedures. Rather, they sought to answer the same questions, using available data, but conceptualizing some of the essential aspects quite differently. For example, all discharged service members were not "calculated equally." That is, if you had one week left in a thirty-year career, the "lost value" of your discharge would be significantly less than if you were discharged one year after enlistment.

The Blue Ribbon Commission calculated that the cost to recruit replacements for enlisted service members was about $79 million, a figure lower than that of the GAO. The commission calculated that the cost to train those in occupations in which separated service members served was about $252 million. Unlike the GAO, the commission included estimates for officers. The commission obtained information for each of the 137 officers separated between 1994 and 2003 and calculated, based on rank, service, etc., that the training costs were close to $18 million. The commission also calculated a cost for separation travel, that is, the cost of out-processing and returning separated service members to their homes, of about $14 million. Using the above analyses, the commission estimated the cost of implementing "Don't Ask, Don't Tell" during the period 1994–2003 to be about $364 million. After considering where they may have overestimated and underestimated the data, the commission concluded that the figure they provide should be considered a conservative estimate.

Not surprisingly, the GAO disagreed with the findings of the commission and, in July 2006, issued a response detailing the methodological differences and standing by their findings. In September 2006, Dr. Belkin responded, detailing the oversights that caused the GAO figure to be so much lower. For example, where the commission calculated training costs for each member by using branch- and occupation-specific data, the GAO used an overall per-person estimate as provided by the branch of service. Belkin cited a different GAO report in which they reported that the Army spends at least $40,000 to train one recruit through basic training. Yet, the GAO, in studying the cost of "Don't Ask, Don't Tell," used the Army figure of $6,400 per person for initial entry training. Whether one is persuaded by the GAO's figure of $190 million or the Blue Ribbon Commission's figure of close to $364 million, that the financial cost of the policy is significant seems undeniable.

The Disproportionate Impact on Women

Women are discharged under "Don't Ask, Don't Tell" at a rate roughly twice their representation. This figure has remained fairly constant since the policy went into effect. In 1994, women comprised 12 percent of the armed forces, yet 26 percent of those discharged under the policy were women. The percentage of women discharged has risen and fallen over the years with a low of 21 percent in 1995 and a high of 33 percent in 2003, the latest year for which data are available. The percentage of women in the military rose from 13 percent to 14 percent in 1997 and stood at 15 percent in 2003. The percentage of discharged personnel that is women is outpacing the overall representation of women in the armed forces. It is interesting to note that while the figure dipped from 31 percent in 1999 to 24 percent in 2000, it rose each year between 2000 and 2003.

In terms of raw numbers, women in the Army seem to be the hardest hit. This is, perhaps, not surprising given the size of the force and the somewhat greater tendency to permit women to serve in nontraditional career fields, a point to which we will return later. In 1999, for example, while women made up only 15 percent of the Army, they constituted 35 percent—over one-third—of those discharged from the Army under the policy. Women constituted 18 percent of those in the Air Force, yet 37 percent of those discharged from the Air Force were women. The most glaring disparity between representation in the branch and percentage discharged was found in the Marine Corps where only 6 percent of the Corps were women, yet women constituted 21 percent of those discharged.

There also appears to be a disproportionate impact on women of color. In 2001, African-American women constituted less than 1 percent (0.84%) of all military personnel. They constituted 3.26 percent of those discharged under "Don't Ask, Don't Tell." Hispanic women are 0.31 percent of those serving, yet were separated at a rate twice that (0.60%). And, other women of color constituted one quarter of 1 percent (0.25%) of those serving, yet were close to 1 percent (0.91%) of those discharged. It is likely that women of color are more likely to be targeted for harassment due to racism and, as we will see, that harassment often takes the form of "lesbian baiting." Other explanations for why women of color would suffer even more than their white counterparts have not been offered by those studying the phenomenon.[5]

It has long been debated whether lesbians are, in fact, overrepresented in the military. That is, is the percentage of lesbians among women in the military greater than those among civilian women? And, more to the point, is the proportion of lesbians to heterosexual women in the military greater than the proportion of gay men to heterosexual men in the military? If the answer is yes, that would partly explain the disproportionate discharge rate.

Two explanations that have often been offered to support an affirmative response to both questions are that lesbians have a greater need for self-sufficiency and that they may find the nontraditional career options more attractive than do heterosexual women. We cannot answer the questions because there are no reliable data about representation in either sector. But, it is very likely that even if there is a tendency toward overrepresentation—either of lesbians compared to heterosexual women or compared to gay men—it is not sufficient to explain the grossly disproportionate discharge rate.

What does serve as a reasonable explanation, and one that can be documented, is the relationship between sexual harassment and "Don't Ask, Don't Tell." It has long been known that women in nontraditional career fields experience a greater degree of harassment than women in traditional career fields. In the military there may be a "double whammy" of sorts. By virtue of being in the military at all, women are in a nontraditional career field. But, when one is a truck driver rather than a clerk, there is a second "layer" of defiance toward a gendered society.

"Don't Ask, Don't Tell" provides service members a mechanism for harassing women in a way that virtually insures that they won't complain about the harassment. There are hundreds, if not thousands, of documented instances in which women who were harassed by being targeted as a lesbian did not complain because they feared that such a complaint would trigger an investigation of their sexual orientation. There are just as many cases in which they did complain and were proved right to have had such fears. While men also experience harassment (i.e., "What are you, a fag?"), this does not occur *because* they are men. Women are targeted simply because they are women. And, men tend not to experience such taunts and threats as retaliation. Women routinely experience harassment as a form of retaliation either for refusing men's advances and/or for not being "woman enough."

The term "lesbian baiting" or "dyke baiting" was coined to describe the situation in which women are taunted, typically about their less feminine appearance or lack of interest in a particular man or men. If a woman declines interest in a man's advances it has not been uncommon for the response to be something like, "So what are you, a dyke?" Under "Don't Ask, Don't Tell" such a comment is both a violation of the policy, per se, and a form of harassment. Nonetheless, women continue to be faced with the dilemma of lying, not answering, and/or filing a complaint and potentially facing more harassment and/or investigation. The "Catch-22" is inescapable. In 1992, the Inspector General, in a pre-"Don't Ask, Don't Tell" report on sexual harassment prepared for the Department of the Army, found that "the prohibition against homosexuals in the Army results in a subtle 'billy club' for anyone to use against single women in the Army. When they turn down a 'date' with another soldier, it is often whispered unjustifiably, that she is a 'lesbian.'"[6] Although the new policy makes clear that such questions or accusations are prohibited, they continue.

One mechanism that men have adopted for countering allegations that they are gay is to date and, in some cases, have sexual relationships with women. While some women have adopted such strategies, they appear to do so far less frequently. In our society, a man who "flaunts" his dating or sexual conquests is rewarded; especially as the number of women he dates increases. A woman is often penalized for the same behavior and is surely penalized if dating or perceived to be dating more than one man. As Marine Captain Guy Richardson stated, "I thank God every day that I am a male Marine in this male Marine Corps . . . If a woman Marine is a little too friendly, she's a slut. If she doesn't smile at all, she's a dyke. I personally believe that a woman Marine in the normal course of a day confronts more stress and more bullshit than a male Marine would in twenty years."[7]

Behind all of these numbers are real people. In all cases they are people whose lives have been put under a microscope. In many cases they have been treated unfairly, if not with hostility. In many cases they have had their careers, their livelihood, terminated prematurely. Who do we find if we look behind the numbers?

The Human Cost[8]

Every gay man and lesbian who has served under "Don't Ask, Don't Tell" has a story to tell. Some are hopeful, some are shocking, and some are saddening.

The service members profiled in the following paragraphs are bound together not only by their shared experience with the military, but also by the fact that they are all plaintiffs in *Cook v. Gates*, the latest legal challenge to the policy.[9] No one story, or dozen stories, can accurately reflect the impact of choosing to serve one's country, only to be fired because of one's identity as a gay man or lesbian. But, these brief descriptions of their service and dismissal provide a glimpse into the experience.

Thomas Cook joined the U.S. Army on April 11, 2001. He sought to change his life and to better himself. Cook excelled and was quickly promoted, attaining the rank of Specialist with an Intelligence specialty, and eventually earning the Army Achievement Medal. Cook deployed to Kuwait in support of military operations in the Middle East from April through September 2002. In late 2003, Cook's company received orders to deploy to Iraq. Preparing for that deployment, Cook conducted a field training exercise with two other enlisted soldiers in his company. One of them was a sergeant and Cook's team leader. On one occasion, the three men saw a man whom they knew to be gay walk by. The sergeant said to Cook that "(i)f I ever found out someone in my crew was gay, I would kill him." The threat worried Cook, because he is gay. Cook knew that he was about to be deployed to Iraq with this sergeant and was worried about what would happen if the sergeant found out Cook was gay. But Cook did not know of any mechanisms through which he could confidentially and without risk of retaliation report the sergeant's threat. Cook decided that the best way to protect his own safety was to inform his commander about the sergeant's threat and explain that he was gay. Thus, in December 2003, Cook told his battalion commander he was gay. Cook's battalion commander thought Cook made that statement solely to avoid deployment to Iraq. He recommended that Cook receive a general discharge rather than an honorable discharge, something that would have hurt Cook's ability to get a job in civilian life. With the help of an attorney, Cook fought the battalion commander's recommendation and the Army issued him an honorable discharge, reflective of his honorable service record. Cook was discharged from the Army on January 22, 2004. He served for nearly three years.

Megan Dresch joined the U.S. Army on August 22, 2001. After basic training and an eight-week military police training course, Dresch was stationed in Kaiserlautern, Germany, and served with the Military Police. Dresch found the burden of lying about her relationship with her girlfriend at home stressful. In an effort to relieve this stress, Dresch sought leave to speak with the chaplain at her base. When told she would need to reveal her reasons for seeing the chaplain, Dresch sought the intervention of a friend and fellow private who had a personal relationship with a non-commissioned officer in her chain of command. Without Dresch's permission, this friend told the non-commissioned officer that Dresch was a lesbian.

The non-commissioned officer then asked Dresch if she was a lesbian. In response to this direct question, Dresch admitted that she was and was honorably discharged from the Army on September 6, 2002. At the time of her discharge, she had served in the Army for just over a year. During her service, she earned the National Defense Service Medal, the Army Service Ribbon, and had attained the rank of Private Second Class with a Military Police specialty.

Laura Galaburda joined the U.S. Air Force on December 10, 1998. Dr. Galaburda participated in the Air Force's Health Profession Scholarship Program as an Air Force Reserve Officer, which provided her a scholarship to attend medical school at Boston University.

During her active duty rotations at Andrews Air Force Base, Dr. Galaburda realized that she was continually forced to lie or only partially answer questions from her colleagues and patients because of her sexual orientation. "Don't Ask, Don't Tell" made it impossible for Galaburda to conceal her sexual orientation and also remain true to her personal sense of honesty and her obligations to her patients. Consequently, Dr. Galaburda decided to tell her commander that she was a lesbian. She submitted a letter to her commander on February 14, 2002. Dr. Galaburda was discharged under "Don't Ask, Don't Tell" because of that statement. She was discharged from both the Air Force and the Health Professional Scholarship Program. Following her discharge, the Air Force began recoupment proceedings against Dr. Galaburda, purportedly seeking to recover the cost of her medical education. That recoupment proceeding is ongoing. At the time of her honorable discharge, Dr. Galaburda had served in the Air Force Reserves for almost four years. She had attained the rank of Second Lieutenant and was a resident physician with training specializing in family medicine.

Jack Glover was a cadet with the U.S. Air Force Reserve Officer Training Corps (ROTC). Glover's dedication and skill were quickly noticed and he received honors and leadership positions typically reserved for the most promising cadets. He was offered his first leadership position—Flight Adjutant—shortly after joining the ROTC program. In the spring of 2001, Glover accepted the position of General Military Corps Advisor. In that position, Glover served as the chief lower classman—a position similar to the Chief Master Sergeant role in the Air Force. In the fall of 2001, Glover served exceptionally well as the Operations Group commander with the rank of Cadet Lieutenant Colonel, in which he was charged with the overall training of the cadets. The following spring, the detachment needed Glover to remain in the operations group to help prepare the cadets for field training. In the fall of 2003, Glover again served as a Cadet Lieutenant Colonel. Glover's talent and dedication also earned him several prestigious training opportunities. In the summer of 2001, Glover attended the Air Force ROTC's five-week field training program. In May 2002, he was selected to go to Vandenburg Air Force Base for three weeks of space program orientation.

In December 2000, Glover had begun dating another University of Alaska student, David Hall. Hall was serving in the Air Force on active duty at the time, but he joined the University of Alaska–Anchorage's Air Force ROTC program in May 2001. In the fall of 2001, Glover, with Hall, helped create a local Arnold Air Society chapter. The Arnold Air Society is an Honor Society in ROTC devoted to community service.

David Hall joined the Air Force on March 6, 1996, following in the footsteps of his father and stepfather, who each had served for over twenty years in the Air Force. After basic training, Hall graduated from tech school with the second highest score in his class and was assigned to the 27th Fighter Squadron at Langley Air Force Base in Hampton, Virginia. At Langley, Hall was one of the top airmen in his flight. He worked as a weapons loader, winning several loading competitions and the Airman of the Quarter Award. While based at Langley, Hall completed a three-month assignment in Saudi Arabia, and was handpicked to go to Kuwait to help fix aircraft.

In the summer of 1998, Hall was assigned to Elmendorf Air Force Base outside of Anchorage, Alaska, where he was selected to work at the Weapons Standardization Section, which employs highly qualified airmen to train and evaluate the load crew on the base. While at the Weapons Standardization Section, Hall won several medals and Airman of the Quarter awards. In his spare time, Hall began taking classes at the University of Alaska–Anchorage, where he met and began dating fellow student Jack Glover. Glover encouraged Hall to join the Air Force ROTC.

After receiving a strong recommendation from his active duty commander, Hall was honorably discharged as an enlisted member from the Air Force in August 2001 following his acceptance to the Air Force ROTC in May 2001. At that time, Hall had served for five years and attained the rank of Staff Sergeant (E-5) with an Aircraft Armament Systems specialty. During his active duty service, Hall received numerous awards including the Air Force Achievement Medal, Air Force Commendation Medal, Air Force Longevity Service Award, Air Force Training Ribbon, NCO Professional Military Education Ribbon, Armed Forces Expeditionary Medal, Air Force Outstanding Unit Ward, and Air Force Good Conduct Medal. With Glover, Hall helped create a local Arnold Air Society chapter. Hall was named the chapter's vice-commander. In March 2002, Hall received a coveted slot to train to be a pilot—an honor given to approximately 500 cadets nationwide each year. At the time Hall received this honor, he had the highest ranking of all the Air Force ROTC juniors in his detachment. In recognition of his talent and dedication, Hall was named a Cadet Captain and flight commander, soon advancing to the position of Operations Officer, Cadet Major, another leadership position. In June 2002, after returning from field training, Hall was called in to speak to a Judge Advocate General and a Staff Sergeant, who told him that they knew of his relationship with Glover. Hall refused to comment about his relationship with Glover, and an investigation ensued. He was disenrolled and honorably discharged from the Air Force ROTC on August 21, 2002. At the time of his disenrollment and discharge, Hall was ranked first in a class of over one hundred cadets. He had served for one year in the Air Force ROTC.

Monica Hill joined the U.S. Air Force on December 21, 1994, having won an Air Force scholarship to medical school. For her residency, Dr. Hill worked at a civilian hospital in Columbus, Ohio. While there, she lived with her partner of fourteen years, Terri Cason, who was a nurse at the hospital. In the summer of

2001, Dr. Hill was scheduled to report to Andrews Air Force Base for her permanent active duty assignment. Dr. Hill arranged for an apartment in Northern Virginia, not far from the base, and made arrangements to have her possessions moved on July 18, 2001. Cason's health deteriorated dramatically in July 2001. In two weeks, Cason went from working at the hospital to being unable even to do household chores. Cason's doctors first thought she had an infectious disease and treated her with antibiotics. On July 14, 2001, Cason's doctors changed their diagnosis. Cason had lung cancer, with additional metastatic brain lesions. That diagnosis meant that Cason had between two months and two years to live. Desperate to remain with her dying partner, and feeling it was irresponsible to move her partner from her treating physician, Dr. Hill decided to seek permission to delay reporting to Andrews Air Force Base by explaining the situation, revealing the nature of her relationship with Cason, and requesting a two-year deferment on July 22, 2001. In response, the Air Force canceled Dr. Hill's orders to report to Andrews Air Force Base. Cason died on September 11, 2001. Several months after her orders were cancelled, the Air Force informed Dr. Hill that discharge proceedings were pending against her based on her statement in her request for deferment that she was a lesbian. The Air Force began an investigation into Dr. Hill's sexual orientation. During the investigation, the investigating officer suggested in hostile and accusatory tones that Dr. Hill had invented the story of Cason's illness, and that Dr. Hill had admitted her sexual orientation solely to escape going on active duty. Dr. Hill was required to provide Cason's death certificate as proof that she had not invented the story. Additionally, the investigating officer repeatedly asked Dr. Hill about her sexual orientation and for details of her sexual history. The investigation concluded that Dr. Hill had made a "homosexual admission" requiring discharge under "Don't Ask, Don't Tell," and that she had made the statement for the purpose of being separated from the military. The Air Force began discharge proceedings. Dr. Hill decided to resign from the Air Force because she felt it was impossible to fight the process and that discharge was inevitable under "Don't Ask, Don't Tell." Dr. Hill was honorably discharged on October 2, 2002. Following her discharge, the Air Force began recoupment proceedings against Dr. Hill, purportedly seeking to recover the cost of her medical education.

Jenny Kopfstein entered the U.S. Naval Academy in 1995 after spending two years at a civilian college. She graduated from the Naval Academy with a bachelor's degree in physics on May 26, 1999, and was selected as a Surface Warfare Officer. She immediately attended the prestigious Surface Warfare Officer's School in Rhode Island—a school dedicated to teaching shipboard systems and operations, similar to the flight training pilots receive at flight school. After graduating from the Surface Warfare Officer's School, Kopfstein was given her first duty station on the U.S.S. Shiloh. The Shiloh's homeport is in San Diego. Serving on board a ship for the first time, Kopfstein realized that concealing her sexual orientation from others was inconsistent with her strong values of honesty and honor. Kopfstein found it difficult to answer casual questions about her personal life without lying or concealing the whole truth. After a few months on board,

Kopfstein gave her commanding officer a letter saying that she was a lesbian, and also saying that she wished to continue service. Despite having made this admission, the Navy did not immediately seek to discharge Kopfstein during her first deployment. Instead, Kopfstein went on a second, six-month deployment in the Western Pacific in support of Operation Enduring Freedom. She completed that deployment, and still no discharge proceedings began. Although Kopfstein had originally been scheduled for an eighteen-month tour of duty on the Shiloh, she was retained on the ship for twenty-two months. Admitting her sexual orientation to others did not harm Kopfstein's job performance. To the contrary, during her deployment and in the months following that deployment, she continued to display a high degree of professionalism and excellence. The Navy recognized this, and gave Kopfstein several awards and honors, including qualifying Kopfstein as Officer of the Deck Underway, which allowed her to take command of the entire ship in certain situations. Kopfstein was promoted to the rank of Lieutenant Junior Grade (O-2) with a Surface Warfare Officer specialty after returning from deployment. Nineteen months after admitting her sexual orientation, a Board of Inquiry finally convened to investigate whether grounds existed for discharging Kopfstein under "Don't Ask, Don't Tell." Although it is highly unusual for a Navy Captain to speak on a subordinate officer's behalf in a Board of Inquiry hearing, both of Kopfstein's captains (command of the U.S.S. Shiloh changed during her tour of duty) volunteered to testify on her behalf. Both captains testified that they understood that Kopfstein was a lesbian, but that Kopfstein was an excellent officer and that she should ideally remain in the Navy. The Board of Inquiry disregarded the recommendations of Kopfstein's captains. Concluding that Kopfstein's statement that she is a lesbian constituted grounds for discharge under "Don't Ask, Don't Tell," the board voted in February 2002 to discharge Kopfstein from the Navy. After a delay, Kopfstein was honorably discharged from the Navy on October 31, 2002. At the time of her discharge, Kopfstein had served in the Navy for nearly three years, not counting her years as a midshipman at the Academy. During her service, Kopfstein received numerous awards, including the Navy Achievement Medal, two Meritorious Unit Commendations, Battle "E" Ribbon, two National Defense Service Medals, Armed Forces Expeditionary Medal, Sea Service Deployment Ribbon, Navy Expert Rifle Medal, Navy Expert Pistol Shot Medal, and Surface Warfare Qualification Breast Insignia.

Jennifer McGinn enlisted in the Army on November 13, 2001. She was motivated by the terrorist attacks on America on September 11, 2001. The Army assigned McGinn to Fort Leonard Wood in Missouri. There, she underwent basic training, followed by Advanced Individual Training as a Military Police officer. During boot camp, McGinn became friends with another female enlisted member. One night in February 2002, McGinn's Drill Sergeant suddenly turned on the barrack lights, ordered a lineup, and announced—incorrectly—that McGinn and her friend had been kissing. An investigation ensued. McGinn's Drill Sergeant sought witnesses and accused the other recruits of lying for not coming forward. McGinn's Drill Sergeant searched her wall locker and read personal letters from her friends and family. McGinn's Drill Sergeant told McGinn that homosexuality is "just wrong," adding that "[m]en and women are made to be together, Private. It says that in the Bible. Do you read the Bible, Private?" McGinn's Drill Sergeant declared, "You can't go to heaven if you're gay," and remarked, "I see that shit on TV and, I'm not saying it's wrong, but I'm a Christian and it makes me sick." Other sergeants made harassing statements and repeatedly asked McGinn about her sexual orientation and sexual history. Due to her Drill Sergeant's allegations, the Army began an investigation into McGinn's sexual orientation. During the investigation, McGinn was asked to fill out a questionnaire that asked several questions about her sexual history. Questions on the form included "Have you experienced difficulties being around other members of your own sex?" "Did you tell your recruiter about your homosexual/bisexual conduct prior to entering the Army?" and "Did you engage in homosexual/bisexual acts as an experiment?" Posing these questions directly to McGinn violated Defense Department and Army regulations. McGinn was honorably discharged from the Army on April 1, 2002. At the time of her discharge, McGinn had served in the Army for five months.

Justin Peacock entered the Coast Guard on September 17, 2001. Following basic training, Peacock reported for duty to Cape Disappointment, Washington. Although Peacock kept his sexual orientation secret, rumors circulated nonetheless. Peacock endured repeated jokes and taunting. The jokes and teasing became progressively worse in the spring of 2002. In fact, during one night of watch duty, Peacock was repeatedly teased by several other Coast Guardsmen about what they perceived to be his sexual orientation. In response to this incessant mockery, Peacock asked, "So what if I am gay?" or words to that effect. Many of the Coast Guardsmen present when this incident occurred later testified that they did not believe that Peacock was making a statement about his sexual orientation and was just trying to sarcastically rebuff the harassment he was enduring. Later that spring, Peacock's civilian roommate, a man, visited the local military exchange with Peacock. The two were not romantically involved. However, another Coast Guardsman falsely alleged that Peacock was seen holding hands at the exchange with his roommate for approximately two seconds. During this time, a fellow seaman began repeatedly harassing Peacock, calling him "a stupid faggot" among other things. Peacock reported this harassment to his executive officer. Peacock's executive officer admonished the seaman who made that remark, but also inappropriately began an investigation into whether Peacock was gay. The executive officer asked the seaman who had harassed Peacock if he had any evidence that Peacock was gay. Peacock's Executive Officer then expanded his investigation, asking other seamen if they had evidence that Peacock was gay. On August 26, 2002, someone reported the alleged hand-holding incident at the military exchange to Peacock's command. Based on this report, an officially sanctioned investigation of Peacock began on September 4, 2002. Peacock requested to defend himself before an administrative discharge board. Peacock presented evidence to the Board that he had been investigated in violation of Defense Department, Department of Homeland Security, and U.S. Coast Guard regulations that, among

other things, forbade investigations based on rumors. Despite testimony contra-
dicting much of the alleged conduct, Peacock lost his case. Peacock was honorably
discharged from the Coast Guard on July 31, 2003. One of the grounds for this
discharge was that Peacock's alleged act of holding hands with another man was
a "homosexual act" under the statute and related regulations.

At the time of his discharge, Peacock had served in the Coast Guard for almost two years. He was promoted from E-3 to E-4 during the investigation into
his alleged homosexual conduct, and earned a Boatswain's Mate specialty and
several awards and commendations, including the Coast Guard Unit Commendation Award, Coast Guard Meritorious Unit Commendation, and National Defense
Service Medal.

James E. Pietrangelo II joined the U.S. Army in 1989. During Operation Desert
Storm in 1991, Pietrangelo led an infantry team in combat as a specialist in the
1st Armored Division. In recognition of that work, he was awarded the Combat
Infantryman's Badge, and received an Army Commendation Medal. Pietrangelo
finished his infantry tour in 1993. He entered law school in 1993 and practiced
law for several years as a civilian. He then took a commission as a judge advocate
general officer with the Army. Pietrangelo served as Chief of Operational Law
with the 10th Mountain Division. He served with that Division when it was deployed in Afghanistan during Operation Enduring Freedom. In February 2003,
Pietrangelo volunteered to deploy to Operation Iraqi Freedom before it began.
He served as an operational law attorney, and then Chief of Operational Law,
in Kuwait and Iraq from February 2003 to August 2003. Pietrangelo's duties included advising commanders on issues of military and international law. He also
deployed forward and served in Iraq, where he helped restart the Baghdad court
system. For his service in Operation Iraqi Freedom, Pietrangelo was awarded a
Meritorious Service Medal and a Joint Service Commendation Medal.

Pietrangelo came off active duty in February 2004, and returned to make his
home in Vermont. There, he began a clerkship with the Vermont State's Attorney's
Office, as part of a process of becoming a member of the Vermont bar. Before his
clerkship was complete, Pietrangelo decided to go back to Iraq. He felt that the
Army needed his expertise and experience as well as more Americans to volunteer
for the Operation at a critical time. Pietrangelo volunteered with the Vermont
National Guard as Chief of Operational Law with the 42nd Infantry Division—
the first National Guard division to be mobilized for Operation Iraqi Freedom.
The Army accepted that offer and ordered Pietrangelo to mobilize on May 24,
2004. Weeks before that reporting date, Pietrangelo met and fell in love with
another man. The two planned to marry in Quebec.

Pietrangelo gave up his lodging in Vermont and reported to Fort Drum, as ordered, to begin his next deployment. Two weeks into the training at Fort Drum,
Pietrangelo decided that he could not keep his relationship with his fiancé secret, due to the fact that he could be injured or killed in Iraq. Pietrangelo wrote
a memo to his commander on June 14, 2004, declaring that he was gay and intended to marry another man. The memo stated that Pietrangelo desired to return

to serve in Iraq, and stated that if the Army would decline to enforce the "Don't Ask, Don't Tell" policy in his case, he would go to Iraq. The Army cancelled Pietrangelo's scheduled deployment to Iraq and began discharge proceedings. Pietrangelo nonetheless continued to provide his expertise and experience to his country. After discharge proceedings began, Pietrangelo created an operational law office from scratch for the 42nd Infantry Division, and prepared the Judge Advocate's Office for deployment. Pietrangelo was honorably discharged from the U.S. Army and the Vermont Army National Guard on October 8, 2004, because of "Don't Ask, Don't Tell." At the time of his discharge, Pietrangelo had served in the Army for more than seven years and in the Army National Guard/Reserves for six years, attaining the rank of Captain (O-3). He had earned the Combat Infantryman Badge, Meritorious Service Medal, three Army Commendation Medals, two Army Achievement Medals, Joint Service Commendation Medal, Army Good Conduct Medal, two National Defense Service Medals, Global War on Terrorism Expeditionary Medal, Global War on Terrorism Medal, Southwest Asia Service Medal with three Bronze Service Stars, Armed Forces Reserve Medal with "M" Device, Liberation of Kuwait Medal, Overseas Service Ribbon, NCO Professional Development Ribbon, Army Service Ribbon, and Expert Infantryman Badge.

Derek Sparks enlisted in the U.S. Navy on October 26, 1987. During his fourteen-and-a-half-year military career, Sparks served on several deployments in several capacities, repeatedly demonstrating his professionalism and skill. Sparks' first command was the U.S.S. Sacramento. In his four years on the Sacramento, Sparks made two deployments, one of them in support of Operation Desert Storm. In recognition of his service, the Navy awarded Sparks a Sailor of the Quarter award. After serving on the Sacramento, Sparks worked for a year and a half in the Navy Absentee Collection Unit, and then transferred to the U.S.S. Cowpens, and then the U.S.S. Hurricane, where in addition to serving as the ship's only signalman, he became qualified as Combat Information Center Watch Officer and served as the Assistant Supply Officer and Information Systems Security Manager. Sparks then worked as a corrections officer at the Naval Consolidated Brig Miramar, and from there transferred to the U.S.S. Bridge after completing Command Career Counselor School. During his long career, Sparks received four Sea Service Ribbons; the COMCARGRU with one letter of commendation; the National Defense Service Medal; the SW Asia Service Medal; a Navy Unit Commendation; the Navy Expert Pistol Medal; the Navy Battle "E" Ribbon; the Kuwait Liberation Medal; three Navy and Marine Corps Achievement Medals; four Navy Good Conduct Awards; a Meritorious Unit Commendation Citation; and the Navy Expert Rifle Medal. Sparks' final deployment was on the U.S.S. Bridge, near Afghanistan, in support of Operation Enduring Freedom. Sparks served as the Bridge's Command Career Counselor. By that time, Sparks had attained the rank of Petty Officer First Class (E-6). One evening during that deployment, Sparks was watching an action movie on the television in his office. Two other service members, both male, were in the office with him. Unknown to Sparks, his

Master Chief observed the three men through a hole in the wall. The Master Chief later alleged he saw Sparks and the other two sailors engaging in homosexual activity. An investigation began based on those allegations. Throughout the investigation into these allegations, all three sailors involved denied committing homosexual acts. Following repeated questioning by investigators, Sparks decided not to fight the Navy any longer. Sparks denied his Master Chief's allegation of engaging in homosexual conduct aboard ship, but admitted to his command that he was gay. Because of that admission, the Navy discharged him on April 9, 2002. Even though Sparks' command recommended he receive an honorable discharge, he was given a general discharge.

Stacy Vasquez joined the U.S. Army in 1991, immediately after high school. She trained as a paralegal and worked in that capacity for about ten years. In 2002, Vasquez was ordered to attend recruiting school. She was selected as the Distinguished Honor Graduate from both recruiting school and advanced noncommissioned officer paralegal studies courses. During Vasquez's annual evaluation in 2002, while she was under investigation, she was cited as the top recruiter in the Army and told she should be promoted ahead of her peers. In January 2003, Vasquez's commander told her that a coworker's wife had seen her kissing a woman at a club in Dallas. Vasquez's commander told her that he liked Vasquez's work as a recruiter and would not tell anybody about the allegation if Vasquez would write a statement saying that she was a lesbian. Several of Vasquez's coworkers tried to convince her not to write such a statement, but Vasquez wrote it anyway. Contrary to her commander's promise, Vasquez was removed from her recruiting job and the Army began an investigation into her sexual orientation based on her letter. Vasquez was forced to sit aimlessly each day for several months in her first sergeant's office. Finally, Vasquez was discharged from the military in August 2003. At the time of her honorable discharge, Vasquez had served in the Army for nearly twelve years. Vasquez earned many awards and commendations during her long Army career, including six Army Commendation Medals, five Army Achievement Medals, three Army Good Conduct Medals, two National Defense Service Medals, Armed Forces Reserve Medal with "M" device, Army Service Ribbon, three Overseas Service Ribbons, three NCO Professional Development awards, Sergeant Audie Murphy Club Member, Physical Fitness Excellence Award, Expert Marksmanship Qualification Badge with Grenade Bar, Marksman Marksmanship Qualification Badge with Rifle Bar, Driver and Mechanic Badge with Driver Bar, U.S. Army Gold Recruiter Badge with three Sapphire Achievement Stars, and the U.S. Army Basic Recruiter Badge with three Gold Achievement Stars. She had attained the rank of Sergeant First Class (E-7) with recruiter and paralegal specialties.

Conclusion

It is true that many of those who have been discharged under "Don't Ask, Don't Tell" have had their careers ended because, in some fashion, they "told." What the stories above only begin to convey is the stress and strain of serving in silence and in the face of harassment. And, in cases like those of Dr. Hill, it is a choice of no choice—forced to choose between duty to one's family and duty to the military. It is no surprise that many exceptional men and women make the decision to leave the military. Yet, the fact that many service members find themselves compelled to "tell," thus violating the policy, does not negate the loss.

Consider the story of former Army Captain Jesse Berglund. In 2000, as he graduated from the University of Minnesota, Berglund received his commission as a lieutenant through ROTC and served on active duty from 2000 to 2005. During this time he was stationed at Fort Bliss, Texas, in Saudi Arabia, and in South Korea. While on active duty, Berglund began to realize that he might be gay. He considered remaining on active duty, but realizing that he was, in fact, a gay man he chose to leave. Now a member of the Individual Ready Reserve, Berglund could still be ordered to active duty. He occasionally receives letters asking if he might consider joining a reserve unit or returning to active duty, but as an openly gay man he is unable to do so. Berglund has stated that if he could serve openly, he would. In fact, Berglund, now a law student, was compelled to turn down an Army program that would have paid for his legal education. The program would have committed him to six more years of active duty, something he would have been quick to do were it not for being forced to live a lie.

Another veteran, "Jack," offered the following:

> Yeah, "don't ask, don't tell," but if we catch you during our witch hunt you're screwed. "Don't ask, don't tell" just means that they don't ask you directly, they ask your buddies, they ask everyone at the gay bars if they've ever seen you in there, and they ask your former spouse if she thinks you are gay and if that might be the reason you split up. That's exactly what happened to a buddy of mine, and when I was asked and adamantly maintained that he wasn't gay, the "investigators" started suggesting that maybe I wasn't willing to give him up because I was gay too and trying to cover for him to protect myself. Well, I'm not gay, I am out of the Army now, married with two kids. And my buddy got out, too, and he's married with kids now. I'm not saying that gays belong in the Army, but the Army policy and the mis-application of it drove him to get out, and the Army lost a good troop.[10]

Regardless of whether one supports or opposes the military service of gay men and lesbians, there can be no argument over whether they have served admirably, nor about the cost of the policy, in organizational, human, and financial terms. Some believe that the ends—keeping gay men and lesbians out of the military— justify the means, and costs. Others argue that the policy is despicable and the costs unconscionable. And, still others may find themselves in general support of the policy, but appalled at the costs, or even just one particular "type" of cost. No matter one's position, there is little doubt that "Don't Ask, Don't Tell"

exacts a great toll on the military, service members and their friends and families, and taxpayers. The debate remains over whether or not that toll is reasonable.

Notes

1. Four service members were granted bad conduct discharges. Data were unavailable
for 417 service members. U.S. Government Accountability Office, February 2005, *Military
Personnel: Financial Costs and Loss of Critical Skills Due to DOD's Homosexual Conduct Policy
Cannot Be Completely Estimated*, p. 7.

2. Ibid., p. 20.

3. Ibid.

4. Ibid., p. 3.

5. All discharge data obtained from SLDN annual reports.

6. Department of the Army's 91st Division (Training), *Sexual Harassment and Sexual
Discrimination*, October 20, 1992, p. 2.

7. Testimony of Captain Guy Richardson, U.S. Marine Corps, at Article 39(a) hearing
of SGT Mary Kyle, 1988, quoted in Michelle M. Benecke and Kirstin S. Dodge, "Military
Women in Nontraditional Job Fields: Casualties of the Armed Forces' War on Homosexuals," *Harvard Women's Law Journal*, 1990, p. 232.

8. All biographical material contained in this section was provided by SLDN
(www.sldn.org) and appears, edited, with their permission.

9. See Appendix I for a summary of the case.

10. http://alexandertheaverage.blogspot.com/2006/02/brokeback-barracks.html.

CHAPTER 4

The International Experience

Aaron Belkin and Melissa Sheridan Embser-Herbert

While many nations across the globe have, in the past, had policies that restricted the military service of gay men and lesbians, many have now either completely eliminated them or modified them considerably. Because of the range of policies, it is, indeed, a complex task to track the status of regulations and customs concerning gays and lesbians in armed forces around the world. Some nations have never had a formal ban. In many instances, especially those where homosexuality is not only condemned but also illegal, this is presumed to be because it simply never occurred to them that it was an issue. If a nation essentially denies that homosexuals are among its citizens, there is no need for a policy banning them from military service. In other nations nothing exists to ban all gays and lesbians from military service, but there have been restrictions on the type of service they can perform.

As best as researchers have been able to determine, countries that allow gays— and lesbians, where women serve at all—to serve in the military are Australia, Austria, Belgium, Canada, Czech Republic, Denmark, Estonia, Finland, France, Germany, Great Britain, Ireland, Israel, Italy, Lithuania, Luxembourg, Netherlands, New Zealand, Norway, Slovenia, South Africa, Spain, Sweden, and Switzerland. Other nations which may or may not be included in this list include, for example, Greece, which bans gay officers, but permits enlisted conscripts who are gay to insist on fulfilling their service obligation, and Portugal, which has no formal ban but may screen out gays during the induction process. As noted above, it is incredibly labor-intensive to determine with great accuracy what a country permits or prohibits by law and what really happens on a day-to-day basis. Not only do laws change, but the application of the law may vary from one location or command to another. It is worth noting that this can also be said of the United States. In addition to the discretion granted commanders, one scholar may interpret "Don't Ask, Don't Tell" as prohibiting the service of gays and lesbians and place the United States in the "no open service" column. Another, however, might interpret the policy as permitting their service, provided that they do not "tell," and place the United States in the "yes" column.[1]

Three nations with which the United States is often perceived as having the most in common are Canada, Australia, and Great Britain. Canada and Australia lifted their bans in 1992; Great Britain did so in 2000. Sociologist Charles Moskos, often considered the primary author of "Don't Ask, Don't Tell," said, "No neat and tidy lessons can be drawn from one country to another."[2] And, during the 1993 Senate hearings, retired Lieutenant General Calvin Waller said that it was a "grave disservice" to draw comparisons between the United States and the armed forces of smaller nations.[3] While it is true that it may not be possible to draw "neat and tidy lessons," and many military leaders, politicians, and jurists deride the notion that the United States might learn from other nations, the fact remains that their experiences may be instructive.

The following sections each provide a brief overview of policies concerning gays and lesbians in the armed forces of Canada, Australia, and Great Britain.

Canada[4]

Prior to 1988, the Canadian Forces' (CF) policy on gays and lesbians was published in Canadian Forces Administrative Order (CFAO) 19-20, entitled "Homosexuality–Sexual Abnormality Investigation, Medical Examination and Disposal." This administrative order stated that "service policy does not allow homosexual members or members with a sexual abnormality to be retained in the Canadian forces.[5] The CF did not permit openly gay men and lesbians to enlist and any soldier later discovered to be gay or lesbian was to be dismissed. The order also required that other military personnel inform on those fellow service members they suspected were homosexual. Investigations of suspected service members' sexual orientation were handled by the Special Investigations Unit of the CF.[6]

After Canada passed the Canadian Human Rights Act (CHRA) in 1978, and later the Canadian Charter of Rights and Freedoms, the policy came under scrutiny by both the judiciary and political bodies. While the CHRA did not explicitly cover sexual orientation, it did require employers to justify their exclusionary or restrictive policies. Although the Charter itself became a part of the Canadian Constitution in 1982, Section 15, the section governing equality, did not come into effect until 1985. The Charter, considered analogous to the U.S. Bill of Rights, also did not include sexual orientation in its enumerated list of prohibited grounds of discrimination. Section 15 of the Charter, did, however, enable the restriction of other forms of discrimination if so ruled by the courts.[7]

In 1985, a review of federal regulations by the Justice Department determined that the CF were potentially in violation of the equal rights provisions of the Charter in a number of areas, including its discrimination against gays and lesbians.[8] In response to the Justice Department's findings, the Department of National Defence conducted a survey of 6,580 soldiers to assess the potential impact of a removal of the ban on homosexual soldiers. Not unlike similar surveys done in the United States in the 1990s, the survey found that military personnel, particularly men, were strongly against removing the ban. Service members expressed concern about all aspects of serving with gays and lesbians; 62 percent of male soldiers stated that they would refuse to share showers, undress, or sleep in the same room as a gay soldier, and 45 percent declared that they would refuse to work with gays. Many also stated that they would refuse to be supervised by a gay or lesbian soldier.[9] The Department of National Defence's Charter Task Force recommended in its final report that the exclusionary policy toward homosexuals be retained, arguing that the unique character and purpose of the armed forces necessitated the restriction of gays and lesbians. Given the aversion toward homosexuals in the military, the report concluded that the "the presence of homosexuals in the CF would be detrimental to cohesion and morale, discipline, leadership, recruiting, medical fitness, and the rights to privacy of other members." It further declared that "the effect of the presence of homosexuals would [lead to] a serious decrease in operational effectiveness."[10]

In response to the Final Report, the new Minister of Defence announced that it was his intention to modify the existing policy only slightly. Under the change, the CF would not knowingly enroll homosexuals. If servicemen or women were discovered or announced themselves to be gay, they would be asked to leave, but they would not be dismissed. Those who chose to stay would not be eligible for training courses, security clearances, transfers, promotions, or reenlistment.[11] Such an approach, of course, would effectively "dismiss" service members, though the date would simply not be as immediate as with an actual dismissal. The CF had, at that point, already removed the obligation of service members to report on suspicions that another solider may be homosexual.[12]

In spite of the measures taken by the Department of National Defence, pressure to change the policy on homosexuals continued to increase. As court decisions extended the rights of gays and lesbians under the Human Rights Act and the Charter of Rights and Freedoms, Lieutenant Michelle Douglas and four others filed separate suits against the CF that directly challenged its policy toward homosexuals. In August 1990, the Security Intelligence Committee ruled that the military ban against homosexuals violated the Charter and found in Douglas' favor. In preparing its appeal in the Douglas case, the Department of National Defence concluded that it could not meet the standard of proof required for a "reasonable limitation" argument under the Charter. That is, they could not justify, within the parameters provided by law, the exclusion of gays and lesbians from the armed forces.

While the Chief of the Defence Staff General John de Chastelain privately informed members of Parliament that the ban was about to be lifted late in 1991, the federal government delayed in the wake of an adamant refusal by some Conservative members of Parliament to support the policy change.[13] Finally, facing a case it knew it could not win and lacking the leadership needed to defend its policy, the Department of National Defence agreed to settle the case against

Douglas in October 1992. In so doing, the military acknowledged that its policy of exclusion violated the Charter of Rights and Freedoms, and it consented to the immediate repeal of that policy.[14]

The policy change in October 1992 concerning gay and lesbian soldiers in the Canadian military was not so much an affirmative order as it was the dismantling of existing policy. General de Chastelain issued a press report that declared, "The Canadian Forces will comply fully with the Federal Court's decision. Canadians, regardless of their sexual orientation, will now be able to serve their country without restriction."[15] In a communiqué entitled "Homosexual Conduct," the Chief of Defence revoked CFAO 19-20 and all related interim policies. The military would no longer draw a distinction between its heterosexual and homosexual soldiers. He expressed his "full support" of the Federal Court's decision and stated his expectations of support of the policy change within the chain of command. General de Chastelain also declared that "inappropriate sexual conduct by members of the forces, whether heterosexual or homosexual," was unacceptable.[16]

Because the courts provided the impetus for change, senior leaders endorsed the change and encouraged the members' sense of duty. Senior political and military leaders believed that reliance on equal standards for the conduct of gays and heterosexuals was the best chance for success of the policy, since it focused on behavior rather than a transformation of individual values or beliefs. The military made no effort at the time to change individual members' attitudes about homosexuality. Instead, the CF promoted the policy change through unequivocal answers to specific questions about appropriate behavior.[17]

In December 1992, the CF issued a new regulation (CFAO 19-36) entitled "Sexual Misconduct." CFAO 19-36 was to be used with an amended version of personal harassment regulations to detail what constituted inappropriate sexual conduct for both homosexual and heterosexual soldiers. Sexual misconduct was defined as "an act which has a sexual purpose or is of a sexual or indecent nature and which . . . constitutes an offence under the Criminal Code or the Code of Service Discipline."[18] Under the personal harassment regulations (CFAO 19-39), sexual harassment was defined as " . . . a type of personal harassment that has a sexual purpose or is of a sexual nature including, but not limited to, touching, leering, lascivious remarks, and the display of pornographic material."[19]

The Canadian military itself did not undertake an initial assessment of the implementation of its new policy concerning homosexuals. Because the idea of allowing gays to openly serve in the military became a volatile issue in the United States soon after Canada's removal of the ban, several analyses were conducted by organizations on behalf of the U.S. Congress and military. These included studies by the National Defense Research Institute (RAND) and the General Accounting Office (GAO), as well as a report by a retired Canadian corporal for the U.S. Army Research Institute. These analyses, as well as journalistic accounts, suggested that the transition was a smooth one. Despite concerns that service members would resign, harassment would increase, and morale would suffer, the reports could find no evidence that any aspect of military life had been negatively affected.

While many heterosexual service members were unhappy with the removal of the ban, they responded professionally in the months following the policy change. Few homosexual soldiers, however, took the opportunity to explicitly state their sexual orientation during this time.

RAND researchers conducted interviews with Canadian military personnel several months after the removal of the ban on gay and lesbian soldiers. They found no evidence that the policy change had had any appreciable effect on any aspect of military life or performance. The officials with whom researchers spoke " . . . kn[e]w to date of no instances of people acknowledging or talking about their homosexual relationships, no fights or violent incidents, no resignations (despite previous threats to quit), no problems with recruitment, and no diminution of cohesion, morale, or organizational effectiveness."[20]

Canadian officials offered several reasons for the smooth transition. First, the military leadership had acknowledged the inevitability of the change in policy. Because the process had occurred over time, the military had been able to acculturate itself to the idea of including openly homosexual soldiers. Second, the military adopted a conscious leadership strategy in the implementation phase. Highest priority was given to ensure compliance with the policy change. Military leaders decided that it was not appropriate to try to change the beliefs or attitudes of individual personnel; they did, however, prioritize acceptance of the policy to minimize possible friction. Third, military officials emphasized the fact that the implementation had been accomplished in a low-profile fashion, without numerous public pronouncements or media scrutiny. Finally, officials cited the content of the policy itself as a reason for the smooth change. Officials pointed out that the policy change itself did not formally institute a policy on gay and lesbian conduct; rather, it established new equitable policies that applied to homosexuals and heterosexuals alike.

The GAO analysis of the first six months of Canada's new policy also found no problems associated with the change. In their interviews with members of Parliament, gay advocacy groups, a veterans' umbrella group, the Canadian Human Rights Commission, the Department of National Defence, and the Department of Justice, the researchers could find no one who had received any reports of resignations, lower recruitment, morale or cohesiveness problems, or gay-bashing incidents. In addition, the GAO found no reports of open displays of homosexual behavior.

CF officials reported that the greatest advantage of the change in policy was that gay and lesbian soldiers no longer had to fear being discovered and discharged from the armed forces. These officials felt, however, that many gay and lesbian soldiers would not publicly express their orientation because they would see no advantage in doing so. The military leadership's public support for the removal of the ban and its unified front were cited as significant reasons for the smooth transition.[21]

At the request of the Deputy Chief of Staff of the U.S. Army, the U.S. Army Research Institute for the Behavioral and Social Sciences issued a report in

January 1994 authored by an outside consultant evaluating early outcomes of the lifting of the ban in Canada. The report surveyed all publicly available literature to describe the original impetus to lift the ban as well as the consequences of the 1992 policy change on a broad array of performance outcomes in the CF. In its summary of findings, the report states, "The impact of the policy change has been minimal. Negative consequences predicted in the areas of recruitment, employment, attrition, retention, and cohesion and morale have not occurred in the 6-month period since revocation of the exclusionary policy."[22]

Although the Canadian military has never undertaken a formal assessment of the policy change toward sexual minorities, a briefing note on the removal of the ban was written by the section head for Human Rights Policy (a bureau of the Canadian Department of National Defence) in 1995. Two and one half years after the removal of the ban, the note still could not find any indication that the policy change had had a negative effect on the CF. The 1995 note was originally prepared in response to a request for information by U.S. lawyers defending a discharged Navy lieutenant under the U.S. military's policy on homosexuals. Although the CF official was ultimately prohibited from offering an affidavit for the U.S. case, he took the opportunity to share the data he had gathered with the CF command. He wanted to let them know that "[d]espite all the anxiety that existed through the late 80s into the early 90s about the change in policy, here's what the indicators show—no effect."[23]

The briefing note also cited a 1993 attitudinal survey on quality of life issues which asked members, among other items, to describe how satisfied they were with the CF's policy on sexual orientation.[24] Out of 3,202 respondents, 43.3 percent were either satisfied or very satisfied with the policy, 24.4 percent stated they were neutral, 28.5 percent were either dissatisfied or very dissatisfied, and 3.8 percent had no opinion. The 1995 note compared these findings to a question on employing women in all units and occupations. In response to the question on female involvement, 44.1 percent stated they were either satisfied or very satisfied, 21.0 percent were neutral, 32.9 percent were either dissatisfied or very dissatisfied, and 2.1 percent had no opinion. The Human Rights policy officer noted that acceptance of the military's policy toward gays and lesbians was quite similar overall to attitudes toward the inclusion of women. Analysis of the 1993 survey further revealed that female service members were generally more accepting than males of the sexual orientation policy (although no figures were provided), and senior officers were overall the most dissatisfied (37.5%) and junior noncommissioned officers were the least dissatisfied (25.7%) with the policy. In his conclusion to the 1995 brief, the CF officer declared that "behavioral and conduct data . . . yield little or no evidence to suggest that allowing homosexuals to serve in the Canadian Forces has been problematic, either in terms of their behavior or their treatment by other members."[25]

The CF removal of the ban on gay and lesbian soldiers occurred only after years of judicial and political struggles. Senior personnel of the Department of National Defence and a sizable number of heterosexual soldiers were worried that a change in policy would seriously compromise the mission of the CF. Fears of sexual harassment by homosexual soldiers, increasing rates of gay-bashing, resignations, and refusals to work with homosexuals had spurred continuing support for exempting the military from the protections proscribed under the Charter of Rights and Freedoms. Because the CF is entrusted with the fundamental task of putting soldiers' lives on the line to protect the interests of Canadian citizens, both at home and abroad, military personnel were wary of a policy change that they felt could compromise the operational effectiveness of the armed services.

Once the demise of the ban was imminent, however, Chief of the Defence Staff General Chastelain and other military leaders took decisive steps to create a smooth transition. They dissolved any distinction in the regulations between heterosexual and homosexual soldiers. They made it clear that the policy change had the full support of the CF leadership. The Department of National Defence outlined the standards of behavior that would be expected of all military personnel, regardless of sexual orientation, and it widely distributed both the standards and the changes in regulations. Perhaps, most importantly, the military leadership emphasized the distinction between beliefs and behavior. The personal attitudes and decisions of individual soldiers would be respected, but soldiers would be expected to put personal feelings aside to accomplish military objectives and to uphold the law.

In the years since the removal of the ban, the CF has continued to move forward in its full integration of gay and lesbian soldiers, and it has done so as part of a larger effort to reduce harassment and discrimination of all types among its personnel. In these efforts, sexual orientation has been neither singled out nor ignored as a potential source of conflict. Among other objectives, the Standards for Harassment and Racism Prevention (SHARP) program strove to overturn common stereotypes about gays and lesbians, and the CF is now developing more sustained antiharassment training. In keeping with federal mandate, the military has also been amending its regulations to ensure equivalent benefits for same-sex soldiers.

The success of these steps has been borne out by all of the available evidence. An examination of all of the studies conducted in the year after the removal of the ban revealed not a single reported case of resignation, harassment, or violence because of the change in policy. Follow-up with the officials in charge of sexual harassment, sexual misconduct, and human rights complaints have reported few if any incidents related to sexual orientation. Sexual and personal harassment rates actually decreased between 1992 and 1998. In research conducted in 2000, CF officials, military scholars, involved nongovernmental and political leaders, and gay soldiers have all concurred that the removal of the ban has had, to their knowledge, no perceivable negative effect on the military. The issue of gay and lesbian soldiers in the CF has all but disappeared from public and internal military debates.

One interesting footnote concerning the CF policy change is that, in 2003, in response to the approval of same-sex marriage, across Canada, province by province, the Interfaith Committee on Canadian Military Chaplaincy issued

"Interim Guidelines for Canadian Forces Chaplains." Chaplains were instructed to treat all couples with respect and dignity, but given permission to act in accordance with their faith and conscience. While chaplains may refuse to officiate, they are obligated to refer the couple to a chaplain or civilian clergy member who can do so. The guidelines state, "In a real sense the ministry provided by the Canadian Forces chaplains is a witness to the culture in which we live. We respond pastorally, prophetically and compassionately to the changing perspectives of culture as an ecumenical team."[26] In May 2005, what is believed to have been the first same-sex wedding on a Canadian military installation took place on Nova Scotia's Greenwood airbase.

While the removal of the ban may not be universally liked among heterosexual soldiers, it does appear to be universally accepted. Despite potential differences, personnel appear to be able to get their jobs done in a manner that does not compromise their effectiveness. For sexual minorities who serve, the change has been less about publicly declaring their sexual or transgender orientation than about being able to do their work well without fear of "being found out" or losing their jobs. The removal of the ban has resulted in a decrease of fear and anxiety and improved access to personnel support systems for soldiers who self-identify as sexual minorities. For the military as a whole, the nondiscrimination policy has also increased its potential pool of qualified recruits.

Australia[27]

Like the armed forces in many other Anglophone countries, the Australian Defence Forces (ADF) maintained both formal and informal rules proscribing the participation of known homosexuals from 1986 to 1992. Prior to 1986, the ADF did not maintain a formal policy regarding the participation of homosexuals. According to a report by the U.S. General Accounting Office (now the Government Accountability Office), recruits were not formally questioned about their sexual orientation before 1986. However, informal efforts frequently were made to identify and document activities of personnel suspected of homosexual conduct, usually followed by the removal of such personnel from duty. Existing state and federal laws proscribing sodomy and homosexual relations usually were invoked to enforce these actions.[28]

In the 1980s, as Australia incorporated international human rights accords into its national laws, federal and state governments actively dismantled existing laws against homosexuality and began to ratify new human rights bills that included protection against arbitrary discrimination. As a result, the ADF could no longer justify antihomosexual practices on the basis of territorial laws and was required to issue its own policy. It did so in September 1986, and the ban on homosexual service became an explicit and formal part of ADF instructions.[29]

In the late 1980s and early 1990s, a number of economic, social, and cultural factors served to undermine the perceived legitimacy and rationale of the ADF ban on homosexual service. To begin, military leaders encountered criticisms of

ADF policies concerning equality of opportunity and racial and ethnic diversity. In 1992, the government examined charges that the ADF was not recruiting a sufficient portion of its soldiers from non-European populations and the result was a major study of the ethnic makeup of the forces.[30] Debates over the status and treatment of women in the ADF also influenced the perceived legitimacy of the ban on gay service. Though women had been able to participate in the Australian military for many years, either directly or through auxiliary branches like the Women's Royal Australian Army Corps, they were not allowed to take combat roles until the late 1980s. Smith points out that the three service branches began to face difficulties in retaining qualified personnel: "The ADF thus had a clear incentive to open more positions to women, thereby expanding the pool of potential recruits."[31]

In the years shortly before government and ADF officials considered lifting the ban on homosexuals, Australia adopted several human rights measures into its laws and codes including the International Covenant on Civil and Political Rights (ICCPR). Article 26 of the ICCPR posits the fundamental equality of all human beings and Article 2 addresses each individual's right to equal treatment before the law. Although sexual orientation is not included explicitly in the ICCPR's list of prohibited justifications for discrimination, Australian Human Rights Commissioner Chris Sidoti says that the ICCPR's list was meant to be inclusive rather than exclusive. Therefore, although not explicitly mentioned, sexual orientation is covered by the spirit of the ICCPR and it cannot serve as the basis of discrimination. Opponents of the ADF ban argued that the military was in violation of these human rights provisions in Australian law.

As civil rights considerations came to play an increasingly important role in the Australian political landscape, the ADF encountered a number of social and international trends that changed the understanding of its own mission and its relationship with civilian society. In particular, the end of the Cold War forced the ADF to reevaluate its role as a fighting force and many Australians came to see military service as a temporary occupation rather than a long-term career. Professor Hugh Smith has argued that during the Cold War, many Australians regarded the military as a calling and a lifetime vocation. According to the old mindset, a career in the armed forces meant that military life always took precedence over other priorities. Smith says that according to the new "occupational" mindset of many Australians, however, a military career is "just another job." Except in extraordinary circumstances like combat, soldiers now expect regular working hours, free weekends, pension and benefits, and other freedoms and privileges associated with the civilian world. In the late 1980s and early 1990s, much of Australian society moved toward an occupational outlook on most careers including military service, and just as the rest of Australian society was moving toward greater tolerance and support for individual rights and freedoms, the military found itself needing to adjust.[32]

As the center-left/left party in Australian politics, the Labour government that controlled Parliament in the late 1980s and early 1990s faced some disagreement within its own ranks over social issues such as the lifting of the ban on gays and lesbians in the military. As Rodney Croome points out, some members of Labour's caucus supported "traditional family values" and opposed lifting the ban. Others were traditional progressives, committed to an expansion of what they argued were equal rights for all Australians.

In a 1990 test of the military ban on homosexuals, a servicewoman made a formal complaint to the Australian Human Rights and Equal Opportunities Commission (HREOC) and contended that her discharge had been partially based upon the fact that she was a lesbian. The HREOC asked the ADF to explain the reasoning behind its ban on homosexual service. In February 1992, the Minister for Defence Science and Personnel informed Parliament that the federal government would review the ADF's ban. In June 1992, however, the Defense Minister told Parliament that following the recommendation of the Chiefs of Staff, the Government would not lift the ban.

The Government formed a special party committee to study the matter, to accept submissions from interested groups, and to make policy recommendations for the government. In September 1992, this committee recommended that the ban be dropped "immediately." The caucus committee also recommended that the ADF undertake a survey of members' attitudes and engage in an education campaign as part of the lifting of the ban. Committee members who favored lifting the ban contended that the military was not significantly different from other organizations and thus should not be exempt from antidiscriminatory policy changes being made elsewhere. Those who opposed the removal of the personnel restrictions contended that such a change would hinder the military's operational effectiveness, combat performance, and morale.

In late November 1992, the Cabinet accepted the Caucus Committee recommendation and the government voted to drop the ban on the service of gays and lesbians in the Australian military. Although the Defense Minister and the service chiefs opposed the removal of the ban, the Attorney General, the Health Minister, and the Prime Minister all supported its removal. The Attorney General argued that Australia's policy violated international human rights agreements not to discriminate against people based upon sexual orientation and the Health Minister said that by pushing military members to keep their relationships "underground," the ban contradicted efforts to fight AIDS. Prime Minister Paul Keating then made the decision to accept the policy change and to order its immediate implementation in the entire ADF.

In place of the previous military regulation banning gays and lesbians from service, the government issued a more general instruction on "sexual misconduct policy." Among other provisions, the new instruction referred to unacceptable conduct without making a distinction between homosexuality and heterosexuality. Rather than define what was unacceptable based upon sexual orientation, in other words, the new instruction prohibited any sexual behavior that negatively impacted group cohesion or command relationships, took advantage of subordinates, or discredited the ADF.[33] Thus, for example, "homosexual advances" were not illegitimate; threatening sexual behavior was. And the policy provided commanders with some latitude to judge whether a certain behavior was acceptable or not in a certain context.

Reaction to the Australian change was swift and severe. The Returned and Services League, Australia's largest veterans group, condemned the policy change and argued that allowing open homosexuals to serve would shatter unit cohesion and lead to a deterioration of trust among soldiers, thus undermining the forces' fighting effectiveness.[34] Other opponents raised the specter of AIDS and said that the battlefield practice of direct blood-to-blood transfers would lead to an increased incidence of HIV infection. Even within the military, however, opinion seemed to be somewhat mixed. As of January 1993, however, no members of the ADF had declared themselves to be gay to military authorities. Early reports generated in the immediate aftermath of the policy change indicated that the ADF did not experience any decline in recruiting or combat performance and media attention to the issue largely disappeared approximately six months after the new policy's implementation.

After the lifting of the ban, the ADF introduced a variety of new programs and training courses to enforce and support the provisions of the Defence Instruction on Discrimination, Harassment, Sexual Offences, Fraternisation and other Unacceptable Behavior in the Australian Defence Forces (2000). In 1997, responsibilities for monitoring, education, and enforcement of the instructions were consolidated into the new Defence Equity Organization (DEO) that reports directly to the Defence Personnel Executive (the head of personnel for the ADF).

In June 1993, seven months after the Australian ban on homosexual service was lifted, the General Accounting Office of the United States conducted interviews with ADF officials to document early outcomes associated with the change. The short overview of the policy change concluded with a summary statement based on comments from an "Australian official," who stated that " . . . although it is too early to assess the results of the revised policy, no reported changes have occurred in the number of persons declaring his or her sexual preference or the number of recruits being inducted. Effects on unit cohesiveness have not yet been fully determined. However, early indications are that the new policy has had little or no adverse impact."[35]

In February 1996, the United Kingdom Ministry of Defence completed a report documenting the findings of its "Homosexuality Policy Assessment Team" that investigated homosexual personnel policies of a number of foreign militaries. The team sent to Australia met with representatives of the Royal Australian Air Force, Royal Australian Army, and Royal Australian Navy, as well as with Dr. Hugh Smith of the ADF Academy and service psychologists at ADF headquarters in Canberra. Regarding implementation of the policy, the British team reported that service staffs believed that the change had not resulted in any notable problems for military functioning. The opinions of personnel drawn from the services, however, varied in their assessments of potential difficulties arising from the policy change. According to the report, male members of a random volunteer group from the Royal Australian Air Force were largely against the new policy and believed that open homosexuals would have a negative effect on unit effectiveness. However, personnel drawn from an Army Logistics unit, as well as a Royal Australian Navy group based in Sydney, emphasized equality and nondiscrimination regardless of personal opinions on homosexuality per se.

The DEO serves as the primary ADF unit responsible for development, implementation, training, and support for all policies regarding equity, diversity, and sexual misconduct in the military. Formed in August 1997 during a widespread reorganization of the ADF, the DEO consolidated responsibilities that had been assigned separately to each service branch as well as a human rights policy area within Defence headquarters (now defunct). In addition to supporting the implementation of ministry policies, DEO handles complaints regarding all matters of sexual misconduct including harassment, bullying, and assault, provides an anonymous advice line for service members and commanders, and directs the training and outreach activities of "Equity Advisors" throughout the forces. The director of DEO, Ms. Bronwen Grey, occupied the analogous directorship in Defence headquarters until 1997.

According to an interview conducted with Director Grey in 2000, all available formal and informal evidence regarding outcomes associated with the 1992 policy change suggested that, in spite of early fears of deleterious consequences, the lifting of the gay ban has had no adverse effects on the capability or functioning of the Defence forces: "I have to say, from that point on [the 1992 change], nothing happened. I mean people were expecting the sky to fall, and it didn't. Now, a number of gay people probably didn't come out at that point, but we've had an X.O. of a ship come out and say to the ship's company, 'I'm gay,' and, quite frankly, no one cared."[36]

When pushed by the interviewer to identify any problems that may have arisen after the ban was lifted, the Director did note that some gay people probably did not feel comfortable revealing their sexual orientation immediately after the change. Nonetheless, she said that a number of individuals had unambiguously come out to peers and commanding officers and that their revelations had no negative consequences for their careers or personal relationships. When asked to clearly specify any other concrete observations of what she termed a virtual "non event," the Director added, "All I can say is, from the organizational point of view, while we were waiting for problems . . . we were ready. Nothing happened. There were no increased complaints or recruiting [problems] at all . . . .I mean nothing happened. And it's very hard to document nothing."[37]

The Australian Human Rights and Equal Opportunities Commission is a statutory body that enjoys a relatively autonomous status in Australian politics that is analogous to courts. The Commission's members are appointed by the government and it receives its budget through the normal budgetary process but it is not accountable to the federal government, the bureaucracy, or political parties. Now retired, Human Rights Commissioner Chris Sidoti had made gay and lesbian equality one of the priorities of his five-year tenure at the Human Rights Commission. Although Sidoti had little authority to force organizations to change their practices, he was responsible for investigating complaints and suggesting legislative reforms to minimize and eliminate discrimination in Australia. Sidoti, agreeing with most of the observations of military and academic experts, when contacted by Belkin and McNichol, indicated that there had been virtually no significant effects of the policy change on the military.

Systematic evidence concerning the lifting of the Australian ban on gays and lesbians in the military is scarce. Work by Belkin and McNichol attempts to redress the gap by drawing together and comparing the findings and observations of informed observers from a variety of vantage points in the policy domain. Taken together, their data make a convincing and credible case that, notwithstanding uneven and partial implementation of the policy, the 1992 inclusion of self-described gay and lesbian soldiers into the ADF has not led to any perceptible decline in operational effectiveness, morale, unit cohesion, retention, or attrition. In fact, ADF officials and a number of other observers, including commanders and soldiers, believe that changes associated with the policy have contributed to a working environment that is freer from the burdensome and unproductive consequences of mistrust, misunderstanding, and misjudgment that at times compromised the integrity of units in the past. As part of a broader commitment to equity in the ADF, then, the policy change has been a success.

One result of the policy change came about in October 2005 when the ADF extended partner and family benefits to service personnel in same-sex relationships. A separate issue, however, is the extension of benefits to veterans. The partners of gay and lesbian veterans are unable to receive the same benefits provided to the spouses of heterosexual veterans. In one interesting turn of events, while the ADF has taken the progressive step of providing benefits to its personnel in same-sex relationships, the Australian Coalition for Equality notes that civilian same-sex couples do not have the same protections. Under most areas of federal law, such as taxation and social security, there is no recognition for same-sex couples.

While the general consensus in the findings above is clear, a close look at the evidence also reveals a number of concerns. Isolated instances of discrimination and harassment still exist, and some service branches may be less proactive in their policies than others. These difficulties may be even more pervasive among the ranks of heterosexual women, who experience higher rates of harassment than gay males. From the perspective of gay and lesbian soldiers and their allies, the failure of the ADF to extend benefits that are accorded to heterosexual spouses to same-sex partners stands as a reminder of a partially fulfilled mission. At the same time, however, the fact that the debate over gays in the military has shifted away from the question of whether homosexual soldiers undermine military performance also stands as a testament to the success of the inclusive policy.

Great Britain[38]

Until January 2000, gay and lesbian soldiers were prohibited from serving in the British armed forces. Prior to 1967, British criminal and military law were congruous with respect to male homosexuality—sodomy was illegal and both civilians and soldiers could be imprisoned for homosexual activity. The 1967 Sexual Offences Act decriminalized private, consensual gay male sex for civilians aged 21 and over, but it included an exemption that allowed the British military to continue to prosecute male service members who engaged in gay sex.[39] However, while criminal law did not cover same-sex female sex acts, the military was able to discharge lesbians under the offense of general misconduct. Offenses for "homosexuality" were usually charged as "disgraceful conduct of an indecent kind," "conduct prejudicial to good order and military discipline," or more rarely "scandalous conduct by officers."[40] That is, it was the meaning imputed to homosexuality, rather than a specific prohibition on certain acts, that allowed lesbians to be discharged as well.[41]

In the wake of considerable Parliamentary debate on the subject during discussions about the 1991 Armed Forces Bill, the government acknowledged that the military exemption from the 1967 Sexual Offenses Act was no longer justifiable. In June 1992, the Ministry of Defense announced an administrative order to immediately halt criminal prosecution for sexual activities that were legal for civilians under the 1967 Act. The British restricted court-martials for homosexuality to those male service members who were found to have had sex in public or with anyone under the age of 21. The legislative reconciliation of military and civilian law occurred later with the passage of the 1994 Criminal Justice Act. The military persisted in maintaining, however, that both male and female homosexuality were incompatible with military service. Gay and lesbian soldiers continued to face discharge if their sexual orientation was discovered.

In 1994, the Ministry of Defense issued Service-wide regulations concerning homosexual soldiers. The new regulations maintained the policy of barring homosexual service, but they standardized policy and provided more detailed protocol. Any recruit who admitted to being gay would not be allowed to enlist, and any service member who was discovered to be homosexual would be discharged from the military. Homosexual sex between adults of consensual age would not be considered a criminal offense, but the military could prosecute a gay or lesbian soldier for otherwise consensual sex if "the act was to the prejudice of good order and Service discipline."[42] All recruits were to be informed that homosexuals were not allowed to serve in the British armed forces. The 1994 policy made it clear that homosexual orientation as well as homosexual behavior would be a bar to enlistment and service: even if a potential recruit admits to being homosexual, but states that he/she does not at present nor in the future intend to engage in homosexual activity, he/she will not be enlisted.[43]

In 1994, four service members discharged for homosexuality began a legal challenge in British courts against the military's ban on gay and lesbian soldiers.

Lawyers for the service members invoked the Wednesbury doctrine and the European Convention on Human Rights to argue that the privacy rights of the soldiers had been violated. In June 1995, the High Court ruled against the discharged service members on the grounds that the British courts did not have the authority to invoke the European Convention on Human Rights. Justices of the High Court signaled, however, that the policy was unlikely to withstand judgment by the European Court. Britain's Court of Appeals upheld the High Court's decision in November 1995.

A legal advisor for the Ministry of Defense also warned military officials that the British Forces were likely to lose their case with the European Court of Human Rights (ECHR), but the Armed Forces Minister and the three Service Chiefs of Staff were said to strongly support a continuation of the exclusion of homosexuals.[44] Instead, Defense Ministers ordered a relaxation of the ban. Military police were instructed not to actively search for gay and lesbian soldiers; they were only to act if a problem was drawn to their attention. The Defense Ministers also made it clear that overzealous investigation, surveillance, and harassment would no longer be tolerated.[45]

On September 27, 1999, the ECHR ruled unanimously that the ban on homosexual military service violated the privacy rights of the plaintiffs. Civil servants suggested that a new code of conduct could be put in place earlier than 2001, presumably because considerable work had already been done on it. A week after taking office, the new Secretary of State for Defense Geoffrey Hoon set aside "at least £4m" to cover pending compensation claims by homosexual ex-service members.[46] The more important question, however, was what model to choose for the new army regulations.

There was considerable opposition from both gay groups and services chiefs to basing the regulations on the American model, which was seen as "a disaster"; services chiefs saw the Dutch and Israeli options as "too liberal."[47] Stonewall recommended the Australian regulations, which bans heterosexual and homosexual public displays of affection, as a possible model.[48] In mid-December, Hoon announced that the new code would be published the following month, and that it would govern "sex not sexuality"—a reference to the Australian rules.

With respect to the model that was chosen, Michael Codner of the Royal United Services Institute explained: "I think both sides of the debate saw 'Don't Ask, Don't Tell' as something which hadn't worked, which was unworkable and hypocritical. The internal advice given to service chiefs by the civilian civil service was in favor of another model . . . . But the Australian model was pushed strongly by Australian service chiefs. Their defense attaches were also very proactive in pushing the success of the Australian option. And I think the British service chiefs saw some logic to it. The two forces have a similar structure and ethos.[49]

On January 12, 2000, the Secretary of State for Defense announced the lifting of the ban to the Commons. He declared that the European Court judgment made the ban "not legally sustainable" and proclaimed that a new code of conduct governing personal relationships, based on that of the Australian armed forces, would be introduced. No legislation was required to effect this change, which went into effect immediately. Discharged homosexuals were also invited to reapply for their jobs. Shadow Defense Minister Iain Duncan-Smith voiced "regret," and he said that if the Conservatives won the next election they would review the decision and allow military chiefs to decide.[50]

In their development of a new policy, the Ministry of Defense emphasized the need for (1) compliance with the ECHR ruling, (2) regulations that were nondiscriminatory; (3) the preservation of operational effectiveness, (4) accordance with the general requirements of the military, and (5) protection of individual rights under the Human Rights Act.[51] Homosexuality is no longer a bar to military service. Gay and lesbian soldiers are not, however, eligible for married accommodations, spousal pension, or other partnership rights. In addition, a code of social conduct establishes rules of behavior that apply equally to heterosexuals and homosexuals. Soldiers, regardless of sexual orientation or sex, are prohibited from engaging in social behavior that undermines, or may potentially undermine, the trust and cohesion, and therefore the operational effectiveness, of the services. Enumerated inappropriate behavior includes unwelcome physical or verbal sexual attention, overfamiliarity with the spouses of other service personnel, displays of affection which might cause offense to others, taking sexual advantage of subordinates, and behavior which damages the marriage or personal relationship of other service personnel. The code of conduct further covers other types of "social misbehavior" that have not been enumerated. Discretion is left up to the commanding officer to determine if behavior constitutes a threat to the cohesion of the unit or the military command chain. Abuse of authority, trust, or rank, or taking advantage of a person's separation, are deemed particularly serious types of misconduct.[52]

The new guidelines for social conduct are general and involve considerable discretion. The code therefore provides a "service test" for commanding officers to use in their assessment of the need to "intervene in the personal lives of personnel."[53] Commanding officers must consider each case in light of the following question: Have the actions or behavior of an individual adversely impacted or are they likely to impact on the efficiency or operational effectiveness of the Service? In the event of an affirmative answer, commanders are instructed to take prompt and decisive action to minimize damage to the effectiveness of the unit. If the misconduct is sufficiently serious, commanders may institute immediate administrative or punitive action. Such action may include a formal warning, official censure, the posting of the parties involved, or other disciplinary action. If the behavior is sufficiently serious, or if the service member has a history of social misconduct, termination of service may occur.

The Ministry of Defense also issued guidelines and speaking notes for commanding officers to help them explain and enforce the new policy. The speaking notes emphasize that the lifting of the ban brings the armed forces into greater concordance with the general society. A person's sexual orientation is to be considered a private matter, and every service member has a right to personal privacy. Commanders were further advised to stress the continuity of the policy: this change is not a major issue, and you should not make it into one. There have always been homosexuals serving in the armed forces. We do not expect that this change will result in a significant increase in the number of homosexuals coming into the Service.[54]

When the new policy was announced by Secretary of State for Defense Geoff Hoon on January 12, 2000, he highlighted the fact that the chiefs of staff were completely involved in the creation of the new policy and endorsed the changes. Secretary Hoon stated that the code would apply to all members of the Forces, regardless of "service, rank, gender or sexual orientation." He further stressed that the code complemented existing policies, including "zero tolerance for harassment, discrimination and bullying."[55]

The British armed forces fought for a number of years to maintain its policy of excluding openly gay and lesbian soldiers. Even after the outcome of the ECHR case appeared inevitable, the armed forces resisted calls to eliminate the ban. While the Ministry of Defense asked commanders to soften their enforcement of the ban in the months before the decision was handed down, it both refused to alter its basic policy and continued to dismiss soldiers for homosexuality. The last gay soldier was discharged from the military just three days before the ruling that overturned the ban on homosexual service. Service officials argued that the inclusion of open homosexuals would engender distrust, splinter working relationships, damage morale, and even harm operational effectiveness. Efforts to overturn the ban were deemed by some military officials to be inappropriate political meddling in military operations and harmful social engineering.

Once the decision was handed down by the European Court, however, the military acted quickly to put in place a policy that would both accord with the ruling and address effectiveness concerns. The armed forces enacted a new policy within three months of the decision by the European Court. It established a nondiscriminatory mandate that focuses on behavior rather than on personal characteristics. It emphasized the importance of equal application of the new social code of conduct and instructed commanders to intervene in soldiers' personal lives only when operational effectiveness might be compromised. It invited discharged soldiers to reapply and accepted back several former service personnel. The Services also reemphasized the policy of zero tolerance for harassment, bullying, and victimization.

Research by Belkin and Evans, conducted shortly after the ban was lifted, indicated that the Services' own internal assessment at six months found that the new policy had "been hailed as a solid achievement."[56] There had been no indications of negative effects on recruiting levels. The social code of conduct had been effectively incorporated into the military's training courses. No mass resignations had occurred. There had been no major reported cases of gay-bashing or harassment of sexual minorities. There had been no major reported cases of harassment or inappropriate behavior by gay or lesbian soldiers. There had been no perceived effect on morale, unit cohesion, or operational effectiveness. The new policy was being well received by soldiers, and the policy change was characterized by a "marked lack of reaction."[57]

Experts in all fields acknowledged that more work remains to be done, and new obstacles could still emerge. Homophobic attitudes persist throughout the Services, and many soldiers therefore feel the need to remain silent about their personal lives. It is possible that some problems will develop as more gay and lesbian service personnel acknowledge their sexual orientation to colleagues, or if the military relaxes its vigilance against harassment and inappropriate behavior of all kinds. Issues of equality such as pension, accommodation, and partnership rights have yet to be addressed. Still, the distance that has been traveled over the past few years is impressive. Concerns of dire consequences have been replaced by a general recognition that the transition has proceeded smoothly.

Conclusion

The experiences of the three nations profiled in this chapter suggest, at a minimum, five main conclusions. First, the attitudes and threats of service members prior to the elimination of any ban are not an accurate indication of what they will actually do once the ban is lifted. Second, while adequate preparation and training is necessary, making a "big deal" about the change may be counterproductive. Third, changing behaviors should not be confused with changing attitudes. That is, personnel need not change what may be deeply held personal convictions about gay men and lesbians. Rather, what they need to do is act in accordance with policy. Fourth, changes in policy would do well not to just address gays and lesbians, but to address issues of equal treatment for all service personnel. And, fifth, such a change may be far more readily accomplished when the sociopolitical and legal foundations of a nation demand, rather than resist, equal treatment under the law.

Some aspects of the American political process lead observers to believe that the lifting of the ban, while inevitable, may not happen for a number of years. There is no judicial or legislative body conceding that equality within the military is an inevitability to which one should begin adjusting. Rather, the U.S. Supreme Court has, as of this writing, refused to hear a case regarding the military policy on gays and lesbians. And, there is no case law holding that sexual orientation constitutes a class of persons protected by the U.S. Constitution. As such, it is true that there is no perfect model with which to compare the U.S. military.

Some argue that, even if the ban is lifted, change within the institution is more challenging because the U.S. military is a considerably larger and, arguably, a far more insular institution than is the case in Canada, Australia, or Great Britain. Yet, the inherent structure of the institution suggests otherwise. The mission of the military requires that those in the chain of command possess the ability to get subordinates to follow orders even when they don't wish to do so. Additionally, a look at the resistance and ultimate successes of the nations profiled here, suggests that when "Don't Ask, Don't Tell" is eliminated, whether by repeal or judicial decision, the U.S. military will not suffer the negative repercussions so many have cautioned us about.

Notes

1. For a more detailed account of the European situation, see Sameera Dalvi's "Homosexuality and the European Court of Human Rights: Recent Judgments against the United Kingdom and Their Impact on Other Signatories to the European Convention of Human Rights," *University of Florida Journal of Law Public Policy*, December 2004.

2. Eric Schmitt, "Gay Soldiers No Problem Elsewhere, Experts Say," *The New York Times*, April 30, 1993, p. A16.

3. Ibid.

4. Material in this section is drawn from "Effects of the 1992 Lifting of Restrictions on Gay and Lesbian Service in the Canadian Forces: Appraising the Evidence," by Aaron Belkin and Jason McNichol, April 2000. Text has been edited to conform, in format and style, to the chapter of which it is a part. This report was prepared for the Center for the Study of Sexual Minorities in the Military, University of California at Santa Barbara, now the Michael D. Palm Center, and is available at its Web site, http://www.palmcenter.org. Portions of the report appeared in "Don't Ask, Don't Tell: Is the Gay Ban Based on Military Necessity?" *Parameters*, Summer 2003, pp. 108–119. A revised version of the report was published as "Homosexual Personnel Policy in the Canadian Forces: Did Lifting the Gay Ban Undermine Military Performance?" *International Journal*, 56(1), Winter 2000–2001, 73–88.

5. David Vienneau, "Human Rights / Key Charter Fights Gay Fights for Career in Military," *The Toronto Star* (Toronto), April 15, 1989, p. D5.

6. For an overview of the history of military policy toward homosexuals in Canada, see Kinsman (1996) and a discussion of Kinsman's work in Bronskill (1998). For an overview of the history of homosexuality in Canada, see Adam (1993): Gary Kinsman, 1996. *The Regulation of Desire*. Montreal: Black Rose Books; Jim Bronskill, 1998. "Study Urges Ottawa Apologize for Gay Purge: Public Careers Ruined During Cold War." *The Gazette* (Montreal), November 24: A11; Barry D. Adam, 1993. "Winning Rights and Freedoms in Canada." In *The Third Pink Book*, edited by A. Hendriks, R. Tielman, and E. Veen. Buffalo, NY: Prometheus Books;

7. Rosemary Park, 1994. "Opening the Canadian Forces to Gays and Lesbians: An Inevitable Decision But Improbable Reconfiguration." In *Gays and Lesbians in the Military: Issues, Concerns, and Contrasts*, edited by W. J. Scott and S. C. Stanley. New York: Aldine de Gruyter.

8. Paul A. Gade, David R. Segal, and Edgar M. Johnson, 1996. "The Experience of Foreign Militaries." In *Out in Force: Sexual Orientation and the Military*, edited by G. Herek, J. B. Jobe, and R. M. Carney. Chicago: University of Chicago Press.

9. R. A. Zuliani, 1986. "Canadian Forces Survey on Homosexual Issues." Charter Task Force, Department of National Defence, Ottawa.

10. National Defense Research Institute (NDRI), 1993. *Sexual Orientation and U.S. Military Policy: Options and Assessment*. Santa Monica: RAND, p. 76.

11. See Farnsworth (1991), Ulbrich (1993), and Lancaster (1992): Clyde Farnsworth, 1991. "Canada Ending Anti-Gay Rules." *The New York Times* (New York), October 11: A3;

John Lancaster, 1992. "Many Allies Allow Gays in the Military; Canada, Australia Are Latest to Drop Exclusionary Policy." *The Washington Post* (Washington, D.C.), May 11: A3; Jeffrey Ulbrich, 1993. "Canada Lifted Ban on Gays in Military Without a Ripple." *The Associated Press* (Toronto), January 29.

12. Park, "Opening the Canadian Forces to Gays and Lesbians."

13. Tim Harper, "Ban on Gays in Military Still in Place, PM Says." *The Toronto Star* (Toronto), October 11, 1991, p. A11.

14. U.P.I., "Canadian Court Says Military Must Accept Gays," October 27, 1992, and Stephen Bindman, "Lesbian Forced to Quit Loses Bid for Old Job: Military Rejects Recommendation to Re-Hire Ex-Air Force Lieutenant," *The Vancouver Sun* (Vancouver),. May 11, 1992, p. A3.

15. See also Norma Greenway, 1993. "Clinton Faces Political Bloodbath Over Gays Issue." *The Gazette* (Montreal), January 28: B6.

16. National Defense Research Institute (NDRI), *Sexual Orientation and U.S. Military Policy*, p. 78.

17. Park, "Opening the Canadian Forces to Gays and Lesbians."

18. National Defense Research Institute (NDRI), *Sexual Orientation and U.S. Military Policy*, p. 423.

19. Ibid., p. 431.

20. Ibid., p. 79.

21. United States General Accounting Office (GAO), 1993. "Homosexuals in the Military: Policies and Practices of Foreign Countries." United States General Accounting Office, Washington, DC.

22. F. C. Pinch, 1994. "Perspectives on Organizational Change in the Canadian Forces." U.S. Army Research Institute for the Behavioral and Social Sciences, Alexandria, VA, pp. vii–viii.

23. Karol Wenek, Civilian, Canadian Forces. Directorate of Policy Analysis and Development, January 20, 2000, personal communication.

24. The survey did not specify or describe the policy.

25. Karol Wenek, "Briefing Note for Director of Public Policy." Ottawa: Canadian Forces, August 25, 1995, p. 3.

26. Same Sex Marriage/Blessing of a Relationship, Interim Guidelines for Canadian Forces Chaplains, http://www.forces.gc.ca/chapgen/engraph/same_sex_marriage_e.asp?cat=7.

27. The material in this section is drawn from "The Effects of Including Gay and Lesbian Soldiers in the Australian Defence Forces: Appraising the Evidence," by Aaron Belkin and Jason McNichol, September 19, 2000. Text has been edited to conform, in format and style, to the chapter of which it is a part. This report was prepared for The Center for the Study of Sexual Minorities in the Military, University of California at Santa Barbara, now the Michael D. Palm Center, and is available at its Web site, http://ww.palmcenter.org. Portions of the report appeared in "Don't Ask, Don't Tell: Is the Gay Ban Based on Military Necessity?" *Parameters*, Summer 2003, pp. 108–119.

28. R. Croome, 1992. A Submission to the ALP Caucus Committee on the Australian Defence Force Policy on Homosexuality, Canberra, Australia, p. 9.

29. Ibid.; H. Smith, 1995. "The Dynamics of Social Change and the Australian Defence Force." *Armed Forces and Society* 21(4): 531–551.

30. Smith, "The Dynamics of Social Change and the Australian Defence Force," 535.

31. Ibid., p. 540.

32. Ibid., pp. 536–539.

33. Ibid., p. 545.

34. Veterans and War Hero Angry Over Lifting of Gay Ban. *Associated Press*. Canberra, Australia, November 24, 1992.

35. *Report of the Homosexuality Policy Assessment Team*, UK Ministry of Defence, London, 1996.

36. Bronwen Grey, Director, Defence Equity Organisation, Interview with Belkin and McNichol, August 17, 2000.

37. Ibid.

38. The material in this section is drawn from "The Effects of Including Gay and Lesbian Soldiers in the British Armed Forces: Appraising the Evidence," by Aaron Belkin and R.L. Evans, November 2000. Text has been edited to conform, in format and style, to the chapter of which it is a part. This report was prepared for the Center for the Study of Sexual Minorities in the Military, University of California at Santa Barbara, now the Michael D. Palm Center, and is available at its Web site, http://www.palmcenter.org. Portions of the report appeared in "Don't Ask, Don't Tell: Is the Gay Ban Based on Military Necessity?" *Parameters*, Summer 2003, pp. 108–119.

39. David Rayside, 1998. *On the Fringe*. Ithaca, NY: Cornell University Press, and Gwyn Harries-Jenkins and Christopher Dandeker, 1994. "Sexual Orientation and Military Service: The British Case." In *Gays and Lesbians in the Military: Issues, Concerns and Contrasts*, edited by Wilbur Scott and Sandra Stanley. New York: Aldine De Gruyter.

40. Ibid.

41. Joan K. F. Heggie, 2003. "Lesbians and the Negotiation of Gender & Sexuality in the British Army since 1950." Unpublished Ph.D. thesis, University of York, York.

42. Ministry of Defense, 1994. "Armed Forces Policy and Guidelines on Homosexuality."

43. Ibid.

44. Owen Bowcott, Ben Stewart, and Chris Zinn, *The Guardian* (London), March 5, 1996, p. 7, and J. Copley, "Services Support Ban on Gays, Says Portillo." *The Daily Telegraph* (London), March 4 1996, www.telegraph.co.uk.

45. Andrew Gilligan and David Wastell, "Soames Tells Troops To Go Softly on Gay Purges." *The Daily Telegraph* (London), May 27, 1996, www.telegraph.co.uk.

46. Rajeev Syal and Andrew Gilligan, "£4m Payout for Gays Sacked from Services." *The Daily Telegraph* (London), November 15, 1999, www.telegraph.co.uk.

47. A. Sparrow, "Sex Code for Forces as Gay Ban is Lifted." *The Daily Telegraph* (London), November 15, 1999, www.telegraph.co.uk.

48. Paul Waugh, "Services Plan to Replace Bar on Gays with Ban on All Sex." *The Independent* (London), November 11, 1999, www.independent.co.uk/news/UK/This_Britain.

49. Michael Codner, Assistant Director (Military Sciences), Royal United Services Institute, personal communication with Belkin and/or Evans, September 26 and October 23, 2000.

50. Paul Waugh, "Military Invites Gays Who Were Forced Out By Bias to Reapply For Old Jobs." *The Independent* (London), 2000, www.independent.co.uk/news/UK/This_Britain.

51. Ministry of Defense, "Background Information," 2000, www.mod.uk/index.php3?page=594.

52. Ministry of Defense, "Armed Forces Code of Social Conduct: Policy Statement," 2000, www.mod.uk/index.php3?page=595.

53. Ibid., p. 1.

54. Ministry of Defense, "Speaking Notes for Commanding Officers," January 2000, p. 2.

55. Ministry of Defense, "Statement by 'Geoff Hoon MP, Secretary of State for Defense,'" 2000, www.mod.uk/index.php3?page=593.

56. Ministry of Defense, "A Review of the Armed Forces Policy on Homosexuality," October 31, 2000, p. 2.

57. Ibid.

CHAPTER 5

The War on Terror

On September 11, 2001, the world, as many in the United States understood it, changed forever. Nine days later, in a speech before the U.S. Congress, President George W. Bush said, "Americans are asking: How will we fight and win this war? We will direct every resource at our command . . . to the disruption and to the defeat of the global terror network."[1]

During 2001, 1,273 service members were discharged under "Don't Ask, Don't Tell." In the next five years, 3,715 service members would be discharged under this policy. If people are a resource, and they surely are, then the military was not using its every resource to defeat the terror. This chapter examines the reality of "Don't Ask, Don't Tell" at a time when the nation's military, arguably, needs every person who is willing to serve.

Military Personnel

Immediately after 9/11, military recruiting Web sites saw a spike in the number of visitors. What they didn't see was a rise in actual enlistments. Many of those who actually made an inquiry with a recruiter were too old, lacked high school diplomas, had criminal records, or were overweight. In most cases they would not qualify. But, in the months that followed, the military did do well enough to meet its recruiting quotas. In May 2002, for example, the Air Force had already met its target for the year. Since that time, recruitment and reenlistment figures have ebbed and flowed. In 2003, a slumping economy was thought to have helped boost recruiting. Two years later things looked more challenging for the military. In October 2004, the Army began the new fiscal year with only 18.4 percent of the year's target of active duty recruits somewhere in the pipeline. With Reserve and Guard personnel experiencing repeated and lengthy deployments, there are challenges there as well.[2]

The military has responded to recruiting challenges in several ways. In 2006, the Army, for example, raised the maximum age for enlistment from thirty-five to forty-two. Earlier, aptitude, educational, and psychological standards had been lowered. For example, the Army has doubled the maximum percentage of recruits who can be admitted with scores in the lowest acceptable category of the military's aptitude test. In 2006, the Army granted waivers to 8,129 recruits with criminal backgrounds. This compares to 4,198 such waivers granted in 2003. Waivers are required for offenses ranging from resisting arrest, public drunkenness, and contempt of court to aggravated assault, robbery, vehicular manslaughter, receiving stolen property, and making terrorist threats. The number of waivers for felony convictions increased from 8 percent of all waivers to 11 percent. The greatest number of waivers (12,313) was for medical conditions, such as asthma, flat feet, or limited hearing loss.[3]

General Barry McCaffrey (U.S. Army, retired) said, "Generally speaking, we've quadrupled the number of lowest mental category recruits, we've quadrupled the number of non-high school graduates, and we're granting 6,000 to 8,000 more moral waivers. When you tell me that you think enlisting a 42-year-old grandmother is the right thing to do, you don't understand what we're doing. We need 19-year-old boys and girls in good health to carry guns and fight."[4]

While the military struggles to attract qualified recruits and changes the meaning of the word "qualified," they continue to deny enlistment to otherwise qualified gay, lesbian, and bisexual recruits. This typically occurs without them knowing who they are "losing" as few individuals have ever shown up at the recruiting office to say, "I'd like to serve, but I'm gay so I cannot." One exception has been those in Soulforce's "Right to Serve" project. Soulforce describes itself as "an LGBT social justice organization dedicated to using nonviolent direct action to expose injustice and call attention to the real costs of homophobia."[5] In 2006, young gay men and lesbians across the nation went to military recruiters seeking to enlist. But, they would enlist only if they could be open about their sexual orientation. According to Soulforce, since the beginning of the Summer of 2006, "43 openly gay young people have attempted to enlist in 17 cities."[6] None were admitted. In addition to denying enlistment, yet facing recruitment and retention challenges, the military continues to discharge experienced personnel simply because they are gay, lesbian, or bisexual.

Though many gay, lesbian, and bisexual service members have been discharged during the time the United States has been fighting in Iraq and Afghanistan, those who have, perhaps, received the greatest attention are those who were trained as Arabic linguists. In November 2002, Dr. Nathaniel Frank reported that seven Arabic language specialists had been discharged. Speakers of Farsi, Korean, and other languages important to national security had also been discharged. In a follow-up to his earlier report, Frank confirmed that "according to Pentagon data, there were at least 73 people discharged from DLI [Defense Language Institute] for homosexuality between 1998 and 2003. At least 37 of these discharges took place after the September 11 attacks."[7] According to Frank, the

Justice Department has acknowledged that the government is unable to translate all the counterterrorism materials it would like because of the lack of translators.

Representative Marty Meehan (Massachusetts) has been very vocal in his opposition to "Don't Ask, Don't Tell," and has addressed the issue of linguists specifically. In September 2004 he wrote to the Department of Defense, asking for information concerning the language specialties of those discharged under the policy. In his response, Under Secretary of Defense David Chu indicated that, in addition to other language specialties, discharges were as follow: Arabic-Modern (16), Korean (16), and Persian-Farsi (6).[8] The Center for the Study of Sexual Minorities in the Military (CSSMM), now the Michael D. Palm Center, utilizing both Chu's response and cases not included in the above data, have concluded that, since 1998 the military has discharged fifty-five service members who were either proficient or training in Arabic. Another six Persian-Farsi linguists have also been discharged.

In 2002, the General Accounting Office indicated that the shortage of language specialists had an adverse impact on military operations. In 2004, then Homeland Security chief Tom Ridge said that the government needed more Arabic speakers as analysts. In their report, the 9/11 Commission indicated that the lack of trained linguists was a primary concern. And, in February 2005, Under Secretary of Defense for Personnel and Readiness Gail McGinn stated that the Department of Defense needed to recruit Arabic speakers and "linguists for other areas of the world that have attracted increased U.S. interest during the war on terror."[9] There seems to be no dispute over the need for trained speakers of Arabic. Dr. Aaron Belkin, director of the CSSMM, said, "When we don't have enough people to read intercepted intelligence cables, sexual orientation should be the last thing on the minds of Pentagon leaders."[10]

Most of the discharged linguists are people whose stories we will never hear. Several, however, have chosen to speak publicly. In 2002, Ian Finkenbinder graduated from DLI as an Arabic linguist. This was at a time when the military knew it was critical that more such personnel be trained. In 2003, Finkenbinder spent eight months serving with the Third Infantry Division in Iraq. As a cryptologist linguist, he was to "translate radio transmissions, to interview Iraqi citizens who had information to volunteer, and to screen native speakers for possible employment in translation units."[11] After his unit returned from Iraq, Finkenbinder had a sense that some unit members were talking about his personal life. One uncomfortable year later, he decided to provide his commander with a written statement in which he acknowledged that he was gay. Finkenbinder said, "I went to Iraq once. I met that challenge. I knew perfectly well I would be able to meet that challenge again." What he wasn't sure about was whether he could or should serve an institution that required him to be silent about his life and whether he could tolerate the, albeit infrequent, incidents of those with whom he served talking behind his back. According to Finkenbinder, his commander was "distraught" at having to discharge him solely because he was gay. But, in December 2004, Finkenbinder was discharged. Ironically, as of this writing, the U.S. Army

Training and Doctrine Command still has an article on their Web site in which Finkenbinder is described as using his experience in Iraq to help in a military intelligence training simulation.[12]

Bleu Copas was a sergeant in the 82nd Airborne Division. In August 2005, someone sent an anonymous e-mail to his unit, alleging that a soldier in the unit had an on-line profile in which he identified himself as gay. The director of the All-American Chorus at Fort Bragg apparently corralled members in the hallway and said, "Which one of you are [sic] gay?" Copas later complained to the director and his platoon sergeant, saying the questions violated the "Don't Ask, Don't Tell" policy. According to Copas, "They said they would watch it in the future." When asked, "Well, you are not gay are you?" he said, "No." The e-mails continued, with the author telling Copas' senior officers that they needed to act or that the author would "inform your entire battalion of the information" that had been provided. Investigators conducted a formal interview with Copas and asked if he understood the military's policy on homosexuals, if he had any close acquaintances who were gay, and if he was involved in community theater. He answered affirmatively. He declined to answer when they asked, "Have you ever engaged in homosexual activity or conduct?" Copas refused to answer nineteen of forty-seven questions before he asked for a lawyer and the interrogation stopped. Copas said he accepted the honorable discharge to end the ordeal, to avoid lying and risking a perjury charge, and to keep friends from being targeted. "It is unfair. It is unjust," Copas has said. "Even with the policy we have, it should never have happened." Although the identity of the person who made the original allegations was never learned, Sergeant Copas was discharged in January 2006.[13]

In maintaining his integrity, in standing up for himself, and ultimately for the many others living under the policy, Copas has faced hardships beyond the loss of his career. He writes,

> The thing that was different about my situation is because I decided to bring the issue of the policy to the American public. My story ended up reaching the far reaches of the world. This has obviously had both its ups and downs. The worst part of the entire situation has come from my family. Before this all happened, I was the son/nephew/grandchild everyone in my family wanted their kid to be. However, as soon as this story broke, those same family members seem to have lost all trust and confidence in me in one instant. I hear accusations that I have disgraced the family name and that it is somehow wrong to be prideful of who I am. It's almost as if I wasn't even a "real" soldier and my service is invalidated. It's all rather unfortunate that those with whom I would love to celebrate the most have made impossible any positive outcomes of my untimely discharge.[14]

Copas is currently completing his master's degree in counseling at East Tennessee State University, a course of study that, after 9/11, he was motivated to put on hold so that he might serve his country.

Since 2001, the majority of those discharged under "Don't Ask, Don't Tell" have not, of course, been linguists. Many are combat veterans. In 2001, Jeff Howe was working as a marketing executive in Silicon Valley and wondering whether there might be something more fulfilling he could pursue. Then, 9/11 happened. As a twenty-nine-year-old openly gay man, he decided to enlist in the Army. He signed up for two years, deciding that it wouldn't be much different from working for a civilian employer to whom he could not be out. Howe served in Iraq, received several commendations, and, having fulfilled his obligation, was planning to leave the military. Shortly before he was to be discharged, Howe was "stop-lossed"[15] and ordered back to Iraq. This time, Howe set up a blog as a way to communicate with friends and family. When his unit was hit by enemy rockets, Howe's company commander asked him to take some photographs of the damage and post them to his blog. He did so. The brigade commander disapproved and ordered Howe to terminate his blog. Completely unrelated to his sexual orientation, an investigation ensued aimed at determining whether Howe might have connections to terrorists. In the course of the investigation, an on-line profile was discovered in which Howe identified himself as a gay man. Because the Internet is considered a public forum and because Howe made a statement via the Internet, he was discharged under "Don't Ask, Don't Tell."

Most of the information concerning the specific circumstances of a discharge comes from the service member. The military does not, as a rule, provide such details. But, everyone seems to agree that the number of discharges under the policy includes not only gay, lesbian, and bisexual service members, but also heterosexual service members wishing to terminate their service. Looking at all the accounts provided by service members, lawyers, advocacy organizations, etc., it appears that about 10 to 15 percent of those discharged are discharged against their will as the result of involuntary discovery. The remaining 85 to 90 percent are those who seek discharge for other reasons. These reasons include, but are not limited to, the stress of living the lie and abuse by other service members.

When heterosexual service members are deployed, their spouses are provided with a range of support services. The deployed service member can also talk about the stress of the separation and, in today's world, send e-mails, communicate by Web cam, etc. The spouse who remains at home has access to services ranging from counseling to financial aid. The same-sex partner of a service member has no access to military support services and has to be very, very careful in his or her communication. Support services continue when the couple or family is reunited. The same-sex couple receives no such support.

In other situations, service members have been subjected to harassment and/or abuse. Though the climate has improved dramatically over the years, harassment—of women and gays, lesbian, and bisexuals—persists. Some service members simply decide that they are not willing to put up with behaviors that, at a minimum, make life unpleasant, and, at the extreme, can be life-threatening. Thus, an unknown number of the discharges are by service members who choose to leave the military rather than serve under those conditions.

Additionally, especially during a time of war, heterosexual service members have been known to claim that they are gay, lesbian, or bisexual to avoid military service. Bleu Copas said that he was aware of both men and women who "faked same-sex attractions" in the hope that they'd be discharged.[16] Because the application of "Don't Ask, Don't Tell" is at the discretion of one's commander, such efforts may or may not be successful. Dr. Aaron Belkin has said that "there is no question" that heterosexuals have used the policy to avoid military service. Other experts, such as Dr. David R. Segal at the University of Maryland, agree. But, it is virtually impossible to know the "true" numbers, because it is highly unlikely that anyone would admit to having lied to leave the service.

The Impact During War

The premature departure of military personnel carries a demonstrable impact on the organization. Less well documented is the fact that those personnel who continue to serve, regardless of sexual orientation, experience the negative effects of the policy and that this, too, has an impact on organizational effectiveness. In his article, "Gays and Lesbians at War: Military Service in Iraq and Afghanistan Under 'Don't Ask, Don't Tell,'" Dr. Nathaniel Frank provides a comprehensive and fascinating account of the experiences of gay, lesbian, and bisexual service members during the first three years of conflict and the impact their experiences have on the military more broadly. This section, framed around his key findings and other supporting information, illustrates the impact of the policy on service members' abilities to perform their duties.

As the result of his in-depth interviews with thirty service members who had served in the Middle East, Frank found that, despite the existence of "Don't Ask, Don't Tell," gays and lesbians have served and are serving in both Operation Enduring Freedom and Operation Iraqi Freedom. In many instances they serve openly or are open with at least some of their fellow service members. Being "out" is positively correlated with a range of factors including morale, professional advancement, access to support services, and retention.

Almost everyone Frank interviewed indicated that the policy had interfered with their ability to create bonds with fellow service members, build trust, deal appropriately with personal issues, and, basically, be as productive as they might otherwise have been. One frequently noted strategy was simply to avoid socializing with other unit members. The result of this strategy is often that the individual is perceived as antisocial, a label that leads to any number of other problems. One Naval lieutenant said that the policy "ends up driving more of a wedge [between gays and straights] than really helping." He said, "I don't socialize much with the people I work with because I can't be out to them and that's not good for cohesion."[17]

While some reported, as above, that the policy itself has a negative effect on unit cohesion, none of Frank's interviewees reported that they believed their openness had a negative effect on unit cohesion. There were incidents of harassment, but they were seen as comparable to the types and level of race and gender-based harassment that continue to exist. In fact, in some instances, it was reported that coming out improved relations. One soldier said that being open "brought me and my soldiers closer together because now they know who I am."[18] Additionally, there was little to suggest that privacy was compromised by the presence of gay and lesbian service members. A "norm of discretion" prevails in which not only do gay and lesbians act selectively in their disclosure, but service members, generally, allow everyone as much privacy as the setting permits.

The saying used to be "If the Army wanted you to have a wife, they would have issued you one." Times have changed and the military now prides itself on the support it provides to spouses and families. A quick Web search reveals hundreds of Web sites and/or organizations aimed at supporting military families. Many of these are official government sites and/or programs. A look at the main page of the Department of Defense contained a story titled, "Boxer Sailor in Gulf Meets Newborn Daughter Via VTC." The article began, "USS Boxer's (LHD 4) Aviation Structural Mechanic 1st Class (AW/SW) Steven Flemens met his newborn daughter for the first time via video teleconference (VTC) Dec. 23 while operating in the Persian Gulf." It goes on to point out that "in the past, Sailors on deployment relied on photographs or waited until the ship returned to homeport to see their newborn children. Communicating with family members was limited to letters, email and occasional phone calls. Onboard VTC systems let Sailors talk to their families in real time using live video and audio. The VTC program is available to all of Boxer's crew and their families." Flemens stated, "VTC is a real morale booster. Nothing is better than being in the presence of family. Even though I can't physically be with them, this is the next best thing."[19] With over 1,000 crewmembers and the capability of berthing over 2,000 troops, it is likely that at least a handful of those aboard the USS Boxer are partnered gay or lesbians, unable, without great risk, to take advantage of this morale booster.

Not surprisingly, Frank found that gay and lesbian service members, in many cases, must decline to take advantage of services such as medical and psychological care and religious support. When it comes to sexual orientation, there is no confidentiality requirement for medical personnel. As Sharra Greer, Director of Law and Policy for the Servicemembers Legal Defense Network (SLDN) notes, "Anything service members reveal to military health professionals can be used against them to start inquiries or investigations, and as evidence in discharge proceedings"[20] Thus, seeking out such help may in fact lead to an investigation and, ultimately, a discharge. One respondent noted that the policy made it very difficult to take care of personal matters such as one's will or next-of-kin notification without raising a red flag. He explained that he had put his partner's name on such paperwork, adding an "e" so that it would appear to be a woman's name, but would easily be considered a mistake if challenged.

According to SLDN, even when a service member seeks treatment outside of military channels, they may be placing themselves at risk. The military requires service members to report when they have received treatment from nonmilitary providers. Failing to do so may result in punishment, but doing so when one is gay or lesbian may place one at risk for investigation under "Don't Ask, Don't Tell." Thus, one result is that some service members simply don't get treatment for various physical and mental health concerns. Frank described one noncommissioned officer who wanted to talk with a chaplain about a "crisis of faith," but failed to do so out of fear that relevant issues regarding his sexuality would come up and the chaplain would report him.[21] The policy prevents service members from getting the medical, psychological, and spiritual support they need. Such a situation is not good for the service member and cannot be good for the military. While this situation holds true in times of peace and in noncombat environments, the need for such support is greatly increased when one is working in a stressful and potentially deadly environment away from the support of friends and family.

Over the years, a lot of discussion about gays and lesbians in the military has centered on sleeping and bathing arrangements. During the 1993 debates, Senator Sam Nunn, chairing the hearings in the Senate, made sure that photographs of the tight quarters of a submarine were taken during a trip to the Naval Station at Norfolk, Virginia. The publication of the photos is believed to have played a significant role in solidifying public support for the ban on gays and lesbians in the military. It is true that in the military, as compared with civilian organizations, there is no denying that privacy is compromised. This is especially true with overseas deployments where accommodations may, at least initially, be constructed hastily and as temporary. But, with everyone's expectation of privacy diminished, it appears that the presence of openly gay and lesbian service members has virtually no impact on privacy. Any lack of privacy is taken as routine, as what one would normally expect of military service.

In addition to a lowered expectation around privacy, Frank found that widespread improvements have been made, including single-stall showers and private bathrooms, such that there appears to be no negative effect on cohesion or mission effectiveness. And, when the actual design of the showers provided little in the way of privacy, service members often created their own means, such as using ponchos as dividers. Additionally, people created ways of dealing with the discomfort of nudity such as joking about it or remaining toweled except when under the water. The overwhelming sentiment was one of it being a nonissue. As one respondent indicated, "When you go in, you just have one thing on your mind: you just want to get clean and go to bed."[22]

It is worth noting that U.S. society has, generally, seen an increase in the accommodation of demands for personal privacy. For example, more and more parents are demanding that their children not be required to use the communal showers prevalent in public schools. In many instances, the schools are accommodating their wishes. In the military, more and more private rooms with private baths are being built. Thus, regardless of sexual orientation, when it comes to one's body, there appears to be a move toward providing a greater degree of personal privacy, both within and outside the military.

As has been described elsewhere, Frank found that, because the enforcement of "Don't Ask, Don't Tell" is at the discretion of the commander, its application is inconsistent and arbitrary. In some instances it appears related to troop strength or unit needs, rather than issues of unit cohesion or privacy. Ironically, when service members observe military leadership failing to enforce military law, it has the potential to create a situation in which respect for military law is diminished. On the other hand, when commanders enforce the law with vigor, emphasizing the stated incompatibility of homosexuality with military service, a climate of homophobia is far more likely to persist. Finally, service members report that there is inconsistency with regard to training on the policy and an uneven understanding of the policy. One Air Force captain remarked, "The whole policy literally became a joke. It still is to this day."[23]

Title 10, Section 654 of the United States Code, or "Don't Ask, Don't Tell," includes the statement: "The presence in the armed forces of persons who demonstrate a propensity or intent to engage in homosexual acts would create an unacceptable risk to the high standards of morale, good order and discipline, and unit cohesion that are the essence of military capability." But, training and other directives try to make clear that one's status as gay, lesbian, or bisexual is not, in and of itself, a bar to service. Only one's actions as a gay, lesbian, or bisexual person are at issue. Thus, the law, and subsequent policy, contends that a person who *demonstrates* the propensity or intent to engage in same-sex sexual behavior creates an unacceptable risk to the military, but that someone who is actually gay and manages to keep it a secret presents no such risk. With the contradiction presented by the language of the policy itself, it is no surprise that service members resort to following the tone set by their commanders, rather than drawing their own conclusions. This is important, because, as Frank found, in units where commanders made it clear that antigay harassment would not be tolerated or where the leadership permitted or encouraged open discussion of the issue, the organizational climate was very positive. In units where the leadership was confused and/or homophobic, the climate was quite negative.

As discussed above, some gay and lesbian service members choose not to reenlist or request discharge because of the hardships they experience as a result of "Don't Ask, Don't Tell." Brian Hughes, an Army ranger who participated in the removal of Jessica Lynch from the hospital where she lay injured, said that he chose not to reenlist because of the impact on family life. As he explained, the policy prevents someone like himself from bringing a partner to unit events and prevents a same-sex partner from taking advantage of support networks while the service member is deployed. Frank described one service member who reported that gays come to resent the military when they realize the sacrifices they are making in order to serve. The service member said, "If the military is not going to let me form normal, happy, healthy relationships; if they're going to discriminate against me, why should I fight for that institution and risk death?"[24]

The story of Army staff sergeant Brian Muller is both disheartening and instructive. Frank writes,

> Muller's commander knew he was gay as a result of both his own suspicions and some third-party disclosures to that effect over the years. After nearly eight years of service and a deployment to Bosnia and Afghanistan . . . Muller felt he had done everything he could do in the military while conforming to the policy. He had celebrated his 18th birthday in Bosnia, had been to war and had twenty-one medals to show for it. He had also heard commanders say "all fags should get AIDS and die," and continued to feel uniquely burdened as he strove to continue service while maintaining a forbidden relationship. So he came out. "I'd done everything I could do in the military," he recalled. "People couldn't say I was trying to get our [sic] of war because I had gone to war, so for me, it was a principle."[25]

The Army lost one noncommissioned officer with eight years of service and combat experience.

Although the current policy has led to the loss of many like SSG Muller, there are indications that both the passage of time and deployments to Iraq and Afghanistan are bringing about change. Respondents to Frank's study report that younger military personnel are more likely to be accepting of their gay and lesbian colleagues than are older and more senior personnel. Those respondents who served both before the policy became effective and after indicate that, at the aggregate level, attitudes toward gays and lesbians appear to have moved significantly in a positive direction. Frank's respondents provided overwhelming evidence that younger service members have little concern with the sexual orientation of their colleagues. "A staff sergeant noted that 'enlisted soldiers are generally younger and more willing to accept new things' while 'officers tend to look to regulations for guidance in soldiering.' "[26]

A number of respondents commented on how attitudes had changed since the policy was created in 1993. Frank offers the comments of a marine who first served in the Navy in 1987. He recounted a recent discussion in his unit about the proposed constitutional amendment to ban same-sex marriage, saying that only one person indicated support for the amendment. The Marine stated that "people care less about sexual orientation and more about performance." A Naval officer agreed noting that "you have to make anti-gay remarks every once in a while in order to really be a guy even though the majority of them don't care."[27] Frank's research is consistent with those, such as SLDN, who report fairly routine harassment, but those findings must be taken hand-in-hand with research that suggests that being openly gay, as opposed to closeted, is a fairly good mechanism for preventing harassment. Regardless, it is clear that attitudes toward the military service of gays and lesbians have changed dramatically since the inception of the policy. Some of this shift is likely due to the state of war and the gay and lesbian veterans who have spoken publicly about their lives and service.

Attitudes

Many other studies and polls have attempted to gauge attitudes toward the military service of gays and lesbians. In June 1992, shortly before the issue would explode as a national debate, Gallup found that 57 percent of those polled believed that homosexuals should have equal employment rights in the U.S. military. Thirty-seven percent said they should not, with the remaining respondents saying "it depends" or that they were unsure. Since that time, the percentage of those supporting the right of gays and lesbians to serve has risen steadily. In May 2003, shortly after the U.S. invasion of Iraq, when asked if homosexuals should be able to serve, 80 percent responded in the affirmative. Thus, national polling data suggested that approximately four out of every five respondents believe that gays and lesbians should be able to serve in the U.S. military.[28] The number of respondents reflecting support has increased fairly steadily from poll to poll, though the gains have not been equal—eight points from 1992 (before the debates) to 1996 (after the policy was implemented); five points from 1996 to 1999; two points from 1999 to 2001. It is worth noting that the increase from May 2001, prior to 9/11, to May 2003, after the U.S. invasion of Iraq, was, again, eight percentage points. This section provides a snapshot of attitudes since that time.

In early 2004, a retired Master chief petty officer in the U.S. Coast Guard, Vincent W. Patton III, visited with U.S. troops stationed in Afghanistan and the Persian Gulf. He was part of a mission seeking to gauge the morale of those stationed in the area. Patton, who was the highest ranking enlisted person in the Coast Guard from 1999 to 2002, also sought to assess their attitudes toward "Don't Ask, Don't Tell." In his conversations with an estimated 700–800 troops, he found that most of them "don't care" about serving with gay and lesbian personnel. Patton, suggesting that attitudes varied by age, said, "I found in my conversations that for the most part they are more culturally exposed to gays. They grew up with it so it's no big deal."[29]

Consistent with Patton's anecdotal findings, in October 2004, the University of Pennsylvania's National Annenberg Election Survey found that 50 percent of junior enlisted service members believed that gays and lesbians should be allowed to serve openly. The survey found that many based their opinion on the belief that sexual orientation was unrelated to job performance. Interestingly, even those who opposed permitting gays and lesbians to serve openly often rejected the most common rationales for the ban, unit cohesion and morale.[30] In March 2005, the Center for Information and Research on Civic Learning and Engagement (CIRCLE) released a poll showing that 85 percent of those aged eighteen to twenty-five were in favor of permitting gays and lesbians to serve in the U.S. military. In 1992, a similar poll had found that 59 percent of those in that age range supported the service of gays and lesbians.[31]

In May 2005, the *Boston Globe* published the results of its poll in which 79 percent of respondents said that gays and lesbians should be able to serve openly. They wrote, "Large majorities of Republicans, regular churchgoers, and (even) people with negative attitudes toward gays think gays and lesbians should be allowed to serve openly in the military."[32] This poll was consistent with a Gallup poll conducted during the same period in which 79 percent agreed that gays and lesbians should be able to serve.[33] It was, however, somewhat different from the results of a poll conducted by the Pew Forum on Religion and Public Life and the Pew Research Center for the People and the Press. In August 2005, Pew found that 58 percent of those polled support permitting gays and lesbians to serve openly. The poll, taken of 1,000 adults, showed that "solid majorities of seculars (72%), white Catholics (72%) and mainline Protestants (63%) believe gays and lesbians should be allowed to serve openly in the nation's military."[34] Less than a year later, a similar poll conducted by Pew found support among 60 percent of respondents.[35] Although the increase of 2 percent falls within the margin of error, polls across the nation continue to reflect increased support for the open service of gays and lesbians.

In the 2006 Pew results, 55 percent of men were supportive of the open service of gays and lesbians, while 66 percent of women held such a view. In age categories of 18–29, 30–49, 50–64, and 65 and over, support was, respectively, 72 percent, 62 percent, 59 percent, and 47 percent within each category. Seventy-one percent of college graduates were supportive compared to 50 percent of those with a high school diploma or less. Forty-six percent of those who identified themselves as Republicans were supportive, though, when characterized as "conservative" or "moderate/liberal" Republicans, the response was quite different—36 percent and 62 percent, respectively. Seventy percent of those identifying as Democrats were supportive with 64 percent of those identifying as "conservative" and 85 percent of those identifying as "moderate/liberal" holding such a view. Finally, a majority of those identifying as Protestant, Catholic, or secular were supportive, with the exception of the subcategory of "white evangelical," where 43 percent indicated support for the open service of gays and lesbians.[36]

In August 2006, the *Fayetteville Observer*, a local paper near Fort Bragg, North Carolina, home of the 82nd Airborne, surveyed twenty soldiers on post. They found little support for "Don't Ask, Don't Tell." Although based on a small convenience sample, finding such lack of support on a military installation remains important. One respondent said, "If you are doing your job, you fall into the same category as anyone else." Another said, "It's political. The Army has to have a public face."[37]

Most recently, in December 2006, The Michael D. Palm Center, as part of their "Don't Ask, Don't Tell" project, released the results of a poll in which Zogby International surveyed 545 U.S. military personnel who had served in Iraq or Afghanistan, or held roles in which they provided direct support to those military operations. The survey was focused on "three key areas—the size and characteristics of the gay and lesbian population in the U.S. military, the views of service personnel regarding the subject, and . . . the impact of gays and lesbians on the military."[38] Not surprisingly, while improving, support for the open service of gays and lesbians was lower than that reflected among the civilian population.

When asked, "Do you agree or disagree with allowing gays and lesbians to serve openly in the military?" 26 percent, or slightly greater than one in every four respondents, indicated that either they strongly agreed (9%) or agreed (17%). Thirty-two percent responded that they were neutral on the issue. This is a particularly high percentage of neutral respondents and one cannot be certain what it means or what impact wording the question differently might have had on the outcome. Sixteen percent disagreed, while 21 percent, or about one in five, strongly disagreed. Five percent were unsure.

Thirty-five percent of those who were veterans (as opposed to currently serving on active duty) and 37 percent of those serving fewer than four years indicated support. The lowest rates of support were found among active duty personnel (23%), officers (23%), those serving between ten and fourteen years (22%), and those serving more than twenty years (19%). Although not provided in the report, there remains the possibility that when controlling for the effects of age, the effect of some of these characteristics would be limited or would entirely disappear. The impact of one's generation on attitudes remains significant.

Zogby also asked about the impact of gays and lesbians on unit morale. While 28 percent indicated that they believed there to be a negative impact (very negative, 8%; somewhat negative, 20%), 66 percent indicated that they believed there to be no impact. Consistent with many studies on this specific issue and homosexuality in general, men were more than twice as likely as women to believe that gays and lesbians had a negative impact on morale. One in every three men (31%) held this view, while only about one woman in seven (14%) did so.

The poll also asked respondents how comfortable they were in the presence of gays and lesbians. Three-quarters of those responding (73%) said that they were very comfortable (29%) or somewhat comfortable (44%). Fewer than one in five (19%) said that they were uncomfortable, with only 5 percent stating that they were very uncomfortable as opposed to somewhat uncomfortable (15%). This is an interesting finding because it suggests that one's attitudes toward the open service of gays and lesbians may be a reflection of more than one's personal comfort level with their presence.

One of the more interesting questions was "Would you have still joined the military if gays and lesbians were allowed to serve openly?" During the 1993 debates, many asserted that one of the problems with allowing gays and lesbians to serve openly was the purported negative impact on recruiting and retention. In response to the above question, 78 percent of those responding to the Zogby poll said definitely yes (42%) or probably yes (35%). Seven percent said probably not and 3 percent said definitely not. Thirteen percent were unsure. While the finding that more than three-quarters of respondents would not change their decision about joining the military is compelling, it is also worth noting that in countries that lifted their bans, anecdotal evidence suggests that none of those who swore they would leave the service if the ban were lifted did so.

Respondents were also asked to indicate which arguments for excluding gays and lesbians they found to be the most compelling. Forty percent said that "open gays and lesbians would undermine unit cohesion." Four responses were in the 20–30 percent range. Twenty-eight percent said that "open gays and lesbians would get beat up or abused," while 26 percent said that "straights would not respect gay or lesbian leaders." Twenty-five percent said that "homosexuality violates religious/moral beliefs" and 22 percent said that "straights should not have to share foxholes, showers, etc., with open gays and lesbians." The remaining arguments for prohibiting the open service of gays and lesbians (e.g., "Gays and lesbians would increase the spread of HIV/AIDS" and "Open gays and lesbians would be more likely to pursue straights") were supported by fewer than 10 percent of respondents. As has been reflected elsewhere, few respondents (less than 1%) attributed their opposition to the notion that gays and lesbians are less capable than their heterosexual counterparts. Finally, 21 percent of those responding to this question said, "There are no strong arguments for keeping gays from serving openly."

Coming to the issue from the other direction, the poll asked respondents to indicate which they felt were the strongest arguments for permitting gays and lesbians to serve openly. Thirty-six percent said that "sexual orientation has nothing to do with job performance" while 30 percent said that "it is wrong to discriminate based on sexual orientation." One-quarter of those responding said that "during wartime, the armed forces need every qualified service member regardless of sexual orientation" and 22 percent said that "discharging service members for being gay is a waste of recruiting, education and training dollars." Nineteen percent, or about one in five, indicated that "there are no strong arguments for allowing gays and lesbians to serve openly."

Public support for allowing gays and lesbians to serve openly has increased dramatically over the years. Support among military personnel has increased, though not nearly as much. Given the trend toward slightly greater conservative views among military personnel, this is not surprising. And, when one considers the impact of the message delivered by military leadership, it is also not surprising that there is less support among military personnel. There exists a "Catch-22" of sorts. The single most important factor in changing attitudes toward gays and lesbians is realizing that someone you know is gay or lesbian. Though more and more military personnel are choosing to be open with their close friends and colleagues in the military, "Don't Ask, Don't Tell" prevents military personnel from having these experiences at a rate on par with those of their civilian counterparts. Thus, while the repeal of "Don't Ask, Don't Tell" may depend on a shift in attitudes among military personnel, so will that shift in attitudes depend on the repeal of "Don't Ask, Don't Tell." But, as more and more veterans of military service in Iraq and Afghanistan choose to "come out" about their gay or lesbian identity, it is likely that there will be a measurable impact on the attitudes of those who continue to serve.

Gay and Lesbian War Veterans Speak Out

We know that many of those who served in World War II, Korea, and Vietnam came home and lived their lives as gay men and lesbians. But, given the times, for most it was a personal decision with little public impact. Only during the debates in 1993 did the stories of gay and lesbian veterans come to play a more dominant role of the public discourse. The increasingly public nature of the debate throughout the late 1990s led to more and more gay and lesbian veterans speaking publicly about their service. Since the U.S. presence in Iraq and Afghanistan, attention has turned from the service of gays and lesbians to the service of gays and lesbians during wartime.

A report issued by the Urban Institute in October 2004 and based on data collected for the 2000 Census estimated that 65,000 gays and lesbians are serving in the armed forces of the United States. Their conservative estimate is that 36,000 gays and lesbians serve on active duty, with the remaining persons serving in the National Guard and Reserve components.[39] Given the arguments of unit cohesion, morale, and a presumed negative impact on the primary mission of the military, it is the stories of these service members that may ultimately have the greatest impact on attitudes, among both the public and military personnel.

Unlike some of those profiled in this chapter, Austin Rooke was not "outed" or discovered. Rather, living the lie just became too much. Rooke had received his commission via the Reserve Officers Training Corps (ROTC) and served as an intelligence officer in the Army. After his four-year obligation was fulfilled, Rooke left the military. He said, "One of the reasons I got out of the Army after they had invested hundreds of thousands of dollars on me is because, at this point, I was an out gay man and had no interest in working for an organization where I couldn't talk about my personal life." As is the case with many service members who complete their active duty obligation, Rooke was assigned to the Individual Ready Reserve (IRR), or inactive reserve. Ironically, after 9/11 Rooke was working for the GLBT advocacy organization, the National Gay and Lesbian Task Force, when he found himself with orders to return to active duty. Rooke was deployed overseas and found himself working in an environment that, he says, was isolating and potentially dangerous. As he points out, when the law mandates discrimination, it's difficult to keep homophobia from being an integral part of institutional culture. Unlike many service members, Rooke was able to complete his tour and returned to the inactive reserve where he remains a captain. It is unlikely that he will be discharged from the IRR under "Don't Ask, Don't Tell." However, should he again receive orders activating him, the Army will be faced with the decision of whether to permit an experienced openly gay veteran to serve his country or to then discharge him.[40]

SGT Robert Stout was wounded while serving in Iraq. His arm, face, and legs were hit by shrapnel, the result of a grenade exploding while he operated a machine gun aboard a Humvee. Stout wanted the opportunity to remain in the military, but he wanted to do so without hiding the fact that he was a gay man. In 2005, he told the Associated Press, "I know a ton of gay men that would be more than willing to stay in the Army if they could just be open." In addition, Stout, who was open to several members of his platoon, said, "We can't keep hiding the fact that there's gay people in the military and they aren't causing any harm."[41] In another interview Stout said, "It's a pretty sad feeling just to realize the fact that I'm sitting here fighting, getting wounded, possibly dying for an organization and even a country that refuses to accept the fact that I even exist."[42] And, in an interview with oral historian, Steve Estes, Stout recalled the first time he told one of his team leaders, "I was E-3, private first class, and he was a sergeant. At that time, all my pronouns were changed. 'He' became 'she,' and the guy I dated at the time, I gave him a feminine name. So my team leader was asking me about her/him. We get talking and it eventually got to the point where I thought, 'This is just not worth it.' So I'm like, 'Hey Sarge, 'she' is a guy.' The only thing he said after that was, 'I need a cigarette.' He got done smoking the cigarette, and he goes, 'Damn it! That means my wife was right.' And shoot, after that we never had any trouble."[43]

Brian Fricke is described by writer Sean Bugg as "[a] tall Tennessean with an easy grin and aw-shucks manner overlaying a strong sense of loyalty and duty." Bugg writes that "Fricke appears every bit the Marine Corps Sergeant. Joining the military as a 19-year-old fresh out of high school, he quickly left his Knoxville roots behind for the more urban and adventurous ports of San Diego and Okinawa."[44] While stationed in Iraq, Fricke realized that if he died, he would die without his family having truly known him. And, worse, his family wouldn't know who his partner was when he showed up at the funeral. When asked why he chose to leave the service, Fricke said, "I didn't want to live that life of secrecy any more. I did my time. I went to Iraq. I would have gone back to Iraq but I was with Brad and I wanted to be with him completely. If it were just me as a single, gay Marine, I might have stayed. But I think I was ready to be done with that kind of suppression."[45]

In January 2005, one lesbian veteran returned from Iraq and spoke out by putting her story to paper. Because she wished to remain in the military she signed her work, "Anonymous." It appeared on the Web site of the Military Education Initiative, now part of the Military Equality Alliance, a "grassroots voice for gay, lesbian, bisexual and transgender service members, veterans and their allies."[46] She wrote, "One night we were getting hit heavy and hard. That is all I can say about that. After it was over and we regrouped, I knew she would hear about it in the news. While others notified their families, I knew I could not. If I heard her sweet scared voice on the other end of the phone, I would have lost my career. So, after making sure my unit was okay, I went alone and cried into my hands."[47] Her partner also told her story. Describing their time apart she wrote, "The day she left, almost a year ago, I went with her and the children and she hugged them and held them and never looked at me. We had said our good byes at home. I looked around at all the couples who could openly show their love and I got angry. . . . Due to the fighting in Iraq, I never turned on the TV or read the paper. The kids would hear about it and they even had a support group for the children, but I could not attend. So, I had no one. I internalized everything. . . . I didn't have a support group I could attend. I didn't have anyone to help me with the kids when they cried for her at night or had nightmares. It was hard to make them to understand why I could not attend the groups with them. I had to listen as other women talked about their spouses being away and how proud they were. I felt the same pride. I felt the same fears, but if I expressed it, we would lose everything and we have worked so hard."[48]

Another veteran, Helen Gerhardt, has published her thoughts in *The New York Times* and as part of a new volume, edited by Andrew Carroll, *Operation Home-coming: Iraq, Afghanistan, and the Home Front, in the Words of U.S. Troops and Their Families*. In the latter she is writing to her friends and family in August 2003, describing some of her first experiences in Iraq. Gerhardt begins, "A few days ago I sat in the passenger seat of a truck with my M16 pointing out the window as I crossed the border into Iraq for the first time."[49] She doesn't mention being in a relationship with a woman. She doesn't need to. Though having to remain closeted did shape aspects of her experience in Iraq, it wasn't the dominant factor in how she experienced the war. The piece in *The New York Times*, published on February 13, 2005, just in time for Valentine's Day, is titled "Back from the Front, with Honor, a Warrior's Truth." This time she describes some of her experiences as a lesbian, serving in silence. After telling of the fictional boyfriend she had created over the course of nearly a year, she writes, "The falsehoods I'd spread to keep my fellow soldiers from knowing the real me were at the same time preventing me from knowing the real them. I could now see that during the time I'd been covering for myself, I'd stood increasingly apart from my unit and my superior officers—friendly, but not a friend. . . . I could never have guessed that the loneliness of maintaining my silence with him and others I cared about would be harder to bear than being shot at or bombed." Gerhardt ends her essay: "I served honorably, remained faithful to my true love and to my country, and I came back in one piece, with even my silence intact. But in the wake of all these deceptions, small and large, innocent and deadly, my ongoing silence eventually became its own burdensome lie—one that I simply could no longer bear. So that is my truth, or at least the best I could do under the circumstances. I know you didn't ask. I had to tell anyway. The fact is, I would very much like to continue to serve as my true self. I hope you'll understand."[50]

Though women are discharged under "Don't Ask, Don't Tell" at a rate twice that of their male counterparts, few women seem to have "gone public" with their stories.[51] Unlike past conflicts, women are serving in the Gulf at a rate proportionate to their presence in the armed forces. Why then are lesbian veterans of service in Iraq and Afghanistan not as visible as gay male veterans? It may be that lesbians are more likely to remain in service than are gay men. It may be that women are less likely to be approached to serve as a "public face" of the issue. It may be that, given society's stereotypes, men have more to gain by going public. It may be that there are simply other, more pressing, issues toward which they put their energy. One such woman is Tina Garnanez, a member of the Navajo nation and a member of Iraq Veterans Against the War. Issues of social class, racism, and peace dominate her efforts. Having served in Kosovo and Iraq as a medic, she is also a lesbian veteran. However, her service as a lesbian appears secondary to her concerns that poor adolescents of color are disproportionately targeted by military recruiters.[52] The likely truth is that the relative absence of lesbian veterans from the public discourse is a reflection of all of the above and more. Regardless of their comparative silence, it must be recognized that lesbian war veterans do exist and that they have the same desire to serve openly as their gay male colleagues.

Conclusion

The United States' invasion of Iraq will, for many decades to come, have repercussions that extend well beyond the borders of Iraq, the institution of the military, the political landscape, and the countless personal tragedies. One potentially positive outcome may well be that we learn that the gays and lesbians not only serve, but can serve openly. During the 1993 debates the issue of unit cohesion focused on war and the perception that in times of war the presence of openly gay and lesbian service members would be disruptive. At the time such comments were largely speculative. Now, four years after the invasion of Iraq, there have been many examples of gay and lesbian service members who, while deployed, were fairly open to their colleagues. More and more service members are returning from the Middle East to tell their stories. Though, for obvious reasons, most remain silent, story after story suggests that today's military personnel are truly professional in that they care more about how well one does his or her job, rather than his or her personal relationships. It is impossible to determine how much change might have occurred just because of the passage of time and the change of societal attitudes generally versus how much has changed because of the experiences of war. But, all indicators are that change may well have been accelerated because of our involvement in Iraq and Afghanistan.

Notes

1. President George W. Bush, "Address to a Joint Session of Congress and the American People," September 20, 2001, http://www.whitehouse.gov/news/releases/2001/09/20010920-8.html.

2. Ann Scott Tyson, "Army Having Difficulty Meeting Goals in Recruiting," *The Washington Post*, February 21, 2005, p. A01.

3. Lizette Alvarez, "Army Giving More Waivers in Recruiting," *The New York Times*, February 14, 2007.

4. Leo Shane III, "Volunteer Force May Be 'Severely Degraded' Soon, Retired General Says," *Stars and Stripes*, November 18, 2006, http://www.estripes.com/article.asp?section=104&article=40613&archive=true.

5. Soulforce, www.soulforce.org.

6. http://www.soulforce.org/article/893.

7. Nathaniel Frank, "Canning Gay Linguists. Stonewalled," *The New Republic*, January 24, 2005, http://www.tnr.com/doc.mhtml?i=20050124&s=frank012405

8. Letter from David S. C. Chu to The Honorable Marty Meehan, U.S. House of Representatives, December 2, 2004.

9. "As Discharge of Gay Linguists Continue, Pentagon Again Acknowledges Shortage of Language Experts," SLDN press release, February 3, 2005, www.sldn.org.

10. Ibid.

11. Ibid., n. 7.

12. "Military Intelligence Soldiers Use Lessons-Learned," November 21, 2003, http://www.tradoc.army.mil/pao/training_closeup/112903.htm.

13. Though this story has appeared in hundreds, if not thousands, of newspapers and on-line sources, the account here is drawn from the story as published by *The Washington Post* on July 27, 2006.

14. Personal communication with Bleu Copas, January 18, 2007.

15. Under a "stop-loss" order, personnel who might have been discharged (e.g., their enlistment obligation is fulfilled) are retained so that troop strength may be maintained.

16. Joshua Lynsen, "Don't Ask" Discharges On The Rise, *Washington Blade*, June 7, 2006, http://www.washblade.com/2006/6-7/news/national/dadt.cfm.

17. Frank, "Gays and Lesbians at War: Military Service in Iraq and Afghanistan Under 'Don't Ask, Don't Tell,'" The Center for the Study of Sexual Minorities in the Military, September 15, 2004. pp. 11–12.

18. Ibid., p. 15.

19. Brian Gaines, "Boxer Sailor in Gulf Meets Newborn Daughter Via VTC," January 1, 2007, http://www.news.navy.mil/search/display.asp?story_id=27210.

20. "National LGBT Health Awareness Week: LGBT Military Personnel Have No Doctor–Patient Confidentiality," SLDN press release, March 14, 2005, http://www.sldn.org/templates/press/record.html?section=2&record=1979.

21. Whether a chaplain is obligated to report an individual who reveals that he or she is gay or lesbian is dependent upon various factors, such as branch of service and whether the guidance sought is recognized as spiritual as opposed to psychological. For additional information, see *SLDN Survival Guide*, Chaplains, http://www.sldn.org/templates/legalhelp/record.html?section=19&record=31.

22. Frank, "Gays and Lesbians at War: Military Service in Iraq and Afghanistan Under 'Don't Ask, Don't Tell,'" The Center for the Study of Sexual Minorities in the Military, September 15, 2004. p. 28.

23. Ibid., p. 39.

24. Ibid., p. 41.

25. Ibid.

26. Ibid., p. 17.

27. Ibid.

28. "Gay and Lesbian Alliance against Defamation," May 25, 2005, http://www.glaad.org/media/guide/infocus/polls.php.

29. SLDN, Retired Master Chief Petty Officer Tours Afghanistan and Persian Gulf, Speaks to Troops About Military's Gay Ban, February 11, 2004, http://www.sldn.org/templates/press/record.html?section=2&record=1384.

30. SLDN, New Poll Shows Shift in Military Attitudes Toward Gays, October 26, 2004, http://www.sldn.org/templates/press/record.html?section=2&record=1674.

31. SLDN, Young Americans Overwhelmingly Support Allowing Gays to Serve in U.S. Armed Forces, March 18, 2005, http://www.sldn.org/templates/press/record.html?section=2&record=1992.

32. SLDN, New Poll Shows Overwhelming Support for Allowing Gays to Serve, May 16, 2005, http://www.sldn.org/templates/press/record.html?section=2&record=2140.

33. Interestingly, when Gallup asked whether "homosexuals" should be permitted to serve, the number of those responding affirmatively dropped slightly to 76 percent.

34. SLDN, Pew Poll Finds Support for Allowing Gays to Serve Openly in Armed Forces, August 31, 2005, http://www.sldn.org/templates/press/record.html?section=2&record=2371.

35. The Pew Research Center for the People and the Press, Less Opposition to Gay Marriage, Adoption and Military Service: Only 34% Favor South Dakota Abortion Ban, March 22, 2006, http://people-press.org/reports/display.php3?ReportID=273.

36. Ibid.

37. SLDN, Fort Bragg Soldiers Express Little Support for "Don't Ask, Don't Tell," August 4, 2006, http://www.sldn.org/templates/press/record.html?section=2&record=3101.

38. *Opinions of Military Personnel on Sexual Minorities in the Military*, submitted to Aaron Belkin, Director, Michael D. Palm Center by Zogby International, Sam Rodgers, writer. December 2006. http://www.palmcenter.org/files/active/0/ZogbyReport.pdf; all the data presented in this chapter are drawn directly from this report.

39. *Gay Men and Lesbians in the U.S. Military*, Urban Institute, September 28, 2004, http://www.urban.org/publications/411069.html.

40. Material on Jeff Howe and Austin Rooke is drawn from "Outed in Iraq: Gay Soldiers Fighting In Iraq Discharged Despite Recruiting Woes; Some Quit Under Pressure," by Melissa McEwan, February 6, 2006, www.rawstory.com.

41. Malia Rulon, "Gay U.S. Soldier Wants To Serve Openly." as reported by the Center for the Study of Sexual Minorities in the Military, http://www.gaymilitary.ucsb.edu/PressClips/05_0407_AP.htm.

42. SLDN, "Remembering a Fallen Hero," November 3, 2006, http://www.sldn.org/templates/press/record.html?record=3271.

43. Steve Estes, Military Education Initiative, "We All Bleed the Same," http://www.military-education.org/stories/story_rstout.html.

44. Sean Bugg, "Secret Service: A Soldier's Life Under 'Don't Ask, Don't Tell'," May 11, 2006, http://www.metroweekly.com/feature/?ak=2112.

45. Ibid.

46. http://www.military-education.org/about/index.html.

47. http://www.military-education.org/stories/story_ActiveDutyIraq1.rtf.

48. Ibid.

49. Helen Gerhardt, "Here Among the Ruins," January 1, 2007, http://www.npr.org/templates/story/story.php?storyId=6693664.

50. Helen Gerhardt, "Modern Love; Back From the Front, With Honor, A Warrior's Truth," *The New York Times*, February 13, 2005, http://select.nytimes.com/search/restricted/article?res=F20D16FE3F5E0C708DDDAB0894DD404482.

51. Though women comprise 15 percent of the armed forces, 30 percent of those discharged under "Don't Ask, Don't Tell" are women.

52. http://www.war-times.org/pdf/WT%20Garnanez.pdf.

CHAPTER 6

Expectations for the Future

In 1993, during the debate over permitting gays and lesbians to serve openly in the U.S. military, political conservative and former Senator Barry Goldwater published a commentary in the *Washington Post* and the *Los Angeles Times*. He wrote, "I served in the armed forces. I have flown more than 150 of the best fighter planes and bombers this country manufactured. I founded the Arizona National Guard. I chaired the Senate Armed Services Committee. And I think it's high time to pull the curtains on this charade of a policy."[1] As he noted, some in Congress thought him wrong. As a result, opposition to the open service of gays and lesbians became enshrined in the law.

In the years since the prohibition on the open military service of gays and lesbians became federal law, and "Don't Ask, Don't Tell" was implemented by the U.S. military, much has changed. Our allies in Great Britain have eliminated their ban. The role of women in the U.S. military continues to expand. Members of the National Guard and Reserve play an increasing role in overseas deployments. Both the presidency and the Congress have changed hands. As of this writing, President George W. Bush seeks to increase both the size of the military and the U.S. military presence in Iraq. The U.S. Supreme Court has two new members and a new Chief Justice. Advocacy groups on both sides of the argument, seeing it as either too permissive or too restrictive, continue to make the case for a change in policy. And, as discussed in Chapter 5, opinions of both military and civilian personnel have shifted toward greater support for the open service of gays and lesbians in the military.

Calls for a Change

In October 2002, former Senator Chuck Robb (Virginia) was the keynote speaker at the Servicemembers Legal Defense Network (SLDN) annual dinner. A longtime supporter of allowing gays and lesbians to serve openly, Robb, a former Marine who served in Vietnam, stated that "this dangerous policy of exclusion . . . must fall."[2] He described why history demands such action and told the stories of gays and lesbians who have served honorably. Others, too, have been long-standing in their opposition to the ban. Some are outspoken supporters like Senators Russ Feingold (Wisconsin) and Ted Kennedy (Massachusetts). Others are gay and lesbian service members, like Colonel Margarethe Cammermeyer, who have been speaking publicly for over a decade. But, in the early twenty-first century, new voices, too, are being heard.

In December 2003, Brigadier General Keith Kerr (U.S. Army, retired), Brigadier General Virgil Richard (U.S. Army, retired), and Rear Admiral Alan Steinman (U.S. Coast Guard, retired) all announced that they were gay. One logical question was why, at that point in time, they chose to speak publicly. General Kerr stated, in an interview on CNN, "It's the 10th anniversary of don't ask, don't tell and the three of us think that don't ask, don't tell is not working. It prohibits and discourages loyal Americans who want to serve their country from doing so . . ."[3] Some have wondered if the fact that the three men had successful careers, including promotion to among the highest ranks, doesn't actually demonstrate that the policy has been successful. All three men described the toll that the policy had taken on their lives. Admiral Steinman said, "I was denied the opportunity to share my life with a loved one, to have a family, to do all the things that heterosexual Americans take for granted. That's the sacrifice I made to serve my country."[4] The following week, fifteen retired military leaders issued a statement calling for the end of "Don't Ask, Don't Tell." The statement ended with this plea: "Our courts, local governments and corporations have affirmed that gays are an integral and valued part of the American family. Our military too should lead in defense of liberty and freedom for all."[5]

In July 2005, and in response to reports that applications at federal military academies were down, five former military officers launched a blog calling on military leaders to support repeal of the law. All five were graduates of U.S. military academies and all were gay. Paula Neira (U.S. Naval Academy, class of 1985) wrote, "Today, when America once again finds itself at war, we continue to let our prejudices—this time homophobia—prevent our military from using the talent of all of our best and brightest in defense of our great country."[6]

In early 2006, newspapers across the United States published editorials calling for an end to "Don't Ask, Don't Tell." In March, *USA Today* called the policy "archaic and hurtful." Major papers such as *The Baltimore Sun*, as well as smaller papers like *The Berkshire Eagle* in Massachusetts, published similar pieces. *The Washington Post* said, "A combination of bigotry and inertia keeps the ban in place."[7] *The Oregonian* wrote, "The law seemed like a reasonable compromise at the time of its passage by Congress, a thousand years ago, in 1993. Today, most people see the law as a costly and indefensible throwback. Two-thirds of Americans say they want the ban lifted, and a small but growing number of military leaders recognize the folly of limiting the pool of able-bodied and qualified recruits. It's time for Congress and President Bush to lift the ban."[8]

In May 2006, Lieutenant General Claudia Kennedy (U.S. Army, retired), the first woman to achieve the rank of three-star general, delivered the keynote at the SLDN annual dinner. In her remarks, she said, "Army values are taught to soldiers from their earliest days in the Army. Those values are: loyalty, duty, mutual respect, selfless service, honor, integrity, and personal courage . . . . I believe that as an institution, our military needs to live up to the values we demand of the service members."[9] Kennedy described "Don't Ask, Don't Tell" as a hollow policy that serves no useful purpose and asserted that the military has outgrown the need for such a policy.

During the following month, June 2006, the White House made the first public comments about the policy since President Bush took office. White House Press Secretary Tony Snow, responding to a question about the Bush administration's policy on "Don't Ask, Don't Tell," responded that the policy is "well-established" and deferred all questions about the policy to the Department of Defense. Ironically, the Department of Defense has gone on record as noting that, as a federal law, they must defer to Congress, the body in which the law originated. Yet, some members of Congress, including Senator John McCain—a veteran and member of the Senate Armed Services Committee—have indicated that they will only take action at the request of the military. In fact, in February 2001, in response to an SLDN request to present a briefing on the issue, Condoleeza Rice, then Assistant Secretary to the President for National Security Affairs, replied that SLDN should contact the Department of Defense directly. C. Dixon Osburn, Executive Director of SLDN, has described this deferral of responsibility as "the keystone cops approach to leadership." Yet, it remained notable that in 2006, for the first time in six years, the White House had been called upon to make public its position on policy.

Public statements calling for an end to "Don't Ask, Don't Tell" continue to appear on a regular basis. But, nowhere, perhaps, was such a public statement more surprising than when it came from a former chair of the Joint Chiefs of Staff. In August 1993, John Shalikashvili was selected to replace Colin Powell as Chair of the Joint Chiefs. After months of debate, the law known as "Don't Ask, Don't Tell" was about to be passed by the Congress. At the time, Shalikashvili was politic in his support of President Clinton's approach. He did not oppose the ban as too progressive, nor did he oppose it as too restrictive. On January 2, 2007, in an op-ed published in *The New York Times*, General Shalikashvili (U.S. Army, retired) wrote that while he still believes that eliminating the ban in 1993 would have been too burdensome on the military, he now believes that "if gay men and lesbians served openly in the United States military, they would not undermine the efficacy of the armed forces." He cautioned that such a change would have to be approached carefully, but that "[b]y taking a measured, prudent approach to change, political and military leaders can focus on solving the nation's most pressing problems while remaining genuinely open to the eventual and inevitable lifting of the ban."[10] The evening that Shalikashvili's piece appeared, former Secretary of Defense William Cohen was interviewed on CNN. He stated, "I think that what we're hearing from within the military is what we're hearing from within society, that we're becoming a much more open, tolerant society . . ." Cohen described the policy as one of discrimination. In light of evidence that both the military and society have seen fairly dramatic shifts in attitudes, both Shalikashvili and Cohen, advocates of the ban a decade ago, now advocate that, at a minimum, the policy be revisited.

And, most recently, on June 13, 2007, Bob Barr published an op-ed in *The Wall Street Journal* titled "Don't Ask, Who Cares." He wrote:

> As a conservative Republican member of Congress from 1995 to 2003, I was hardly a card-carrying member of the gay-rights lobby. I opposed then, and continue to oppose, same-sex marriage, or the designation of gays as a constitutionally protected minority class. Service in the armed forces is another matter. The bottom line here is that, with nearly a decade and a half of the hybrid "don't ask, don't tell" policy to guide us, I have become deeply impressed with the growing weight of credible military opinion which concludes that allowing gays to serve openly in the military does not pose insurmountable problems for the good order and discipline of the services . . . . The fact is, equal treatment of gay and lesbian service members is about as conservative a position as one cares to articulate.[11]

In response to statements such as these, newspapers around the country are again addressing the issue. Some, like the *Houston Chronicle*, note that while caution seems wise, we shouldn't wait too long. Others, like the *Seattle Post-Intelligencer*, citing the president's desire to increase troop levels in Iraq, point out that this may be a case of doing the right thing for the wrong reason. But, most are calling for repeal, in whatever fashion it occurs. Of course, there are those who continue to oppose military service by gays, lesbians, and bisexuals. Some oppose even the notion of "serving in silence." It is those voices to which we now turn.

Supporting a Policy of Exclusion

Discrimination, in and of itself, is not a bad thing. We all discriminate. Some prefer pepperoni to sausage. Others have a preference for bright clothing over dark or Coke over Pepsi. When the term "discrimination" is applied in that manner, there is little debate over its acceptance. Even with regard to employment, situations exist where it is not only legitimate, but also legal to prefer an employee of one faith tradition to another. For example, a kosher butcher shop is permitted to hire only Jewish butchers. And, viewed by many as more exceptional, but still permissible under law, is the case where an employer successfully demonstrates the need to hire a person of one sex rather than another. For example, a filmmaker may require that the "male lead" in a movie in fact be male.[12]

As discussed earlier in this volume, the military has a history of successfully discriminating on the basis of both race and sex. While, in the military, racial discrimination by law or regulation is no longer permissible under any condition, legal discrimination on the basis of sex persists. There are some jobs in the military that women are simply forbidden by law to perform. The military also discriminates on the basis of age, health, weight, and mental capacity, to name a few. In some military specialties, such as a pilot, one's vision or height may serve as a disqualifying factor. Few would quibble over the need of the military to discriminate on these bases.[13]

Putting aside the debate over whether "Don't Ask, Don't Tell" actually forbids all military service by gays, lesbians, and bisexuals or whether it merely restricts their service, the question is not whether the government may ever discriminate, but whether, in this case, it is justified in doing so. This volume has sought to explore the history, implementation, and impact of the policy that prohibits gays, lesbians, and bisexuals from serving openly. The voice of those who favor such a policy, or one more stringent, has been largely absent. This is not because such individuals do not exist. Chapter 1 presented their views as expressed during the Congressional hearings that took place in 1993. But, while individual opposition remains, there has been little in the way of ongoing, organized support for "Don't Ask, Don't Tell."

The most obvious reason for this lack of organizational voice is that the policy is the law. When successful at establishing one's position as law, many perceive there to be little over which to continue arguing. That role falls to those who advocate for change. It is those who advocate for change who collect the data, lobby Congress, file the lawsuits, and so forth. Thus, in this volume, material is drawn almost exclusively from advocacy organizations such as SLDN, research organizations like the Michael D. Palm Center,[14] and individuals, like Bleu Copas, who have seen their careers terminated against their will.

Military organizations were very vocal during the debates in 1993. For example, the Non Commissioned Officers Association (NCOA), the Reserve Officers Association (ROA), and the Retired Officers Association (TROA)[15] all communicated to members of Congress their organizational support for a ban on the military service of gays, lesbians, and bisexuals. Representing the NCOA in his capacity as the Deputy Director of Legislative Affairs, Michael Ouellette (Sergeant Major, U.S. Army, retired) testified before the Senate that "if [the Department of Defense] should, by chance, succumb to public pressure on the issue, NCOA will not alter its position" and that "NCOA firmly believes that this is a social issue and not one of discrimination as some would lead us to believe." None appear to have made public an organizational position on the issue since that time. If they have, an exhaustive search of their Web sites failed to reveal such evidence. These organizations are focused primarily on personnel issues such as health care, taxes, survivorship, etc.

In 2003, Hofstra University School of Law held a conference titled *Don't Ask, Don't Tell: 10 Years Later*. Conference organizers sought representatives from the Department of Defense and from those public figures most vociferous in their defense of the policy. "Despite repeated invitations and offers to give them an exclusive platform to air their views," none attended.[16] While there does not appear to be an organization whose sole mission is to keep "Don't Ask, Don't Tell," there are organizations in which such efforts do exist as a part of the overall mission and it would be an oversight not to address their place in the debate. One such organization is Elaine Donnelly's Center for Military Readiness (CRM). It describes itself as "an independent, non-partisan 501(c)(3) educational organization formed to take a leadership role in promoting sound military personnel policies" and "the only organization that concentrates on military personnel issues full-time."[17]

Its guiding principles include the statement that "[t]he armed forces should not be used for political purposes or social experiments that needlessly elevate risks, detract from readiness, or degrade American cultural values." To get a sense of what this involves, consider that, though purporting to support women in uniform, CMR seeks the review of what it characterizes as "Clinton-era social engineering." This includes the assignment of women soldiers in or near land combat units, co-ed basic training, and "gender-based recruiting 'goals' and quotas that hurt morale and increase costs."[18] On the issue of gays, lesbians, and bisexuals, CMR is actually in agreement with organizations like SLDN. "If the goal is to allow homosexuals to serve, Clinton's . . . [Don't Ask, Don't Tell] regulations do not go far enough."[19] That, however, is where any similarity ends.

The position of CMR on the issue is clear, yet inarticulate. That is, it is clear that they oppose any military role for gays, lesbians, and bisexuals. What is less clear is the rationale they provide in support of their position. In brief, their position appears to be support for what they believe to be the law, but not the policy that resulted from the law. That is, they argue that the military regulations are inconsistent with Section 654, Title 10 of the United States Code.

Regarding Public Law 103-160, the legislation that became the Code, CMR states, "The flawed cornerstone principle of 'don't ask, don't tell,' to the effect that homosexual orientation is not a bar to military service, is conspicuously absent." They are correct that the law does not explicitly state that orientation is not a bar to service. The language of the law focuses affirmatively on what it purports to address—homosexual conduct—rather than what it does not—homosexual orientation. Ironically, both sides in the debate acknowledge the fallacy of drawing this distinction.

CMR continues, "Instead, the plain meaning of the law and legislative history affirmed the classic principle that 'Homosexuality is incompatible with military service.'"[20] By this they understand, correctly, that the language of the law implicitly affirms the notion of incompatibility, while not explicitly stating that homosexuality is not a bar to service. What the law actually says is that "homosexual conduct is a long-standing element of military law that continues to be necessary in the unique circumstances of military service." As above, the conundrum, for both sides in the debate, is that, under both the law and the policy, conduct, not status, is alleged to serve as the bar to service. Thus, while inherent in the law is the position that homosexuality—conduct and status—is incompatible, CMR is correct in its assertion that the law does not, as did earlier regulations, state that homosexuality, as a status characteristic, is incompatible. The irony is that while many agree that the law is flawed, and even come to some agreement on the nature of the flaw, there is no agreement as to the remedy.

Additionally, CMR argues that the exceptions listed in the regulation are contrary to the law. The exceptions under the regulations include, for example, the provision under which the accused can rebut the presumption that his or her statement of "being" gay, lesbian, or bisexual presumes the prohibited "homosexual acts." Yet, contrary to what CMR appears to believe, the law itself does provide exceptions. For example, "Nothing ... shall be construed to require that a member of the armed forces be processed for separation from the armed forces when a determination is made in accordance with regulations prescribed by the Secretary of Defense that ... separation of the member would not be in the best interest of the armed forces." It is clear that CMR seeks a full prohibition on the military service of gays, lesbians, and bisexuals, a prohibition they believe exists in the law, but not in the regulations that implement the law. What remains debatable is whether that law, given the way it uses status—including speech—as a proxy for conduct, can really be interpreted as permitting the service of gays, lesbians, and bisexuals at all.

Following the line of argument that the law demands a prohibition, regardless of status or conduct, CMR calls on President Bush to eliminate the regulations and enforce the law. "President Bush," they write, "has a constitutional responsibility to enforce the 1993 statute that excludes homosexuals from the military. He has no obligation to retain administrative regulations put in place by the previous administration."[21]

CMR believes that the law has a greater likelihood, than do the regulations, of surviving a constitutional challenge. They write, "Legal challenges to America's law, citing foreign court decisions that activists want to use in overruling the U.S. Constitution, pose a real threat. Current and future challenges can be defeated, however, by sound legal strategy that defends the law, not the convoluted DADT policy."[22]

They assert, accurately, that the federal courts have a tradition of deferring to the military in personnel issues. They believe that *Lawrence v. Texas* is unlikely to have any impact because "there is no such thing as 'privacy' in the military."[23] This is an open question as while personal privacy is certainly compromised in a military setting, it is not true that military service involves accepting an absolute concession of one's right to privacy.

Finally, they believe that since the military prohibition on sodomy, an area of law that remains largely untouched by *Lawrence*, applies to all service members, there is no valid equal protection claim. In an example of the confusion evidenced in their writings, CMR states, "[t]he 1993 exclusion law and the Uniform Code of Military Justice (UCMJ) ban on sodomy apply to men and women in precisely the same way...."[24] The issue is not whether they apply to men and women in the same way. Opposition to "Don't Ask, Don't Tell" does not rest on sex or gender discrimination, but on discrimination on the basis of sexual orientation. Thus, at issue is whether the law or the UCMJ justifiably discriminates between heterosexual service members and those who are gay, lesbian, or bisexual. Again, it is important to note that challenges to the UCMJ are completely distinct from challenges to the law known as "Don't Ask, Don't Tell."[25]

Thus, relative to the growing demand to eliminate "Don't Ask, Don't Tell," there has been little public voice demanding that gays, lesbians, and bisexuals be prohibited from serving in the military. But, loud or not, such voices do exist. As public outcry for the repeal or overturn of the law grows louder, it can be expected that the voice of the opposition may rise accordingly. Yet, as more and more of those who supported "Don't Ask, Don't Tell" change their position, it is also likely that those voices will find themselves fewer and fewer in number.

Congressional Efforts to Repeal

On March 2, 2005, Representative Marty Meehan (Massachusetts) introduced legislation to repeal "Don't Ask, Don't Tell" and replace it with a policy explicitly prohibiting discrimination on the basis of sexual orientation. Meehan has long been opposed to the policy restricting the military service of gays and lesbians. In 1993, his first piece of legislation as a new member of Congress had been an amendment to eliminate "Don't Ask, Don't Tell," a policy he has described as "as senseless and counterproductive militarily as it is un-American," from the fiscal year 1994 Defense Authorization bill.[26]

The Military Readiness Enhancement Act of 2005 (H.R. 1059) stated that "[t]he Secretary of Defense, and the Secretary of Homeland Security with respect to the Coast Guard when it is not operating as a service in the Navy, may not discriminate on the basis of sexual orientation against any member of the armed forces or against any person seeking to become a member of the armed forces."[27] The bill further stated that "[n]othing in this section prohibits the Secretary of Defense, and the Secretary of Homeland Security with respect to the Coast Guard when it is not operating as a service in the Navy, from prescribing or enforcing regulations governing the conduct of members of the armed forces if the regulations are designed and applied without regard to sexual orientation."[28] That is, the legislation would not prevent the military from regulating the conduct of its personnel, provided that such regulation did not discriminate on the basis of sexual orientation.

In addition, the legislation addressed the issues of reentry and dependent benefits. Service members who were discharged under previous policies barring the service of gays, lesbians, and bisexuals would, if otherwise qualified, not be prohibited from reentering the armed forces solely because of the earlier separation. And, responding to an issue of great concern to many who support the ban, the legislation directed that "[n]othing in this Act, or the amendments made by this Act, shall be construed to require the furnishing of dependent benefits in violation of Section 7 of Title 1, United States Code (relating to the definitions of 'marriage' and 'spouse' and referred to as the 'Defense of Marriage Act')."[29] The bill was also careful to note that the term sexual orientation includes heterosexuality, homosexuality, and bisexuality, both real and perceived, as well as statements and consensual sexual conduct taken as indicative of heterosexuality, homosexuality, or bisexuality. At its core, the legislation, had it passed, would have repealed the law, Section 654, Title 10 of the United States Code, that serves as the foundation for the military policy known as "Don't Ask, Don't Tell."

In response to the introduction of this legislation, Representative Meehan was contacted by people across the country, including military personnel and veterans. Patrick Heusner wrote, "As an openly gay veteran of Operation Iraqi Freedom, I was incredibly encouraged to hear that legislation had been introduced to repeal 'Don't Ask Don't Tell'... I was an enlisted (Specialist) servicemember of the U.S. Army for $3^1/_2$ years, having served as a combat medic both in Bosnia and Iraq... [M]y fellow soldiers judged me as a soldier, and most could not have cared less about my 'orientation.' They cared about whether I could remain alert on a 36-hour convoy, use my weapon efficiently, and perform my medical tasks successfully."[30]

On March 17, 2005, the bill was referred to the Subcommittee on Military Personnel where it remained for the session. At the close of the 109th Congress in December 2006, 122 members of the U.S. House of Representatives had signed on as cosponsors of the legislation. The legislation, not having passed during the previous session, was reintroduced as H.R. 1246 on February 28, 2007. In an end-of-the-year letter to his constituents, Meehan had written, "I'll be working tirelessly to bring new members of both parties onboard our campaign to lift the ban. I will also be asking for the first congressional hearings on gays in the military since 1993. I know that when my colleagues see and understand the evidence against 'don't ask, don't tell,' they will be motivated to join me in the fight for repeal."[31]

Cook v. Gates

In December 2004, twelve plaintiffs, aided by SLDN and the pro bono work of a law firm with offices in Boston and Washington, DC, filed suit against then Secretary of Defense Donald Rumsfeld, then Secretary of Homeland Security, Tom Ridge, and the United States. In the complaint, filed in U.S. District Court for the District of Massachusetts, they challenged the constitutionality of Section 654, Title 10 of the United States Code, the law known as "Don't Ask, Don't Tell."

The plaintiffs first claimed that they had been denied due process. The complaint asserted that the "Fourth, Fifth, and Ninth Amendments to the U.S. Constitution guarantee and protect vital interests in liberty and privacy" and that these interests include "a fundamental liberty interest in private adult consensual intimacy and relationships, including consensual intimacy and relationships between adults of the same sex."[32] Since "Don't Ask, Don't Tell" deprives gay, lesbian, and bisexual service members from pursuing such relationships, the complaint asserted that they were, by definition, deprived of liberty, privacy, and due process of law.

Questions of constitutional law require that the court apply a particular standard of review. Depending upon the group asserting that their rights are being infringed, or the right being asserted, the court may use one of several standards of review. The classification "sexual orientation" has generally been granted review only at the level of rational basis. This is the lowest hurdle for the government and deprivation of rights may, in fact, be permissible. That is, the government need only show that its action is rationally related to serving a legitimate state interest. In *Cook*, the plaintiffs asserted that under no standard of review was there a government interest that permits the deprivation of rights they asserted exist under "Don't Ask, Don't Tell."

The plaintiffs also claimed that the law violated their rights under the First Amendment. Under Section 654 of Title 10, service members are prohibited from stating that they are gay, lesbian, or bisexual or from making any statement that might suggest a propensity to engage in same-sex acts. The plaintiffs claimed that the law violates their freedom of speech, right to assemble, and the right to expressive association. As with the first claim, the plaintiffs asserted that there is no government interest, at any level of review, which should allow such a violation of the rights granted by the Constitution.

In the third claim, the plaintiffs in *Cook* asserted that the law violates the Fifth Amendment guarantee of equal protection under the law. Heterosexual service members are not discharged for their sexual orientation. Gay, lesbian, and bisexual service members are discharged because of their sexual orientation. Service members who identify as heterosexual are not prohibited from speaking openly and engaging in actions that indicate their heterosexuality. Service members who identify as gay, lesbian, and bisexual are prohibited from such speech or actions. The complaint alleged that the law "reflects an improper animus based on sexual orientation."[33] That is, the law is motivated by hostility toward a particular class of persons. Again, the plaintiffs asserted this type of discrimination is impermissible under the Constitution, regardless of the standard of review that is applied.

The plaintiffs in *Cook* sought an order declaring the law unconstitutional and declaring that the application of the law to each plaintiff was also unconstitutional. They sought an order declaring that the regulations issued in compliance with the law are unconstitutional and were unconstitutionally applied to each plaintiff. They sought to prohibit the defendants from enforcing the law. In addition to requesting any other relief the court would have found appropriate and the granting of costs and attorneys' fees, the plaintiffs sought to be reinstated, provided that they met all other eligibility requirements for doing so (e.g., weight, health).

Two months later, in February 2005, the government filed a motion to dismiss the case. The government's motion first cites the tradition of deference to the military as a rationale for dismissal. In essence, the defendants argue, the unique nature of the military and military life requires that the court defer to the knowledge of Congress on the majority of issues involving military personnel.

The government also claims that the law is neither a denial of equal protection nor a violation of the First Amendment. The government argues that the appropriate level of review is rational basis, the lowest hurdle for establishing the legitimacy of discriminatory practices. Then, having only to establish a rational basis for the policy, the government cites the unique nature of military life and the need for unit cohesion and privacy as sufficient justification for the exclusionary policy. With regard to the First Amendment, the government proffers the argument that the policy does not forbid speech, but merely the conduct for which the speech serves as evidence. The memorandum supporting the government's motion to dismiss ends by requesting that the court enter judgment in their favor and dismiss the suit.

After the filing of additional motions by both plaintiffs and defendants, the District Court for Massachusetts issued its ruling in April 2006. With regard to the issues of both due process and equal protection, the court did not find persuasive the plaintiffs' argument that the case called for a heightened level of judicial review. Rather, the level of rational basis, giving the government the most leeway to justify discrimination, was found to be appropriate. The court held that the plaintiffs' claims on both due process and equal protection must be dismissed. With regard to the alleged violation of rights under the First Amendment, the court held that this claim, too, was without merit and must be dismissed. As discussed throughout the opinion, the court held that "the policy rationally serves the important government interest of maintaining an effective national military."[34]

In November 2006, the plaintiffs in *Cook* filed an appeal of the District Court's decision with the First Circuit Court of Appeal in Boston. Michael Chertoff replaced Tom Ridge as a defendant in his capacity as the Secretary of Homeland Security. The appeal asserts that the District Court applied the wrong legal framework to the due process and equal protection claims. Specifically, the appellate brief provides that the court misread the holding of the U.S. Supreme Court in *Lawrence v. Texas*. It also states that the court applied the wrong standard of review to the equal protection claim, asserting that animus can never serve as a legitimate government interest. With regard to the legal framework, the appellants also argue that the doctrine of deference to the military should not be understood as carte blanche denial of constitutional protections. The appellants also assert that the District Court misunderstood their challenge and made several errors by ignoring key elements of their claims. With regard to the First Amendment, appellants argue that the law does require a heightened level of review because it is directed at protected speech. In addition, they argue that the rebuttable presumption aspect of the law imposes an unconstitutional condition on protected speech. It is, they claim, in all practicality, impossible to effectively rebut the presumption and that the law therefore has a "chilling effect" on all statements and expressions that one might make related to gay, lesbian, or bisexual issues.[35]

Since that filing, amicus briefs in support of the plaintiffs have been filed by the American Civil Liberties Union, Lambda Legal Defense and Education Fund, Inc., and Gay and Lesbian Advocates and Defenders. Six professors of law have filed an amicus brief speaking to the proper application of the doctrine of military deference. Fourteen military leaders, including former Assistant Secretary of Defense Lawrence J. Korb, Carolyn Becraft, former Assistant Secretary of the Navy, and Admiral John D. Hutson, (U.S. Navy, retired), President and Dean of Franklin Pierce Law School, have signed on to a brief supporting the plaintiffs. And, the American Sociological Association and five social scientists submitted a brief regarding the social science research supportive of the plaintiffs' case.[36]

In late December 2006, the government filed its response to the appeal. Robert Gates replaced Donald Rumsfeld as a defendant in his capacity as Secretary of Defense. As is the convention, the government response addresses those points made in the appellate brief. The government asserts that substantial deference to the military is appropriate. Claiming that neither a fundamental right is infringed nor that a suspect or quasi-suspect class is involved, the government asserts that a rational basis level of review is appropriate. The response contends that the District Court acted appropriately when it dismissed the complaint. Finally, the government claims that using speech as evidence for prohibited activities does not implicate the First Amendment and that the arguments made to the contrary by the amici lack merit. For example, the response finds no merit in the American Sociological Association and social scientists' contention that the open service of gays and lesbians does not impair military performance.[37] The First Circuit heard oral arguments on March 7, 2007. As of this writing, no decision has yet been announced.

Conclusion

As I write this conclusion, in March 2007, the 110th Congress has convened. The Democrats, generally more in favor of eliminating "Don't Ask, Don't Tell" than their Republican colleagues, hold a majority in both houses. The U.S. Court of Appeals in the First Circuit will likely issue its opinion in *Cook* before the summer ends. The Bush administration seeks to increase U.S. troop presence in Iraq, yet the military continues to face challenges with recruitment and retention. Public support for the open service of gays and lesbians continues to increase. A lot could change by the time this volume is in your hands.

All indicators suggest that "Don't Ask, Don't Tell" will disappear. The question is how and when. It is unlikely that, even with a Democratic majority, there will be enough support to override the veto that President Bush would be expected to sign. But, with a presidential election on the horizon, and candidates from many sides unwilling to take a strong stand in favor of the policy, repeal may be possible.

If the First Circuit finds in favor of the plaintiffs, the government will surely appeal to the U.S. Supreme Court. And, with the government requesting a hearing, there is a good chance that the Court will accept the case. On the other hand, if the First Circuit finds in favor of the government, leaving the plaintiffs to appeal to the Supreme Court, history suggests that the Court will decline to review the case. Whether by Congressional repeal or judicial decision, the outcome of efforts to end "Don't Ask, Don't Tell" is anyone's game.

There is the possibility that the law will remain the law and that, over time, the military will ignore it. There is ample evidence that this was the case under previous regulations and there is evidence that many current commanders already choose to look the other way. But, that does little to assuage the very real concerns of gay, lesbian, and bisexual military personnel. They are still not safe.

Until "Don't Ask, Don't Tell" is officially removed from the U.S. Code, whether by repeal or being declared unconstitutional, gay, lesbian, and bisexual service members will continue to serve their country while not having the same freedoms as do their heterosexual counterparts. This is not a political statement. The difference of opinion is not in whether it is true or not. The difference of opinion centers on whether or not the discrimination is justified.

One anonymous author, a graduate of the U.S. Military Academy at West Point and former secretary of the Cadet Honor Committee, wrote these words to Representative Meehan: "As the military valiantly battles terrorists in Iraq and Afghanistan, many officers, non-commissioned officers, and soldiers are fighting soulful, internal battles of their own between the concepts of honor and duty. How does one balance one's sexual orientation against one's desire or perceived duty to serve one's country through honorable service in the United States Armed Forces?"[38]

"Don't Ask, Don't Tell" doesn't explicitly prohibit gay, lesbian, and bisexual citizens from serving in the U.S. armed forces. Yet, such a prohibition is inherent. The law, and related policies, requires that gay, lesbian, and bisexual service members—and potential service members—lie. It prevents them from establishing the kind of relationships with their peers that aid the military in performing its assigned mission. Thoughtful citizens are beginning to understand that while "Don't Ask, Don't Tell" might have been the only option in 1993, times have changed. What remains to be seen is how the changing times will lead to a change in the law.

Notes

1. "Barry Goldwater on Gays in the Military," SLDN Law Library, http://www.sldn.com/templates/law/record.html?section=33&record=289.

2. "Senator Chuck Robb: 'Don't Ask, Don't Tell' Must Fall," SLDN Law Library, http://www.sldn.org/templates/law/record.html?section=33&record=627.

3. "American Morning: Gays in the Military," CNN transcript, December 11, 2003, http://transcripts.cnn.com/TRANSCRIPTS/0312/11/ltm.10.html.

4. John Files, "Gay Ex-Officers Say 'Don't Ask' Doesn't Work," *The New York Times*, December 10, 2003, p. A18.

5. "Senior Retired Military Leaders Call for Dismantling 'Don't Ask, Don't Tell,'" SLDN press release, December 16, 2003, http://www.sldn.org/templates/press/record.html?section=2&record=1335.

6. "As Enrollment Declines, Military Academy Grads Call on Services to Support Repeal of 'Don't Ask, Don't Tell,'" SLDN press release, July 11, 2005, http://www.sldn.org/templates/press/record.html?section=2&record=2279.

7. "Newspapers Call for Repeal of 'Don't Ask, Don't Tell,'" SLDN press release, March 8, 2006, http://www.sldn.org/templates/press/record.html?section=2&record=2759.

8. "A Better Way to Fight 'Don't Ask, Don't Tell,'" *The Oregonian*, March 8, 2006, http://www.oregonlive.com/editorials/oregonian/index.ssf?/base/editorial/1141782905405 10.xml&coll=7.

9. "Three Star Army General Calls for Repeal of 'Don't Ask, Don't Tell,'" SLDN press release, May 16, 2006, http://www.sldn.org/templates/press/record.html?section=2& record=2958.

10. John M. Shalikashvili, "Second Thoughts on Gays in the Military," *The New York Times*, January 2, 2007. © 2007 The New York Times, Inc. All rights reserved. Used by permission and protected by the Copyright Laws of the United States. The printing, copying, redistribution, or retransmission of the Material without express written permission is prohibited.

11. Bob Barr, "Don't Ask, Who Cares," *The Wall Street Journal*, June 13, 2007, http://www.bobbarr.org/default.asp?pt=newsdescr&RI=860.

12. "Law and the Workplace," in *ABA Family Legal Guide*, Chapter 11, http://www.abanet.org/publiced/practical/books/family_legal_guide/chapter_11.pdf. Race, however, is never permitted to function as a bona fide occupational qualification.

13. Thanks to Dr. Aaron Belkin for suggesting the clarification of the concept of discrimination.

14. Formerly the Center for the Study of Sexual Minorities in the Military at the University of California, Santa Barbara.

15. As of September 2002, TROA is now the Military Officers Association of America.

16. James A. Garland, *Symposium Introduction*, Hofstra Lab. & Emp. L. J. 325, 326 (2005).

17. What this actually means is unclear since many organizations, such as those addressed above, exist solely to address the concerns of service members, veterans, and their families. With the exception of a volunteer board of advisors, it appears as though Elaine Donnelly *is* CMR. However, lacking confirmation of this possibility, but as no authorship is provided for the CMR materials cited herein, this chapter refers to CMR, rather than Donnelly, as the author.

18. "CMR Launches Americans for the Military Campaign," September 8, 2003, http://www.cmrlink.org/activities.asp?docID=213.

19. "The Homosexual Exclusion Law vs. the Clinton 'Don't Ask, Don't Tell' Policy," January 7, 2002, http://www.cmrlink.org/HMilitary.asp?docID=103.

20. "A Law Worthy of Public Support: Public Law 103-160, Section 654, Title 10," September 17, 2001, http://www.cmrlink.org/HMilitary.asp?docID=29.

21. "Bush Enforces Law—Clarity Still Needed," September 7, 2004, http://www.cmrlink.org/HMilitary.asp?DocID=229.

22. Ibid.

23. Ibid.

24. Ibid.

25. A number of military cases have addressed Article 125, the Uniform Code of Military Justice's prohibition on sodomy. Given the facts of the cases, some have found the law to have been applied unconstitutionally. Article 125 remains a part of military criminal law, distinct from military regulations regarding the service of gay, lesbian, and bisexual service members.

26. "Meehan Introduces Legislation to Repeal 'Don't Ask, Don't Tell,'" Congressman Martin T. Meehan press release, March 2, 2005, http://www.house.gov/list/press/ma05_meehan/NR050302DADT.html.

27. http://www.govtrack.us/congress/billtext.xpd?bill=h109-1059.

28. H.R. 1059, 109th Congress, http://thomas.loc.gov/cgi-bin/query/D?c109:2:./temp/~c109pQDEr7::, March 2, 2005.

29. Ibid.

30. "Ending the Ban on Gays in the Military," Web site of Representative Marty Meehan, http://www.house.gov/meehan/issues-dadt.html.

31. "Meehan to push for repeal of gay soldier ban," Advocate.com, December 29, 2006, http://www.advocate.com/news_detail_ektid40713.asp.

32. *Cook v. Rumsfeld*, complaint filed in the U.S. District Court for the District of Massachusetts, December 6, 2004, http://www.sldn.org/binary-data/SLDN_ARTICLES/pdf_file/1864.pdf.

33. Ibid.

34. *Cook v. Rumsfeld*, Civil Action No. 04-12546-GAO, U.S. District Court for the District of Massachusetts, Memorandum and Order, April 24, 2006, http://pacer.mad.uscourts.gov/dc/cgi-bin/recentops.pl?filename=otoole/pdf/cook%20v%20rumsfeld%20mem%20ord.pdf.

35. The synopses of documents in *Cook v. Rumsfeld/Cook v. Gates* are intentionally brief. The appellate brief submitted by the plaintiffs/appellants is over sixty pages in length. The government's response to the appeal exceeds eighty pages. Materials are available as pdf files at http://www.sldn.org/templates/law/index.html?section=92.

36. Amicus briefs can also be found at http://www.sldn.org/templates/law/index.html?section=92. It should be noted that the author of this volume is a named social scientist in that brief.

37. The response states, "As we have explained, Congress heard and credited ample evidence to the contrary. Under rational basis review, courts cannot second-guess Congress's rational assessment of conflicting evidence . . . . To the contrary, legislative choices subject to rational basis review 'may be based on rational speculation unsupported by evidence or empirical data,' . . . ." What the response fails to note is the potential for the underlying evidence to simply no longer hold merit. This, of course, would undermine the position they are trying to establish.

38. "Ending the Ban on Gays in the Military," Web site of Representative Marty Meehan, http://www.house.gov/meehan/issues-dadt.html.

Key Legal Decisions

Long before the passage of "Don't Ask, Don't Tell" (DADT), courts had been faced with litigation challenging various military policies that excluded gay and lesbian service members. The rulings in these cases are complex. In this volume it is not possible to provide a thorough telling of all of the decisions, appeals, remands to a lower court, partial victories, etc. But, it is fair to say that, typically, a result favoring the plaintiff applied only to that plaintiff. That is, no successful challenge has been broadly applied to similarly situated service members, but to only the individual who brought the suit. As discussed in Chapter 1, for example, Leonard Matlovich and Vernon "Copy" Berg were reinstated, but the court's ruling did not open the doors for other gay and lesbian service members to serve openly.

A good number of significant cases occurred prior to DADT, but remain relevant for how the courts interpreted different aspects of the legal challenges. In the 1980s, Miriam Ben-Shalom had success before the District Court, though she ultimately lost when the Seventh Circuit reversed the decision of the District Court, holding that the regulations making homosexuality a disqualifying factor did not violate the First Amendment. The court also held that gays and lesbians were not a suspect class; thus, a deferential rational basis standard of review applied. Under such a standard, they found no violation of Equal Protection.[1] James Dronenburg filed suit challenging his discharge from the Navy. His case also affirmed that discharges for homosexual conduct are a rational means of achieving a legitimate interest, that is, the maintenance of discipline, order, etc.[2] Dusty Pruitt was discharged for having acknowledged her lesbianism in a newspaper interview. Her case, which she ultimately lost, is often cited in DADT cases because of its ruling that the deference courts must afford the military does not preclude judicial review of military decisions and the holding that First Amendment protections do not preclude speech from serving as evidence of one's propensity for same-sex sexual conduct.[3] Other cases include, though are not limited to, those of Mel Dahl, Keith Meinhold, Joseph Steffan, and Perry Watkins.[4] Although none of these cases proved decisive in terms of the exclusionary policies overall, they remain important as part of the history and for understanding the rationales used by the courts to, for the most part, uphold discrimination on the basis of sexual orientation.

Litigating "Don't Ask, Don't Tell"

A number of cases were initiated just prior to the passage of DADT, but were resolved after its passage. In these cases the court often had to consider both previous and current policies. Other cases began after the law's passage and are strictly DADT cases. Both are addressed here. These summaries warrant a word of caution. Again, it is not possible, within the limitations of this volume, to do justice to the details of each case. Provided here is a very brief snapshot of each case with particular attention paid to the holding of the court and the rationale for that holding.[5]

Cammermeyer v. Aspin, 850 F. Supp. 910, W.D. Wash. 1994

Plaintiff Margarethe Cammermeyer, a Colonel and a nurse, had served over twenty years in the U.S. Army, Army Reserve, and the National Guard. In 1985 she had been selected by the Department of Veteran's Affairs as the Nurse of the Year. In 1988 she was the Chief Nurse of the Washington State National Guard. Les Aspin was the Secretary of Defense during the Clinton administration. Other defendants were unnamed.

In 1989, Cammermeyer was interviewed as part of the process to upgrade her security clearance. In the course of that interview, she admitted that she was a lesbian. In 1992, the Army discharged her on those grounds. Even the governor had tried to intervene, protesting the dismissal of someone with such a long and distinguished career. Cammermeyer immediately filed suit, claiming that her discharge, based on Army Regulation 135–175, violated her rights to Equal Protection, Due Process, privacy, and freedom of speech. She also claimed that the Army regulation was an invalid exercise of executive power in that it violated the separation of powers and the principles of federalism. Army Regulation 135–175 was the Army's ban on homosexuals, in place prior to the implementation of DADT. It explicitly linked homosexual orientation to conduct.

The court ruled in Cammermeyer's favor on her Fifth Amendment Equal Protection and Due Process claims. The defendants were ordered to reinstate her, expunge her record, and were enjoined from taking further action against her. The court also declared the Army's action and the regulation unconstitutional. The court's determination on the Equal Protection claim rested on their finding that the government proffered no rational basis for discharging members based solely on their sexual orientation.

In the time between Cammermeyer's filing and the court's ruling, DADT was implemented. Nonetheless, Cammermeyer was reinstated in the National Guard in June 1994 and resumed her previous position as Chief Nurse. In March 1997, after thirty-one years of dedicated service, she retired with full military privileges.

Elzie v. Aspin, 841 F. Supp. 439, DDC 1993; 897 F. Supp. 1, DDC 1995

Plaintiff Justin Elzie served as a sergeant in the U.S. Marine Corps. Throughout his eleven years of service, he had received numerous honors including Marine of the Year for both his battalion and group. Les Aspin was the Secretary of Defense during the Clinton administration. Defendants also included John Dalton, Secretary of the Navy, and Carl Mundy, Jr., Commandant of the Marine Corps.

Elzie had submitted his paperwork for an early retirement program and was waiting to begin out-processing. Then, President Clinton announced his intention to eliminate the ban on gay and lesbian service members, calling for an interim policy under which the Attorney General had power to suspend discharges. In January 1993, the U.S. District Court in the Central District of California ruled in the case of sailor Keith Meinhold, permanently enjoining the Department of Defense from discharging or denying enlistment to any person based on sexual orientation in the absence of sexual conduct which interferes with the military mission of the armed forces of the United States. It was *after* these two events that Elzie made statements about his sexual orientation, believing that the interim policy would prevent him from discharge. Elzie came out as a gay Marine on ABC's *World News Tonight* and was honorably discharged the following month.

After spending six months in a standby reserve status, Elzie filed suit against the Department of Defense claiming that the Marine Corps unlawfully recommended him for discharge and denied him access to the retirement benefits program. Elzie's discharge was based solely on statements he made about his sexual orientation. He sought a preliminary injunction that would restore him to active duty, enjoin the parties from discharging him solely on the basis of his sexual orientation, and restore him to full participation in the retirement benefits program.

On November 10, 1993, Judge Stanley Sporkin, in the U.S. District Court for the District of Columbia, granted an injunction barring the defendants from taking any adverse action toward the plaintiff based on his sexual orientation. Significantly, using a rational basis standard of review, the court ruled that the removal of service members based on their sexual orientation alone does not meet a legitimate government purpose. Justin Elzie served as an openly gay member of the Marine Corps until retiring in February 1997.

Selland v. Aspin, 832 F. Supp. 12, 1993; 905 F. Supp. 260, 1995

Plaintiff Richard Selland was a lieutenant in the Navy. Defendants included Secretary of Defense Les Aspin (later replaced by William Perry). There are two separate cases involved. The first was filed and heard in U.S. District Court for the District of Columbia. The second was filed and heard in U.S. District Court for Maryland.

In 1993 procedures were initiated to separate Selland from the Navy. However, due to the interim policy put in place before DADT, the Attorney General suspended his discharge until October 1, 1993, when the interim policy would expire and the new policy would begin. Selland was alerted that on this date the Navy would most likely finalize his separation without further consideration. In 1993 he filed for a temporary injunction in district court and was granted it. However, this first suit was dismissed when the new policy took effect. In 1995 Selland initiated the second case challenging his discharge under DADT. The Maryland District Court ruled that because DADT creates only an incidental burden on speech, the policy does not violate the First Amendment. Also, the court ruled that DADT did not violate Equal Protection, Due Process, or the Administrative Procedure Act (APA). They also said that the policy was not an unconstitutional sanction on status.

Holmes v. California Army National Guard, 920 F. Supp. 1510, 1996

Plaintiff Andrew Holmes was a First Lieutenant in the California Army National Guard (CANG) and, thus, the U.S. Army National Guard (USANG), with an exemplary service record. Defendants included the CANG, Major Tandy Bozeman, Governor Pete Wilson, the USANG, the United States, and Secretary of Defense William Perry.

The case was filed and decided in U.S. District Court for the Northern District of California. This included Holmes' challenge to his discharge and multiple motions for dismissal or summary judgment from the defendants. Holmes filed claims on both the state and federal levels. There were seven claims directed at the CANG, including the grounds of Equal Protection and free speech under the California state constitution, privacy under the California state constitution, California Labor Code §§ 1101, 1102, and 1102.1, California government code § 18500 (c)(5), and Executive Order B-54-79, and Equal Protection as provided in the Fourteenth Amendment of the U.S. Constitution. There were six other claims based in the U.S. Constitution including Equal Protection, free speech/expression, vagueness/over breadth, intimate associations, Due Process, and privacy. Holmes sought a reinstatement, restoration of his officer status, an injunction preventing DADT from being applied to him, and a pronouncement that DADT was unconstitutional.

The court dismissed all state law claims based on the Eleventh Amendment rule that federal courts cannot decide state law claims against a state or its officials. The California defendants asserted that the case was moot, but this was denied by the court. The court also rejected the California defendants' argument that they had no choice but to discharge Holmes from the CANG because he had lost federal recognition in the USANG. The California defendants relied on a section of U.S. Code that says members who lose federal recognition should be discharged from the National Guard. The court rejected their preemption argument because states have the sole responsibility for personnel decisions at the state level, for example in the California Guard. The court also rejected a similar California claim that they had no choice over Holmes' discharge because the federal DADT policy controls state National Guard action. The court did allow Holmes' federal claims against the state because of an exception to the Eleventh Amendment in which a suit against a state official seeking relief from unconstitutional state action is not a suit against the state. Significantly, the court agreed with Holmes' Equal Protection argument, saying DADT discriminates against homosexual service members based on sexual orientation, not conduct; that DADT does not rationally further a legitimate government interest, and that DADT is irrational because it is founded on prejudices. The court held DADT to violate Equal Protection because it equates a statement of status (homosexual orientation) with conduct, and allows this statement to be grounds for dismissal. They also rejected the assertion that using a rebuttable presumption allows service members to prove that their conduct does not align with their status. The court found that the presumption was in fact irrebuttable. Also, they found the rebuttable presumption strategy to violate Equal Protection because it presumes that conduct follows status, which the Supreme Court has, in other non-DADT cases, uniformly disallowed. Maintaining an effective military is certainly a legitimate government interest, but the court did not find DADT to be rationally related to this purpose. The defendants first claimed a privacy justification, but this was rejected because homosexuals are still allowed to serve in the military as long as they do not announce their status as such. The court also stated that unit cohesion cannot be used as justification because they believe DADT works against unit cohesion. The court also found that DADT violated Holmes' right to free speech because a mere statement of status was given significant evidentiary weight to his conduct. The court dismissed Holmes' Due Process claim saying it was covered better by his Equal Protection claim. The court also dismissed some of Holmes' claims based on privacy, vagueness, and intimate associations. Holmes' cross-motion for summary judgment was granted with regard to his federal Equal Protection and freedom of speech claims. Holmes was ordered to be reinstated in the CANG and as an officer in the USANG. The court ordered that no further proceedings based on DADT could be taken against Holmes. The government appealed and the Ninth Circuit Court upheld the constitutionality of DADT. Though one judge dissented, the three-judge panel concluded that the court was not in a position to "judge the wisdom, fairness or logic" of a policy set by Congress and military leaders.

Richenberg v. Perry, 909 F. Supp. 1303, 1995; 73 F.3d 172, 1995; 97 F.3d 256, 1996

Plaintiff Richard Richenberg was a captain in the Air Force. William Perry, Secretary of Defense, was named as the defendant. Also named as a defendant was Sheila Widnall, Secretary of the Air Force.

Richenberg first filed suit in the U.S. District Court for the District of Nebraska. The final decision on the case was made by the U.S. Court of Appeals for the

Eighth Circuit. The Eighth Circuit denied Richenberg an injunction while the appeal was pending and denied rehearing the case en banc in January 1997.

Richenberg sought review of his discharge under DADT. His arguments were grounded in the First Amendment, the Fifth Amendment, and the APA. Richenberg argued that his Equal Protection claim under the Fifth Amendment should receive heightened scrutiny from the courts because homosexuals are a suspect class. Richenberg also argued that the "presumption" created by DADT takes away Due Process because it is irrebuttable. Richenberg also used a bill of attainder claim, meaning he argued DADT was passed to punish a particular group of people without trial. The court held that the district court was correct in granting summary judgment to the defense, that DADT does not violate the First or Fifth Amendments or the APA, and that Richenberg failed to "rebut the presumption." The Eighth Circuit followed the trend of rejecting all First Amendment claims because the policy targets actions, not speech. The court rejected Richenberg's suspect class claim and confirmed that only a rational basis test must be used.

One judge, Richard Arnold, dissented in the case, saying that Richenberg should not have been discharged because he met the burden to rebut the presumption. While Richenberg did admit to being homosexual, he swore under oath not to act on any sexual feelings. If the government is going to make the assumption that he would act, Arnold said that there needs to be a realistic way to prove them wrong. Multiple testimonies were given that if Richenberg said he would not act, he would keep to his word. No government testimony refuted his adamancy that he would not act on homosexual feelings.

Thomasson v. Perry, 895 F. Supp. 820, 1995; 80 F.3d 915, 1996

Plaintiff Paul Thomasson, a lieutenant in the U.S. Navy and Naval Reserve, had received numerous commendations, including a Joint Service Commendation Medal issued under General Colin Powell as Chair of the Joint Chiefs of Staff. William Perry, Secretary of Defense, was named as a defendant. Also named as a defendant was John Dalton, Secretary of the Navy.

On March 4, 1994, the day following the Navy's implementation of DADT, Thomasson provided four Navy admirals for whom he worked with statements acknowledging that he was gay. The Navy immediately began separation proceedings. During the administrative board of inquiry, the Navy acknowledged both that Thomasson possessed a distinguished record of service and that there was no evidence that Thomasson had engaged in homosexual acts. Thomasson, however, refused to present evidence rebutting the presumption that a statement that one is gay is equivalent to acknowledging one's participation in, or propensity to engage in, homosexual acts. The board recommended that he be discharged.

In February 1995, Thomasson filed for an injunction in U.S. District Court for the Eastern District of Virginia, Alexandria Division. The court granted the injunction, thereby preventing the Navy from further action. In 1996, the Court of Appeals for the Fourth Circuit affirmed the ruling of the lower court. Thomasson claimed that DADT was unconstitutional and violated the APA. He based his claims on the rights to Equal Protection, Due Process, and free speech. Thomasson argued that the law violates the First Amendment because it places a content-based restriction on free speech. He argued that, unlike the old policy, DADT accepts that homosexuals may serve in the military, as long as they don't acknowledge their orientation. Therefore, Thomasson argued that the acknowledgment itself should have no evidentiary value, since the military should know that gay members are serving. The court ruled for the defendants saying that DADT was constitutional and that it did not violate the APA. The court rejected Thomasson's free speech argument, saying it was not the speech itself that caused the discharge, but that the speech was merely evidence of conduct, and the conduct the reason for the discharge. The court settled on a rational basis test to evaluate the law and noted that a challenge to the military creates a greater burden for the plaintiff. They concluded that the law meets a legitimate government purpose in maintaining unit cohesion and readiness, along with abating concerns for privacy and sexual tension. Additionally, they ruled that DADT and the rebuttable presumption method are rational means to achieve the government purpose.

Thorne v. Department of Defense et al., 916 F. Supp. 1358, 1996; 945 F. Supp. 924, 1996

Plaintiff Tracy Thorne was a lieutenant in the Navy with an exemplary service record. Defendants were the Department of Defense and other unnamed persons. The complaint was originally filed in the District Court for the Eastern District of Virginia. The judge called for clarification of whether, as implemented, DADT permits rebuttal, short of recantation, of the presumption that a declared homosexual has a propensity to engage in forbidden conduct. If not, the judge indicated he would find the statute and regulations to be unconstitutional restrictions on speech. In the interim, *Thomasson* was decided and the court granted summary judgment for the defendants. On appeal, the U.S. Court of Appeals for the Fourth Circuit upheld the decision of the lower court. In 1997 the U.S. Supreme Court refused to hear an appeal.

Watson v. Perry, 918 F. Supp. 1403, 1996

Plaintiff Richard Watson was a Navy lieutenant with fourteen years of exemplary military service. Defendants were Secretary of Defense William Perry, Secretary of the Navy John Dalton, and the United States.

The case was filed and decided in U.S. District Court for the Western District of Washington. Watson claimed that DADT was unconstitutional on the grounds of Due Process, Equal Protection, and free speech. He also claimed his discharge violated the APA as he only received 50 percent of the normal separation pay. His Equal Protection claim said DADT was based on prejudice and discriminated against homosexuals for their status alone. Watson also argued that DADT is aimed at suppressing protected speech. He claimed that DADT is facially invalid because there is no rational basis for presuming that a statement of orientation is paramount to propensity for prohibited conduct.

The court found for the defendants and said it could not reach the issue of whether DADT is unconstitutional on its face because it was constitutionally applied to plaintiff. They maintained that only statements that implied conduct would be used as means for discharge. The court found that DADT was constitutionally applied to Watson because discharges for homosexual conduct are permissible and his statement that he would not rebut the presumption could be interpreted to imply conduct. The court found the Equal Protection argument to be unpersuasive, saying that homosexual conduct can be constitutionally prohibited and that statements can serve as evidence to propensity to engage in homosexual acts/conduct. They similarly rejected all Due Process claims. Although Watson expressed that he had not and would not ever engage in homosexual acts with military personnel while on duty or on any military installation, the court found it telling that he omitted any reference to off-duty actions with non-military personnel, which are also prohibited. He was discharged not for his status, but for his propensity. Watson's First Amendment claims were rejected because although DADT affects speech, it does not seek to punish speech alone, but the conduct that speech can imply.

The opinion included a paragraph stating that the decision was not to be read as an endorsement of DADT and that the court found it regrettable that honorable men and women were discharged in such a way. But they maintained that they could not rule on the wisdom of the policy, only on whether it was constitutionally applied. The court noted that gay and lesbian service members have served and still serve this country honorably. They went on to say that they could not substitute their judgment for that of Congress and that they were compelled to give deference to the military.

Philips v. Perry, 883 F. Supp. 539, 1995; 106 F.3d 1420, 9th Cir. 1997

Plaintiff Mark Philips was a Navy machinist's mate second class with an excellent service record. William Perry, Secretary of Defense, was named as a defendant. Other defendants included John Dalton, Secretary of the Navy, and M.B. Margosian, Philips' Commanding Officer.

In November 1992 Philips acknowledged his homosexuality to his division officer and the Navy began proceedings for discharge. Because of the interim policy that had gone into effect in January 1993, Philips' discharge was placed on hold, pending the outcome of Congressional action and other lawsuits. After DADT was implemented in February 1994 the Navy began a second administrative process for separation. A hearing board recommended that Philips be discharged, and in December of that year, Philips moved for a temporary restraining order. Philips claimed he had been wrongfully discharged on the basis of his sexual orientation. He argued, in addition to other constitutional claims, that his discharge violated the First Amendment because his statements were political speech. The court based much of its ruling against Philips on Ninth Circuit precedent. The Ninth Circuit had rejected claims based on Equal Protection and Due Process because discharges based on homosexual acts pass the rational basis test. The court distinguished Philips' case from others in that he admitted to homosexual acts. They maintained that the status of being homosexual is not enough to substantiate a discharge, but in accordance with all policies, homosexual acts are enough. The court did not consider Philips' challenge to the "Don't Ask" section of DADT because his statements were made before the policy was created. The decision in the lower court was upheld upon appeal to the Ninth Circuit.

Able v. United States, 847 F. Supp. 1038, 1994; 44 F.3d 128, 1995; 1995 WL 116322, 1995; 880 F. Supp. 968, 1995; 88 F.3d 1280, 1996; 968 F. Supp. 850, 1997; 155 F.3d 628, 1998

Plaintiffs included Lieutenant Colonel Jane Able, Petty Officer Robert Heigl, First Lieutenant Kenneth Osborn, Sergeant Steven Spencer, Lieutenant Richard von Wohld, and Seaman Werner Zehr. Defendants included Secretary of Defense William Perry, Secretary of Transportation Frederico Pena, and the United States.

The case was originally heard in U.S. District Court for the Eastern District of New York. This court first granted a preliminary injunction in 1994 while the litigation was pending. The Second Circuit reviewed this determination in 1995, decided the wrong standard had been used to grant the preliminary injunction, and remanded this decision to be reheard with the rest of the case. The Eastern District of New York held a hearing about plaintiffs' standing in 1995 and decided they only had standing to challenge one section of DADT, 10 U.S.C. § 654 (b) (2). The plaintiffs had wanted to challenge Sections 1–3. Later in 1995, the court heard the case and found for the plaintiffs. The Second Circuit remanded this decision in 1996, saying plaintiffs should have been allowed to challenge Section 1 as well. The Eastern District reheard the case in 1997 and found again for the plaintiffs.

The Second Circuit heard the case again in 1998 and reversed. Plaintiffs claimed that the law that authorized DADT was a violation of both the First Amendment and Equal Protection. The district court had rejected the government's justifications for the legitimate purpose of DADT, including unit cohesion, privacy, and sexual tensions, saying that these reasons just reflect heterosexual prejudices. That court also thought that gays and lesbians should be afforded heightened scrutiny in equal protection deliberations. The Second Circuit was the last court to speak on this case. They ruled that neither Section 1 nor 2 of 10 U.S.C. § 654(b) was unconstitutional reversing the decision of the district court.

McVeigh v. Cohen, 983 F. Supp. 215, 1998

Plaintiff Timothy McVeigh was a senior chief who had served seventeen years in the Navy. Defendants included Secretary of Defense William Cohen and Secretary of Navy John Dalton.

The case was filed and decided in U.S. District Court for the District of Columbia. McVeigh claimed that the Navy had violated his rights by discharging him under DADT. He contends that the Fourth Amendment, Fifth Amendment, APA, Electronic Communications Privacy Act (ECPA), and the Navy's own policy were violated.

The district court granted McVeigh a preliminary injunction pending litigation, and later made this injunction permanent, ordering his reinstatement and enjoining the Navy from taking further action against him.

In granting the preliminary injunction, the court had to find that the plaintiff had a likelihood of success on the merits of his case. They easily found this likelihood, noting that the Navy had violated not only DADT, but more than likely ECPA as well. A member of the Navy had solicited AOL for private information about McVeigh without stating he was from the Navy. The court noted that although the constitutionality of DADT had already been questioned, this was the first case to probe into what DADT literally means. For example, what questions or tactics when taken by the military prove to be "asking" or "pursuing"?

Turner v. U.S. Navy, 2002

Plaintiff Jim Turner was an operations specialist second class and had served in the Navy for seven years. Defendants were the U.S. Navy, Secretary of Defense William Cohen, and Secretary of the Navy John Dalton.

The complaint was originally filed in U.S. District Court for the District of Columbia. The case was remanded to the Navy. In Turner's original complaint in district court, he claimed that the Navy had violated the APA and denied him Due Process, Equal Protection, and freedom of speech.

In 1998 the court granted Turner's motion for summary judgment on the count of violating the APA, dismissed on all other counts, and remanded the case to the Navy for further consideration. None of Turner's constitutional claims were addressed. The Navy refused to correct Turner's Navy record, the issue at question in the remand. Once again the two parties headed to the district court, both filing motions for summary judgment. At this time Turner declined to raise any constitutional claims. The only issue still raised was whether the Navy violated the APA, or on a smaller scale, whether the Deputy Assistant Secretary of the Navy acted arbitrarily or capriciously, or abused her discretion in upholding minority findings from the Navy Board for the Correction of Naval Records (BCNR). A majority of the BCNR upon review of Turner's discharge recommended it be overturned and changed to an honorable discharge because none of the charges against him had been proven. But the Deputy Assistant Secretary assigned to review the case upheld the minority findings, approving his discharge, without explanation.

The court, the second time around, found that the Deputy Assistant Secretary did not act arbitrarily or capriciously or abuse her discretion in upholding the minority findings. The Navy's motion for summary judgment was granted.

This case may not be particularly relevant to the policy per se, but it did mention DADT in one interesting way. Turner alleged that the Navy violated DADT when they questioned one of his accusers. This particular witness did not come forward on his own, but was brought in for questioning and asked if he would like to accuse Turner. There were further allegations of coercion of the witness. However, the court ruled that because the Department of Defense had said it would not be procedurally or substantively bound by DADT, Turner had no procedural or substantive rights under the policy that could be enforced by the court.

Hensala v. Department of the Air Force, 343 F.3d 951, 2003

Plaintiff John Hensala received his medical education at the expense of the U.S. Air Force. Upon completion of his training, Hensala advised the military that he was gay and that he did not feel that this infringed upon his ability to serve. Nonetheless, he was discharged in accordance with DADT. The government then sought to recover approximately $70,000, the cost of his education, as was stipulated in the contract he had signed. Hensala lost before the lower court, but on appeal the Ninth Circuit ruled that the district court would have to revisit several of the issues. Ultimately, the parties reached an out-of-court settlement.

Loomis v. United States, United States Court of Federal Claims, 2005

Plaintiff Loren Loomis was a lieutenant colonel who had served in the U.S. Army and Army Reserve for twenty-nine years, from 1967 to 1996. Defendant was the U.S. government. In 1996, LTC Loomis was involved in an investigation as the result of the arson of his home. The investigation revealed videotape of his participation in same-sex sexual activity. As a result of this discovery, separation proceedings were initiated.

Loomis asked the court to set aside the Army's internal rulings that authorized and characterized his discharge. Most of Loomis's grounds dealt with the procedures taken by the Army in their internal proceedings. However, he also contended that the Army's punishment of consensual sodomy was unconstitutional and that DADT violates both Due Process and Equal Protection.

The court found that the Army erred procedurally in their discharge of Loomis and remanded his case to the Secretary of the Army to be reconsidered in light of their decision. However, the pertinent part of the ruling was that they upheld DADT. Despite having considered Loomis's challenge to the Army's sodomy prohibition in light of *Lawrence v. Texas*, the court found that sodomy is still not a fundamental right, and, as such, Due Process had not been violated. They also said that DADT is rationally related to a legitimate end in military success, and so it passes the rational basis test for Equal Protection.

Pending Litigation

Log Cabin Republicans v. United States

On October 12, 2004, the Log Cabin Republicans (LCR), a GLBT Republican organization, filed suit challenging DADT. This challenge, filed in U.S. District

Court for the Central District of California, is on behalf of their members who are currently serving in the military. They are basing their challenge on the 2003 Supreme Court ruling in *Lawrence v. Texas* as well as the rights of Due Process, Equal Protection, and freedom of speech. They seek a preliminary and permanent injunction enjoining the government from enforcing DADT as well as a declaration that the policy is unconstitutional. In March 2006, the district court dismissed LCR's suit for lack of standing. LCR had not named any persons as plaintiffs, and so they did not prove to the court that their members had the right to sue, and that they, thus, had the right to sue on their behalf. The court dismissed the claim without prejudice, saying that LCR could submit an amended complaint naming a plaintiff by April 28, 2006. In May, LCR filed an amended complaint with the court. The government then moved to dismiss the amended complaint and LCR opposed that motion. As of this writing, they are awaiting the court's decision on the motion.

Cook v. Rumsfeld/Cook v. Gates

On December 6, 2004, twelve veterans, aided by the Servicemembers Legal Defense Network, filed suit in the U.S. District Court for the District of Massachusetts. This challenge to the constitutionality of DADT alleges violations of the rights of free speech, Due Process, and Equal Protection. Plaintiffs sought a declaration that the policy is unconstitutional as well as an injunction against its enforcement and reinstatement for the twelve plaintiffs. On April 24, 2006, the court dismissed the suit for the procedural failure to state a claim on which relief could be granted. While the plaintiffs had argued that there is a fundamental liberty interest in private, adult, consensual intimacy, and relationships between homosexuals, the court found that, even in light of *Lawrence v. Texas*, there is no such fundamental interest. They also confirmed that homosexuals are not a suspect class, and so in evaluating an Equal Protection claim, only the rational basis standard need be used. In this case they found DADT to meet that standard. That is, given its goals, the policy is a rational restriction on rights. The court also dismissed the First Amendment freedom of speech claim saying that the policy only regulates speech incidentally and is aimed at conduct, not speech. The case was appealed to the U.S. Court of Appeals for the First Circuit. Oral arguments were heard on March 7, 2007. This case is discussed in greater detail in Chapter 6.

Conclusion

The legal history of DADT and the regulations that predate it are long and complex. At its core is a series of questions about the constitutionality of denying gays, lesbians, and bisexuals participation in the military. Another important question is the degree to which the judiciary can and should defer to the expertise of military leadership. The answers to these questions are themselves in a state of evolution. The study of relevant case law is as instructive with regard to the operation of the judicial system as it is the substantive question of sexual orientation and the military. Until the U.S. Supreme Court rules on the issue, no conclusions can really be drawn and no lower court opinion will have a widespread impact on those gays, lesbians, and bisexuals serving, or wishing to serve, in the U.S. military.

Notes

1. See *BenShalom v. Secretary of the Army*, 489 F. Supp. 964, 1980; 826 F.2d 722, 1987, and *BenShalom v. Marsh*, 703 F. Supp. 1372, 1989; 881 F.2d 454, 1990.

2. See *Dronenburg v. Zech*, 741 F.2d 1388, 1984.

3. See *Pruitt v. Cheney*, 659 F. Supp. 625, 1987; 963 F.2d 1160, 1991.

4. See *Dahl v. Secretary of the Navy*, 830 F. Supp. 1319, 1993; *Meinhold v. U.S. Department of Defense*, 62 Empl. Prac. Dec. p. 42, 619, 1993; 114 S. Ct. 374, 1993; 34 F.3d 1469, 1994; *Steffan v. Cheney*, 733 F. Supp. 121, 1989; 920 F.2d 74, 1990; 780 F. Supp. 1, 1991; 8 F.3d 57, 1993; 41 F.3d 677, 1994; and *Watkins v. U.S. Army*, 551 F. Supp. 212, 1982; 721 F.2d 687, 1983; 847 F.2d 1329, 1988; 875 F.2d 699, 1989.

5. It is difficult to present the cases in perfect chronological order because while "Case A" might have been initiated prior to "Case B," "Case A" might also have been resolved *after* "Case B." Thus, cases are presented here only in roughly chronological order.

Key Documents

Thousands and thousands of pages of documentation are relevant to the issue of "Don't Ask, Don't Tell." Using the term "Don't Ask, Don't Tell" and the dates January 1, 1993, through December 31, 2002—roughly the first decade of both the debate and implementation of the policy—a search of the *New York Times* archive reveals 440 documents. While results do include minor documents such as news summaries, the count remains conservative as it does not include relevant documents that appeared prior to May 12, 1993, the date on which the expression "Don't Ask, Don't Tell" first appeared in the *Times*. Nor does it include articles on the issue that don't use that particular phrase. Steve Jackson, in his memo to Janet Halley regarding the legislative history of the policy, describes the record as extensive, in excess of 3,000 pages of text.[1] This figure includes only those documents that appear in federal legislative records. The report of the RAND Corporation alone, a study commissioned by the Department of Defense, exceeds 500 pages. Thus, the selection of "key documents" posed quite a challenge. The documents that appear in this appendix were chosen either for their critical relevance or for the fact that they are less likely to be discovered by one making a more casual inquiry into the subject matter.

A. The first inauguration of President Clinton was held on January 20, 1993. Nine days later he gave a press conference in which he described his views toward military policy on gays, lesbians, and bisexuals in the U.S. military and took questions on the issue. The text of that event is provided here.

The President's News Conference, January 29, 1993[2]

Gays in the Military

The President. Good afternoon, ladies and gentlemen. I'm sorry, we had a last-minute delay occasioned by another issue, not this one.

The debate over whether to lift the ban on homosexuals in the military has, to put it mildly, sparked a great deal of interest over the last few days. Today, as you know, I have reached an agreement, at least with Senator Nunn and Senator Mitchell, about how we will proceed in the next few days. But first I would like to explain what I believe about this issue and why, and what I have decided to do after a long conversation, and a very good one, with the Joint Chiefs of Staff and discussions with several Members of Congress.

The issue is not whether there should be homosexuals in the military. Everyone concedes that there are. The issue is whether men and women, who can and have served with real distinction, should be excluded from military service solely on the basis of their status. And I believe they should not. The principle on which I base this position is this: I believe that American citizens who want to serve their country should be able to do so unless their conduct disqualifies them from doing so. Military life is fundamentally different from civilian society; it necessarily has a different and stricter code of conduct, even a different code of justice. Nonetheless, individuals who are prepared to accept all necessary restrictions on their behavior, many of which would be intolerable in civilian society, should be able to serve their country honorably and well.

I have asked the Secretary of Defense to submit by July the 15th a draft Executive order after full consultation with military and congressional leaders and concerned individuals outside of the Government, which would end the present policy of the exclusion from military service solely on the basis of sexual orientation and at the same time establish rigorous standards regarding sexual conduct to be applied to all military personnel.

This draft order will be accompanied by a study conducted during the next 6 months on the real, practical problems that would be involved in this revision of policy, so that we will have a practical, realistic approach consistent with the high standards of combat effectiveness and unit cohesion that our armed services must maintain.

I agree with the Joint Chiefs that the highest standards of conduct must be required. The change cannot and should not be accomplished overnight. It does require extensive consultation with the Joint Chiefs, experts in the Congress and in the legal community, joined by my administration and others. We've consulted closely to date and will do so in the future. During that process, interim measures will be placed into effect, which, I hope, again, sharpen the focus of this debate. The Joint Chiefs of Staff have agreed to remove the question regarding one's sexual orientation from future versions of the enlistment application, and it will not be asked in the interim.

We also all agree that a very high standard of conduct can and must be applied. So the single area of disagreement is this: Should someone be able to serve their country in uniform if they say they are homosexuals, but they do nothing which violates the code of conduct or undermines unit cohesion or morale, apart from that statement? That is what all the furor of the last few days has been about.

And the practical and not insignificant issues raised by that issue are what will be studied in the next 6 months.

Through this period ending July 15th the Department of Justice will seek continuances in pending court cases involving reinstatement. And administrative separation under current Department of Defense policies based on status alone will be stayed pending completion of this review. The final discharge in cases based only on status will be suspended until the President has an opportunity to review and act upon the final recommendations of the Secretary of Defense with respect to the current policy. In the meantime, a member whose discharge has been suspended by the Attorney General will be separated from active duty and placed in stand-by reserve until the final report of the Secretary of Defense and the final action of the President. This is the agreement that I have reached with Senator Nunn and Senator Mitchell.

During this review process, I will work with the Congress. And I believe the compromise announced today by the Senators and by me shows that we can work together to end the gridlock that has plagued our city for too long.

This compromise is not everything I would have hoped for or everything that I have stood for, but it is plainly a substantial step in the right direction. And it will allow us to move forward on other terribly important issues affecting far more Americans.

My administration came to this city with a mission to bring critical issues of reform and renewal and economic revitalization to the public debate, issues that are central to the lives of all Americans. We are working on an economic reform agenda that will begin with an address to the joint session of Congress on February 17th. In the coming months the White House Task Force on Health Care, chaired by the First Lady, will complete work on a comprehensive health care reform proposal to be submitted to Congress within 100 days of the commencement of this administration. We will be designing a system of national service to begin a season of service in which our Nation's unmet needs are addressed and we provide more young people the opportunity to go to college. We will be proposing comprehensive welfare reform legislation and other important initiatives.

I applaud the work that has been done in the last 2 or 3 days by Senator Nunn, Senator Mitchell, and others to enable us to move forward on a principle that is important to me without shutting the Government down and running the risk of not even addressing the family and medical leave issue, which is so important to America's families, before Congress goes into its recess. I am looking forward to getting on with this issue over the next 6 months and with these other issues which were so central to the campaign and, far more importantly, are so important to the lives of all the American people.

Q. Mr. President, yesterday a Federal court in California said that the military ban on homosexuals was unconstitutional. Will you direct the Navy and the Justice

Department not to appeal that decision? And how does that ruling strengthen your hand in this case?

The President. Well, it makes one point. I think it strengthens my hand, if you will, in two ways. One, I agree with the principle embodied in the case. As I understand it—I have not read the opinion—but as I understand it, the opinion draws the distinction that I seek to draw between conduct and status. And secondly, it makes the practical point I have been making all along, which is that there is not insignificant chance that this matter would ultimately be resolved in the courts in a way that would open admission into the military without the opportunity to deal with this whole range of practical issues, which everyone who has ever thought about it or talked it through concedes are there. So I think it can—it strengthens my hand on the principle as well as on the process.

Q. Mr. President, there's a glass of water there, by the way, while I ask the question. Do you think, since you promised during the campaign—your literature put out a very clear statement: lift the ban on homosexuals in the military immediately—do you think you didn't think through these practical problems? What have you learned from this experience in dealing with powerful members of the Senate and the Joint Chiefs? And how much of a problem is this for you to accept a compromise which doesn't meet your real goals?

The President. Well, I haven't given up on my real goals. I think this is a dramatic step forward. Normally, in the history of civil rights advancements, Presidents have not necessarily been in the forefront in the beginning. So I think the fact that we actually have the Joint Chiefs of Staff agreeing that it's time to take this question off the enlistment form, that there ought to be a serious examination of how this would be done, even though they haven't agreed that it should be done; that the Senate, if they vote for the motion advocated by Senators Nunn and Mitchell, will agree; Senators who don't agree that the policy should be changed are agreeing that we ought to have a chance to work through this for 6 months and persuade them of that, I think, is very, very significant. Now, I would remind you that any President's Executive order can be overturned by an act of Congress. The President can then veto the act of Congress and try to have his veto sustained if the act stands on its own as a simple issue that could always be vetoed. But I always knew that there was a chance that Congress would disagree with my position. I can only tell you that I still think I'm right; I feel comfortable about the way we have done this; and I'm going to maintain the commitment that I have.

Q. But do you think that you hadn't examined the practical problems-

Q. Sir, I just wonder, do you think in retrospect that—obviously, you didn't intend the first week—I'm sorry, you want to -

The President. No, I had always planned to allow some period of time during which policies would be developed to deal with what I think are the significant practical problems. This, in effect, may reverse the process over what I intended to do, but there has to be a time in which these issues, these practical issues are developed and policies are developed to deal with them.

Q. Obviously, you didn't intend the first week of your administration, given your promise to have the laser focus on the economy, to be seen around the country as military gay rights week. I wonder if in retrospect you think you could have done things differently to have avoided that happening?

The President. I don't know how I could have done that. The Joint Chiefs asked for a meeting about a number of issues, in which this was only one. We spent a lot of time talking about other things. This issue was not put forward in this context by me; it was put forward by those in the United States Senate who sought to make it an issue early on. And I don't know how I could have stopped them from doing that.

Q. You don't think that in making the promise and then in promising to follow through on it early that you might have given rise to this, do you, sir?

The President. Well, I think it was pretty clear to me that we were talking about some sort of 6-month process days and days ago. And the people who wanted it debated now were not deterred by that, and probably a lot of them won't be deterred by the agreement announced today. I think that we must—they have the perfect right to do this. But the timing of this whole issue was clearly forced by the people in the Senate who were opposed to any change of the policy no matter what the facts are. And I think that was their right to do, but they control the timing of this, not me.

Q. Two questions. First of all, just to make sure that we're clear on this: July 15th this happens, period, regardless of what comes out at these hearings, is that correct? The ban will be issued, or will be lifted, rather?

The President. That is my position. My position is that I still embrace the principle, and I think it should be done. The position of those who are opposed to me is that they think that the problems will be so overwhelming everybody with good sense will change their position. I don't expect to do that.

Q. So you definitely expect to do it. And secondly-

The President. I don't expect to change my position, no.

Q. What do you think is going to happen in the military? There have been all sorts of dire predictions of violence, of mass comings-out, whatever. What do you think the impact of this is going to be, practically?

The President. For one thing, I think if you look at the last 10 years of experience here, according to the reports we have, this country spent $500 million in tax dollars to separate something under 16,500 homosexuals from the service and has dealt with complaints, at least, of sexual abuse, heterosexual abuse, largely against women, far greater volumes. But during this period, we have plainly had the best educated, best trained, most cohesive military force in the history of the United States. And everybody, ask anybody, and the Joint Chiefs will tell you that. They agreed that we should stop asking the question. This single thing that is dividing people on this debate, I want to make it very clear that this is a very narrow issue. It is whether a person, in the absence of any other disqualifying conduct, can simply say that he or she is homosexual and stay in the service. I do not expect that to spark this kind of problem. And I certainly think in the next 6 months, as people start to work it through and talk it through, a lot of legitimate, practical issues will be raised and dealt with in a more rational environment that is less charged. That is certainly what I hope will happen. Thank you.

B. Of the thousands of pages of testimony before Congress, no one person, day, or issue truly stands out against the others. Yet, the issue of the "rebuttable presumption" continues to be an important part of debate over the policy. Is it possible to rebut the presumption that one is gay, lesbian, or bisexual and, in particular, to effectively establish that one does not have the propensity or intent to engage in homosexual acts? The following excerpt from the final day of testimony before the Senate Committee on Armed Services illustrates the difficult nature of the issue.

Policy Concerning Homosexuality in the Armed Forces, Hearings Before the Committee on Armed Services, United States Senate, July 22, 1993

Ms. Gorelick. Thank you, Senator.

Let me summarize for you. First, let me describe what the working group did. The working group looked at the operation of our old policy and determined that some aspects of it were, indeed, misunderstood.

I believe you are calling it the current policy versus the July 19 policy. Under the current policy, we discharge for conduct, not for homosexuality per se. That decision was made and clarified in 1981 when status was rejected as a basis for discharge.

Also, people who have made a statement that they are homosexual currently are allowed to rebut that conclusion that they engage in acts or that they have a propensity to do so.

Thus, we kept the legal structure with respect to discharge and with respect to rebuttable presumption, but we are clarifying those two key elements of the discharge policy.

The second thing the working group did was assess our investigative approach and the way we ask questions and determined, (a) that there is no need to ask about orientation at accession or at any other point, because orientation is not a basis for discharge or other action, and (b) we do not need to have witch hunts.

The issue does not justify the use of scarce investigative resources. And commanders had, at times, been confused as to what their goals were in the investigative process because, as I mentioned before, there was some lack of clarity in whether they were investigating for "homosexuality" or for conduct.

So let me summarize what is old and what is new: Do not ask. We no longer ask, that is new. Do not tell. The basis for discharge is the same. The rebuttable presumption was there. It was a little hard to understand. We will make it clearer. And I believe I have articulated and will continue to articulate today what the rebuttable presumption is.

Also, for clarity, we have eliminated, as points in the discussion, the terms "homosexuality" and "homosexual" as unnecessary to the analysis. Let me just give you one brief example so that you can understand what I mean.

We used to say, in the old policy, "If you say you are a homosexual, we will presumptively conclude that you are." What is a homosexual under our policy? Someone who engages in acts or has a propensity or intent to do so.

So we say now, "If you say you are a homosexual, we presumptively conclude that you engage in acts or have a propensity or intent to do so."

We have simply taken out the intervening point of: What is a homosexual?

Chairman Nunn. And the homosexual definition is someone who by statement, by conduct, or by marriage so indicates.

Ms. Gorelick. A homosexual is someone who engages in homosexual acts or has a propensity or intent to do so. Under the old policy, that is the definition. And that is what we presume someone means when they say they are homosexual.

Chairman Nunn. So then if, basically, they convince you they have erred in that understanding of what the word means, and they do not meet that definition, then they are not, by your definition, homosexual.

Ms. Gorelick. They may rebut that presumption by saying –

Chairman Nunn. Right.

Ms. Gorelick. They may rebut the presumption by proving that they do not engage in acts and that they do not have a propensity or an intent to do so.

Chairman Nunn. Which means –

Ms. Gorelick. And that is the same –

Chairman Nunn. Which means they may prove they do not meet your definition –

Ms. Gorelick. That is correct.

Chairman Nunn. – Or the definition under the policy of homosexuality.

Ms. Gorelick. That is correct. The showings remain the same. Second, with respect to marriages, the policy is the same.

Third, with respect to acts, our definition will remain the same.

We have used shorthand for engaging in acts in our policy statement of July 19th. The definition, which currently includes soliciting or attempting homosexual acts, will remain the same. We have had a lot of discussion about the fourth category; other activities. Since 1981, there has been a recognition that certain associational activities are themselves not a basis for discharge, because of concerns raised in a number of cases, not the least of which is the Ben-Shalom case, where the issue was: If you speak in a way that homosexual might speak, if you say something a homosexual might say, does that make you a homosexual?

And I expect we will continue to face challenges. I feel that the current proposed policy, the policy of July 19, is on stronger legal ground.

C. The U.S. Code is a compilation, by subject matter, of all general and permanent laws of the United States. It is divided by broad subjects into fifty titles and published by the Office of the Law Revision Counsel of the U.S. House of Representatives. When, on November 30, 1993, the U.S. Congress passed the legislation that became known informally as "Don't Ask, Don't Tell," it was as Public Law 103-160. This law was then codified as Section 654 of Title 10 of the U.S. Code.

U.S. Code, Title 10, Section 654

U.S. Code, Title 10, Section 654. Policy Concerning Homosexuality in the Armed Forces

(A) Findings. Congress makes the following findings:

(1) Section 8 of Article I of the Constitution of the United States commits exclusively to the Congress the powers to raise and support armies, provide and maintain a Navy, and make rules for the government and regulation of the land and naval forces.
(2) There is no constitutional right to serve in the armed forces.
(3) Pursuant to the powers conferred by Section 8 of Article I of the Constitution of the United States, it lies within the discretion of the Congress to establish qualifications for and conditions of service in the armed forces.
(4) The primary purpose of the armed forces is to prepare for and to prevail in combat should the need arise.
(5) The conduct of military operations requires members of the armed forces to make extraordinary sacrifices, including the ultimate sacrifice, in order to provide for the common defense.
(6) Success in combat requires military units that are characterized by high morale, good order and discipline, and unit cohesion.
(7) One of the most critical elements in combat capability is unit cohesion, that is, the bonds of trust among individual service members that make the combat effectiveness of a military unit greater than the sum of the combat effectiveness of the individual unit members.

(8) Military life is fundamentally different from civilian life in that -
  (a) the extraordinary responsibilities of the armed forces, the unique conditions of military service, and the critical role of unit cohesion, require that the military community, while subject to civilian control, exist as a specialized society; and
  (b) the military society is characterized by its own laws, rules, customs, and traditions, including numerous restrictions on personal behavior, that would not be acceptable in civilian society.
(9) The standards of conduct for members of the armed forces regulate a member's life for 24 hours each day beginning at the moment the member enters military status and not ending until that person is discharged or otherwise separated from the armed forces.
(10) Those standards of conduct, including the Uniform Code of Military Justice, apply to a member of the armed forces at all times that the member has a military status, whether the member is on base or off base and whether the member is on duty or off duty.
(11) The pervasive application of the standards of conduct is necessary because members of the armed forces must be ready at all times for worldwide deployment to a combat environment.
(12) The worldwide deployment of United States military forces, the international responsibilities of the United States, and the potential for involvement of the armed forces in actual combat routinely make it necessary for members of the armed forces involuntarily to accept living conditions and working conditions that are often spartan, primitive, and characterized by forced intimacy with little or no privacy.
(13) The prohibition against homosexual conduct is a longstanding element of military law that continues to be necessary in the unique circumstances of military service.
(14) The armed forces must maintain personnel policies that exclude persons whose presence in the armed forces would create an unacceptable risk to the armed forces' high standards of morale, good order and discipline, and unit cohesion that are the essence of military capability.
(15) The presence in the armed forces of persons who demonstrate a propensity or intent to engage in homosexual acts would create an unacceptable risk to the high standards of morale, good order and discipline, and unit cohesion that are the essence of military capability.

(B) Policy. A member of the armed forces shall be separated from the armed forces under regulations prescribed by the Secretary of Defense if one or more of the following findings is made and approved in accordance with procedures set forth in such regulations:

(1) That the member has engaged in, attempted to engage in, or solicited another to engage in a homosexual act or acts unless there are further findings, made and approved in accordance with procedures set forth in such regulations, that the member has demonstrated that -
  (a) such conduct is a departure from the member's usual and customary behavior;
  (b) such conduct, under all the circumstances, is unlikely to recur;
  (c) such conduct was not accomplished by use of force, coercion, or intimidation;

(d) under the particular circumstances of the case, the member's continued presence in the armed forces is consistent with the interests of the armed forces in proper discipline, good order, and morale; and

(e) the member does not have a propensity or intent to engage in homosexual acts.

(2) That the member has stated that he or she is a homosexual or bisexual, or words to that effect, unless there is a further finding, made and approved in accordance with procedures set forth in the regulations, that the member has demonstrated that he or she is not a person who engages in, attempts to engage in, has a propensity to engage in, or intends to engage in homosexual acts.

(3) That the member has married or attempted to marry a person known to be of the same biological sex.

(C) Entry Standards and Documents.

(1) The Secretary of Defense shall ensure that the standards for enlistment and appointment of members of the armed forces reflect the policies set forth in subsection (B).

(2) The documents used to effectuate the enlistment or appointment of a person as a member of the armed forces shall set forth the provisions of subsection (B).

(D) Required Briefings. The briefings that members of the armed forces receive upon entry into the armed forces and periodically thereafter under Section 937 of this title (Article 137 of the Uniform Code of Military Justice) shall include a detailed explanation of the applicable laws and regulations governing sexual conduct by members of the armed forces, including the policies prescribed under subsection (B).

(E) Rule of Construction. Nothing in subsection (B) shall be construed to require that a member of the armed forces be processed for separation from the armed forces when a determination is made in accordance with regulations prescribed by the Secretary of Defense that -

(1) the member engaged in conduct or made statements for the purpose of avoiding or terminating military service; and

(2) separation of the member would not be in the best interest of the armed forces.

(F) Definitions. In this section:

(1) The term "homosexual" means a person, regardless of sex, who engages in, attempts to engage in, has a propensity to engage in, or intends to engage in homosexual acts, and includes the terms "gay" and "lesbian."

(2) The term "bisexual" means a person who engages in, attempts to engage in, has a propensity to engage in, or intends to engage in homosexual and heterosexual acts.

(3) The term "homosexual act" means -

(a) any bodily contact, actively undertaken or passively permitted, between members of the same sex for the purpose of satisfying sexual desires; and

(b) any bodily contact which a reasonable person would understand to demonstrate a propensity or intent to engage in an act described in subparagraph (A).

D. On July 19, 1993, President Clinton announced the new policy on gays and lesbians in the military at National Defense University, Fort McNair, Washington, D.C. He provided a brief overview of the events leading to the policy change and acknowledged that many would likely be unhappy with the outcome of the debate. One of the puzzling aspects of his announcement was emphasis on the role of the Uniform Code of Military Justice (UCMJ) and the goal of addressing misconduct in an evenhanded fashion. While the UCMJ does prohibit sodomy, whether occurring between same-sex or other-sex individuals, many of the acts (e.g., kissing) that would lead to someone being discharged under the policy do not constitute sodomy. President Clinton stated that the policy would protect those who wished to serve and who obeyed the military's rules against misconduct. However, it is not at all clear from his remarks what constitutes misconduct. And, if misconduct is those behaviors outlined in or suggested by the policy (e.g., stating one's sexual orientation, holding hands, or marrying someone of the same sex), yet falling outside the purview of the UCMJ, it is not clear how such a policy can be evenly applied to both heterosexual and homosexual personnel. While his remarks were certainly necessary and many good points were made, his remarks also left many questions unanswered.

President Clinton's Remarks Announcing the New Policy on Gays and Lesbians in the Military

Thank you very much. Secretary Aspin, General Powell, members of the Joint Chiefs, Admiral Kime, to our host, Admiral Smith, ladies and gentlemen, I have come here today to discuss a difficult challenge and one which has received an enormous amount of publicity and public and private debate over the last several months: Our Nation's policy toward homosexuals in the military.

I believe the policy I am announcing today represents a real step forward, but I know it will raise concerns in some of your minds. So I wanted you to hear my thinking and decision directly in person because I respect you, and because you are among the elite who will lead our Armed Forces into the next century, and because you will have to put this policy into effect and I expect your help in doing it.

The policy I am announcing today is, in my judgment, the right thing to do and the best way to do it. It is right because it provides greater protection to those who happen to be homosexual and want to serve their country honorably in uniform, obeying all the military's rules against sexual misconduct. It is the best way to proceed because it provides a sensible balance between the rights of the individual and the needs of the military to remain the world's number one fighting force. As President of all the American people, I am pledged to protect and to promote individual rights. As Commander in Chief, I am pledged to protect and advance our security. In this policy, I believe we have come close to meeting both objectives.

Let me start with this clear fact: Our military is one of our greatest accomplishments and our most valuable assets. It is the world's most effective and powerful fighting force, bar none. I have seen proof of this fact almost every day since I became President. I saw it last week when I visited Camp Casey, along the DMZ in Korea. I witnessed it at our military academies at Annapolis and West Point when I visited there. And I certainly relied on it three weeks ago when I ordered an attack on Iraq after that country's leadership attempted to assassinate President Bush.

We owe a great deal to the men and women who protect us through their service, their sacrifice, and their dedication. And we owe it to our own security to listen hard to them and act carefully as we consider any changes in the military. A force ready to fight must maintain the highest priority under all circumstances.

Let me review the events which bring us here today. Before I ran for President, this issue was already upon us. Some of the members of the military returning from the Gulf war announced their homosexuality in order to protest the ban. The military's policy has been questioned in college ROTC programs. Legal challenges have been filed, including one that has since succeeded. In 1991, the Secretary of Defense, Dick Cheney, was asked about reports that the Defense Department spent an alleged $500 million to separate and replace about 17,000 homosexuals from the military during the 1980's, in spite of the findings of a Government report saying there was no reason to believe that they could not serve with distinction. Shortly thereafter, while giving a speech at the Kennedy School of Government at Harvard, I was asked by one of the students what I thought of this report and what I thought of lifting the ban. This question had never before been presented to me, and I never had the opportunity to discuss it with anyone. I stated then what I still believe, that I thought there ought to be presumption that people who wish to do so should be able to serve their country if they are willing to conform to the high standards of the military and that the emphasis should be always on people's conduct, not their status.

For me, and this is very important, this issue has never been one of group rights but rather of individual ones, of the individual opportunity to serve and the individual responsibility to conform to the highest standards of military conduct. For people who are willing to play by the rules, to be able to serve and make a contribution, I believed then and I believe now we should give them a chance to do so.

The central facts of this issue are not much in dispute. First, notwithstanding the ban, there have been and are homosexuals in military service who serve with distinction. I have had the privilege of meeting some of these men and women, and I have been deeply impressed by their devotion to duty and country.

Second, there is no study showing them to be less capable or more prone to misconduct than heterosexual soldiers. Indeed, all the information we have indicates that they are not less capable or more prone to misbehavior.

Third, misconduct is already covered by the laws and rules which also cover activities that are improper by heterosexual members of the military.

Fourth, the ban has been lifted in other nations and in police and fire departments in our country with no discernible negative impact on unit cohesion or capacity to do the job, although there is, admittedly, no absolute analogy to the situation we face and no study bearing on this specific issue.

Fifth, even if the ban were lifted entirely, the experience of other nations and police and fire departments in the United States indicated that most homosexuals would probably not declare their sexual orientation openly thereby making an already hard life even more difficult in some circumstances.

But as the sociologist Charles Moskos noted after spending many years studying the American military, the issue may be tougher to resolve here in the United States than in Canada, Australia, and in some other nations because of the presence in our country of both vocal gay rights groups and equally vocal antigay rights groups who believe that lifting the ban amounts to endorsing a lifestyle they strongly disapprove of.

Clearly the American people are deeply divided on this issue, with most military people opposed to lifting the ban because of the feared impact on unit cohesion, rooted in disapproval of homosexual lifestyles and the fear of invasion of privacy of heterosexual soldiers who must live and work in close quarters with homosexual military people. However, those who have studied this issue extensively have discovered an interesting fact. People in this country who are aware of having known homosexuals are far more likely to support lifting the ban. In other words, they are likely to see this issue in terms of individual conduct and individual capacity instead of the claims of a group with which they do not agree and also to be able to imagine how this ban could be lifted without a destructive impact on group cohesion and morale.

Shortly after I took office and reaffirmed my position, the foes of lifting the ban in Congress moved to enshrine the ban in law. I asked that congressional action be delayed for 6 months while the Secretary of Defense worked with the Joint Chiefs to come up with a proposal for changing our current policy. I then met with the Joint Chiefs to hear their concerns and asked them to try to work through the issue with Secretary Aspin. I wanted to handle the matter in this way on grounds of both principle and practicality.

As a matter of principle, it is my duty as Commander in Chief to uphold the high standards of combat readiness and unit cohesion of the world's finest fighting force, while doing my duty as President to protect the rights of individual Americans and to put to use the abilities of all the American people. And I was determined to serve this principle as fully as possible through practical action, knowing this fact about our system of government; While the Commander in Chief and the Secretary of Defense can change military personnel policies, Congress can reverse those changes by law in ways that are difficult, if not impossible, to veto.

For months now, the Secretary of Defense and the Service Chiefs have worked through this issue in a highly charged, deeply emotional environment, struggling to come to terms with the competing consideration and pressures and, frankly, to work through their own ideas and deep feelings.

During this time many dedicated Americans have come forward to state their own views on this issue. Most, but not all, of the military testimony has been against lifting the ban. But support for changing the policy has come from distinguished combat veterans, including Senators Bob Kerrey, Chuck Robb, and John Kerry in the United States Congress. It has come from Lawrence Korb, who enforced the gay ban during the Reagan administration, and from former Senator Barry Goldwater, a distinguished veteran, former chairman of the Senate Armed Services Committee, founder of the Arizona National Guard, and patron saint of the conservative wing of the Republican party.

Senator Goldwater's statement, published in *The Washington Post* recently, made it crystal clear that when this matter is viewed as an issue of individual opportunity and responsibility rather than one of alleged group rights, this is not a call for cultural license but rather a reaffirmation of the American value of extending opportunity to responsible individuals and of limiting the role of Government over citizens' private lives.

On the other hand, those who oppose lifting the ban are clearly focused not on the conduct of individual gay service members but on how nongay service members feel about gays in general and in particular those in military service.

These past few days I have been in contact with the Secretary of Defense as he has worked through the final stages of this policy with the Joint Chiefs. We now have a policy that is a substantial advance over the one in place when I took office. I have ordered Secretary Aspin to issue a directive consisting of these essential elements: One, service men and women will be judged based on their conduct, not their sexual orientation. Two, therefore the practice, now 6 months old, of not asking about sexual orientation in the enlistment process will continue. Three, an open statement by a service member that he or she is a homosexual will create a rebuttable presumption that he or she intends to engage in prohibited conduct, but the service member will be given an opportunity to refute that presumption; in other words, to demonstrate that he or she intends to live by the rules of conduct that apply in the military service. And four, all provisions of the Uniform Code of Military Justice will be enforced in an even-handed manner as regards both heterosexuals and homosexuals. And thanks to the policy provisions agreed to by the Joint Chiefs, there will be a decent regard to the legitimate privacy and associational rights of all service members.

Just as is the case under current policy, unacceptable conduct, either heterosexual or homosexual, will be unacceptable 24 hours a day, 7 days a week from the time a recruit joins the service until the day he or she is discharged. Now, as in the past, every member of our military will be required to comply with the Uniform Code of Military Justice, which is Federal law, and military regulations at all times and in all places.

Let me say a few words now about this policy. It is not a perfect solution. It is not identical with some of my own goals. And it certainly will not please everyone, perhaps not anyone, and clearly not those who hold the most adamant opinions on either side of this issue.

But those who wish to ignore the issue must understand that it is already tearing at the cohesion of the military and it is today being considered by the

Federal courts in ways that may not be to the liking of those who oppose any change. And those who want the ban to be lifted completely on both status and conduct must understand that such action would have faced certain and decisive reversal by the Congress and the cause for which many have fought for years would be delayed, probably for years.

Thus, on grounds of both principle and practicality, this is a major step forward. It is, in my judgment, consistent with my responsibilities as President and Commander in Chief to meet the need to change current policy. It is an honorable compromise that advances the cause of people who are called to serve our country by their patriotism, the cause of our national security, and our national interest in resolving an issue that has divided our military and our Nation and diverted attention from other matters for too long.

The time has come for us to move forward. As your Commander in Chief, I charge all of you to carry out this policy with fairness, with balance, and with due regard for the privacy of individuals. We must and will protect unit cohesion and troop morale. We must and will continue to have the best fighting force in the world. But this is an end to witch hunts that spend millions of taxpayer dollars to ferret out individuals who have served their country well. Improper conduct, on or off base, should remain grounds for discharge. But we will proceed with an even hand against everyone, regardless of sexual orientation.

Such controversies as this have divided us before. But our Nation and our military have always risen to the challenge before. That was true of racial integration of the military and changes in the role of women in the military. Each of these was an issue, because it was an issue for society as well as for the military. And in each case your military was a leader in figuring out how to respond most effectively.

In the early 1970's, when President Nixon decided to transform our military into an all-volunteer force, many argued that it could not work. They said it would ruin our forces. But the leaders of our military not only made it work, they used the concept of an all-volunteer force to build the very finest fighting force our Nation and the world have ever known.

Ultimately, the success of this policy will depend in large measure on the commitment it receives from the leaders of the military services. I very much respect and commend the Joint Chiefs for the good-faith effort they have made through this whole endeavor. And I thank General Powell, the Joint Chiefs, and the Commandant of the Coast Guard for joining me here today and for their support of this policy.

I would also like to thank those who lobbied aggressively in [sic] behalf of changing the policy, including Congressman Barney Frank; Congressman Gerry Studds; and the Campaign for Military Service, who worked with us and who clearly will not agree with every aspect of the policy announced today, but who should take some solace in knowing that their efforts have helped to produce a strong advance for the cause they seek to serve.

I must look now to General Powell, to the Joint Chiefs, to all the other leaders in our military to carry out this policy through effective training and leadership. Every officer will be expected to exert the necessary effort to make this policy work. That has been the key every time the military has successfully addressed a new challenge, and it will be key in this effort, too.

Our military is a conservative institution, and I say that in the very best sense, for its purpose is to conserve the fighting spirit of our troops, to conserve the resources and the capacity of our troops, to conserve the military lessons acquired during or Nation's existence, to conserve our very security, and, yes, to conserve the liberties of the American people. Because it is a conservative institution, it is right for the military to be wary of sudden changes. Because it is an institution that embodies the best of America and must reflect the society in which it operates, it is also right for the military to make changes when the time for change is at hand.

I strongly believe that our military, like our society, needs the talents of every person who wants to make a contribution and who is ready to live by the rules. That is the heart of the policy that I have announced today. I hope in your heart you will find the will and the desire to support it and to lead our military in incorporating it into our Nation's great asset and the world's best fighting force.

Thank you very much.

E. Professor Emeritus Charles Moskos, Northwestern University, is often described as the "chief architect" of "Don't Ask, Don't Tell." In an op-ed for *The Washington Post*, published on January 31, 1993, Moskos wrote,

> Despite widespread resistance within the U.S. military, Clinton has committed himself to rescind the gay ban. One can of course argue that the United States now has such a decisive strategic advantage over any potential enemy that it can well afford to advance the cause of equal opportunity at possible cost to military effectiveness. Still, such a risk must be acknowledged. We must decide, for example, whether we will be willing to restore compulsory national service if dropping the gay ban makes recruitment even more difficult than it now is. (Most nations without such a ban do have obligatory national service, the military being an option in many cases.) Unless such realities are faced, we can only hope that our postmodern military never has to face the uncivil reality of war.

Since that time, Professor Moskos has provided expert testimony on the issue, has been publicly recognized for his contributions, and has often been interviewed concerning his role in and opinion of the policy. In October 2000, Moskos was interviewed for an article in *Lingua Franca*, and in October 2003, for an article in *The Northwestern Chronicle*, a self-described "conservative college weekly." Excerpts from these interviews appear below.

What's Love Got to Do with It? The Real Story of Military Sociology and 'Don't Ask, Don't Tell,'—Nathaniel Frank, *Lingua Franca*, October 2000

Charles Moskos is proud of his contribution to the American language: the introduction of the catchphrase "don't ask, don't tell." A professor of military sociology at Northwestern University, Moskos staked his authorship claim in a 1998 radio show when he called himself the "architect" of the 1993 policy, which allows gays to serve in the U.S. military so long as they remain celibate and do not disclose their sexuality. "The phrase and the policy just came to me one night at my house when I was at the watercooler," he writes via e-mail....As it happens, Moskos and the military leadership differ as to why they think the armed forces should ban out-of-the-closet gays. Military leaders maintain that the presence of gays threatens "unit cohesion," which they believe is necessary for an effective fighting force. But Moskos defends the ban on the grounds that in the military's close quarters, openly gay soldiers would violate straight soldiers' right to privacy....As if tacitly acknowledging the difficulties in the unit-cohesion argument, Moskos prefers to take another tack entirely. "Fuck unit cohesion," he says. "I don't care about that." The distinction between social and task cohesion strikes him as hairsplitting. "To me it's all psychobabble...." Rather, for Moskos, the ban on openly gay soldiers is a matter of "modesty rights for straights." Invoking the analogy of sex integration, Moskos likens the toleration of openly gay soldiers in combat units to allowing straight men in an all-female unit.... "I should not be forced to shower with a woman. I should not be forced to shower with an open gay." Moskos feels so strongly about the privacy issue that he views mandatory gay–straight cohabitation as inhumane. "I would not want to fight for a country in which privacy issues are so trampled upon," he says. "Those are the conditions of concentration camps." "I think," says Moskos of the ban on gays, "that it's going to end." He gives it five to ten years.

The *Chronicle* Interview: Charles Moskos, Father of "Don't Ask, Don't Tell," October 30, 2003

The Northwestern Chronicle: Harvard Professor Janet E. Halley called the "Don't Ask, Don't Tell, Don't Pursue" policy "the institutionalization of anti-gay animus." Do you think your policy has been successful?

Professor Charles Moskos: Well, it's what Winston Churchill said about democracy: "it's the worst system possible, except for any other."

What's interesting is, it's not a military policy. Everybody, including the law professors of America, has their head up their ass. It's a congressional law...If anything, the military is more, you might say, benign to gays than the law.

The law specifically states, "homosexuality is incompatible with military service." Well, the military has just gone to "don't ask, don't tell," which is a little milder form of it. If you really take the law literally, you should go out and ask people, "are you gay, or not gay?" and then kick them out or whatever....[3]

To me, the issue comes down to privacy. Prudes have rights, too. There are three times in life when you are forced to live with people you might not otherwise choose in most situations: the military, jail—which I don't think gays want to use as a model for gay relations—and number three, the freshman dorm. And about the only way you can get out of a freshman dorm situation is when you have a gay and a straight, and one wants out.

Otherwise, you have to grin and bear it for a year. So the universities are hypocrites on this—they preach to the military, asking the military to do something the universities won't practice.

Anybody who's for doing away with "don't ask, don't tell" should therefore also be opposed to separate-gender toilets. Sexual orientation is sexual
orientation, and at my age, I wish I had any sexual orientation.

F. Op-ed., General John M. Shalikashvili, *The New York Times*, January 2, 2007

Second Thoughts on Gays in the Military

Two weeks ago, President Bush called for a long-term plan to increase the
size of the armed forces. As our leaders consider various options for carrying
out Mr. Bush's vision, one issue likely to generate fierce debate is "don't ask,
don't tell," the policy that bars openly gay service members from the military.
Indeed, leaders in the new Congress are planning to re-introduce a bill to
repeal the policy next year.

As was the case in 1993—the last time the American people thoroughly
debated the question of whether openly gay men and lesbians should serve
in the military—the issue will give rise to passionate feelings on both sides.
The debate must be conducted with sensitivity, but it must also consider the
evidence that has emerged over the last 14 years.

When I was chairman of the Joint Chiefs of Staff, I supported the current
policy because I believed that implementing a change in the rules at that time
would have been too burdensome for our troops and commanders. I still
believe that to have been true. The concern among many in the military was
that given the longstanding view that homosexuality was incompatible with
service, letting people who were openly gay serve would lower morale, harm
recruitment and undermine unit cohesion.

In the early 1990s, large numbers of military personnel were opposed
to letting openly gay men and lesbians serve. President Bill Clinton, who
promised to lift the ban during his campaign, was overwhelmed by the
strength of the opposition, which threatened to overturn any executive action he might take.

The compromise that came to be known as "don't ask, don't tell" was
thus a useful speed bump that allowed temperatures to cool for a period of
time while the culture continued to evolve. The question before us now is
whether enough time has gone by to give this policy serious reconsideration.
Much evidence suggests that it has.

Last year I held a number of meetings with gay soldiers and marines,
including some with combat experience in Iraq, and an openly gay senior
sailor who was serving effectively as a member of a nuclear submarine crew.
These conversations showed me just how much the military has changed,
and that gays and lesbians can be accepted by their peers.

This perception is supported by a new Zogby poll of more than 500 service members returning from Afghanistan and Iraq, three quarters of whom
said they were comfortable interacting with gay people. And 24 foreign nations, including Israel, Britain and other allies in the fight against terrorism,
let gays serve openly, with none reporting morale or recruitment problems.

I now believe that if gay men and lesbians served openly in the United
States military, they would not undermine the efficacy of the armed forces.
Our military has been stretched thin by our deployments in the Middle East,

and we must welcome the service of any American who is willing and able to do the job.

But if America is ready for a military policy of nondiscrimination based on sexual orientation, the timing of the change should be carefully considered. As the 110th Congress opens for business, some of its most urgent priorities, like developing a more effective strategy in Iraq, share widespread support that spans political affiliations. Addressing such issues could help heal the divisions that cleave our country. Fighting early in this Congress to lift the ban on openly gay service members is not likely to add to that healing, and it risks alienating people whose support is needed to get this country on the right track.

By taking a measured, prudent approach to change, political and military leaders can focus on solving the nation's most pressing problems while remaining genuinely open to the eventual and inevitable lifting of the ban. When that day comes, gay men and lesbians will no longer have to conceal who they are, and the military will no longer need to sacrifice those whose service it cannot afford to lose.

Notes

1. Jackson's memo focused primarily on two issues, "the intent to discriminatorily censor speech," and "the intent to accommodate troop prejudice," http://dont.stanford.edu/hearings/memo.pdf.

2. Jan. 29/Administration of William J. Clinton, 1993, http://dont.stanford.edu/regulations/pres1-29-93.pdf.

3. In fact, while previous policy, that is, Department of Defense Directive 1332.14, January 28, 1982, "Enlisted Administrative Separations," stated, "Homosexuality is incompatible with military service," no "Don't Ask, Don't Tell" documents (i.e., neither Public Law 103-160 nor associated Code or branch regulations) use that language.

Chronology of Events

1991   October 28—Candidate Bill Clinton, responding to a question at a forum at Harvard's Kennedy School of Government, states that, if elected, he will issue an executive order permitting gay men, lesbians, and bisexuals to serve openly in the U.S. military.

1992   October 27—Petty Officer Allen R. Schindler is murdered by his shipmates on the U.S.S. Belleau Wood in an antigay hate crime.

October 27—A federal court in Canada rules that the Canadian policy prohibiting the military service of gays violates Canada's Charter of Rights and Freedoms.

November 3—William Jefferson Clinton wins the presidential election.

1993   January—With the knowledge that Clinton is about to be inaugurated, members of Congress and military leadership express their objection to an outright lifting of the ban.

January 20—Clinton is inaugurated as the 42nd President of the United States.

January 21—It is reported that the president has agreed to delay lifting the ban for a six-month period during which the impact of such a change can be studied and the Department of Defense can play a role in drafting the policy.

January 28—In *Meinhold v. U.S. Department of Defense*, in the U.S. District Court for the Central District of California, Judge Terry Hatter finds that the Navy regulation on gays and lesbians violates the equal protection guarantee of the Fifth Amendment to the U.S. Constitution.

January 29—President Clinton directs Secretary of Defense Les Aspin to draft an executive order ending discrimination on the basis of sexual orientation with regard to military service.

March to July—House and Senate Armed Services Committees hold hearings on allowing gays to serve openly in the military.

July 19—Clinton issues a "Don't Ask, Don't Tell, Don't Pursue" policy that allows gays to serve as long as they do not reveal their sexual orientation. He calls it "an honorable compromise."

July 19—The RAND Corporation issues an independent report which concludes that there is no reason to continue the ban on gay service members. Although requested by the Department of Defense, the report is largely ignored by Congress and plays little to no role in the debate.

November 30—Bill Clinton signs Public Law 103–160, the legislation that would become known as "Don't Ask, Don't Tell" (DADT).

1994   June—The Navy Manpower Analysis Center issues a memo implying that public support for gay activities (e.g., participation in a gay choir) by Navy members may be "inconsistent with good military character" and a violation of DADT.

November 3—Richard Peterson, Deputy Chief, General Law Division, Office of the Judge Advocate General, U.S. Air Force, issues a memo encouraging the questioning of parents, siblings, counselors, roommates, and close friends of suspected gay service members.

December 1—A Navy retention hearing board, agreeing that stating "I am a lesbian" is not a statement regarding conduct, votes unanimously to retain Lieutenant Zoe Dunning in service.

1995   August 4—President Clinton issues Executive Order 12968 prohibiting discrimination based on sexual orientation in the issuing of security clearances.

August 18—In response to the Dunning case, Department of Defense General Counsel Judith Miller issues a memo requiring service members who state a homosexual orientation to prove they do not have the propensity to engage in homosexual acts.

1996   January 25—Officials at Hawaii's Hickam Air Force Base reduce the sentence of a service member facing rape charges if he agrees to name military men with whom he had sexual relations. He accuses seventeen men.

July 31—A bill is introduced in Congress which would revert to pre-DADT regulations and allow the military to ask and pursue suspected gay service members. The bill passes in the House, but fails in the Senate.

1997   January 10—In a 700-page report concerning the case at Hickam Air Force Base, the Air Force Inspector General concludes that sentence reduction in exchange for the provision of names does not constitute a violation of DADT, which expressly prohibits "witch hunts."

March 24—Under Secretary of Defense Edwin Dorn issues first of its kind guidance on how to handle reports of harassment by service members suspected of being gay. This memo explained that service members have the ability to report without retaliation or further investigation.

1998   April—The Department of Defense issues a report reviewing DADT, concluding that, in spite of an increase in discharges and reports of harassment, the policy is working.

1999   July—The Navy removes material from its online General Medical Officer Manual that has instructed medical personnel to turn in gay service members.

July 5—Soldiers at Fort Campbell, Kentucky, murder Private First Class Barry Winchell in his sleep because they believed him to be gay.

August 12—Under Secretary of Defense Rudy de Leon issues a memo reinforcing the prohibition on antigay harassment in the military.

September 27—The European Court of Human Rights declares unanimously that Great Britain's ban on gays in the military is a violation of the basic right to privacy.

October 6—President Clinton issues Executive Order 13140 strengthening military sentencing for antigay hate crimes. He also provides for limited psychotherapist–patient privilege for service members facing criminal charges.

2000   January 6—At a debate in New Hampshire, presidential candidate George W. Bush states, "I'm a don't ask, don't tell man." All democratic candidates support a repeal of DADT.

January 12—Great Britain ends its ban on the military service of gays.

March 16—The Department of Defense issues report showing overwhelming antigay harassment throughout the military.

July 21—The Department of Defense issues Anti-Harassment Action Plan and directs all branches to implement it.

2001   October 7—Operation Enduring Freedom begins. After the invasion of Afghanistan, gay discharges dropped by 30 percent. U.S. troops serve alongside openly gay service members from countries without a gay ban on their military.

2002   January 9—The Army Judge Advocate General Corps conducts training on the Homosexual Conduct Policy for about eighty-five military attorneys. Their presentation includes clips of the television character "Tinky Winky" and the words "faggot" and "queers."

April 4—At Twentynine Palms, California, the Marine Corps issues a memo saying, "Homosexuals can and do serve honorably in the Marine Corps. Homosexuals can and do make some of the best Marines."

July—In violation of DADT, the Air Force is found using forms that ask recruits if they are homosexual or bisexual and if they intend to engage in homosexual acts.

2003   March 20—Operation Iraqi Freedom begins. The number of gay discharges drops by 40 percent from what it was before the Afghanistan invasion.

July 9—The Urban Institute publishes a report that estimates there are 1 million lesbian, gay, or bisexual veterans in the United States.

October 6—Former President Bill Clinton calls for an end to the military's ban on homosexuals on the tenth anniversary of DADT.

December 10—Two retired generals and one retired admiral come out in *The New York Times* and condemn DADT.

December 16—Fifteen retired senior military leaders issue a statement calling for a repeal of DADT.

2004   September 15—The Center for the Study of Sexual Minorities in the Military, now the Michael D. Palm Center, releases a study showing the contributions of GLBT (lesbian, gay, bisexual, and transgender) service members during the wars in Afghanistan and Iraq. Among participants is Brian Hughes, a gay Army Ranger who was part of the task force that rescued prisoner of war (POW) Jessica Lynch.

2005   January—The Department of Defense reports that between 1998 and 2003, twenty-six Arabic or Farsi language experts were separated from the military.

February—According to a Government Accountability Office report, the first ten years of DADT cost the government about $191 million.

March 2—Representative Martin Meehan introduces HR 1059, the Military Readiness Enhancement Act, into Congress. This would effectively repeal DADT by instituting a policy of nondiscrimination on the basis of sexual orientation in the military.

September 13—The Center for the Study of Sexual Minorities in the Military, now the Michael D. Palm Center, issues a news release revealing the existence of a 1999 regulation, FORSCOM 500-3-3, that allows for the active duty deployment of Army Reservists and National Guard troops who say they are gay or who are accused of being gay.

2006   February 14—A Blue Ribbon Commission determines that DADT cost the Pentagon at least $363.8 million to implement during its first ten years.

March 22—Polling data from the Pew Research Center shows that a majority of Americans—including across age, geography, and religious denomination—support allowing lesbian and gay Americans to serve openly in the armed forces.

2007   January 2—In an editorial, published in *The New York Times*, former Chair of the Joint Chiefs of Staff, General John Shalikashvili, wrote, "I now believe that if gay men and lesbians served openly in the United States military, they would not undermine the efficacy of the armed forces."

February 28—Representative Martin Meehan reintroduces HR 1059, the Military Readiness Enhancement Act, into Congress. Now HR 1246, this legislation would effectively repeal DADT by instituting a policy of nondiscrimination on the basis of sexual orientation in the military.

March 7—The U.S. Court of Appeals for the First Circuit, Boston, Massachusetts, hears oral arguments in *Cook v. Gates*, formerly *Cook v. Rumsfeld*.

Glossary of Terms

Amicus curiae brief—or amicus brief; a "friend of the court brief"; a document stating the facts and points of law of a client's case filed with the court by someone who is not a party to the case.

Commissioned officer—person in any of the armed forces who holds grade and office under a commission issued by the president; for example, in the Army, a person who has been appointed to the grade of second lieutenant or higher is a commissioned officer; also referred to simply as an officer.

Defendant—person against whom a charge is brought in a court of law.

Department of Defense (DOD)—executive department of the government consisting of the Secretary of Defense and his or her office, the War Council, the Joint Chiefs of Staff, Joint Staff and joint agencies, as well as the departments of the Army, the Navy, and the Air Force.

Discharge—term applicable to military personnel whose military service will be terminated other than through death or termination of a specific status; also applied to the document that effects the discharge, i.e., a discharge certificate.

Dyke baiting/lesbian baiting—labeling a woman as a lesbian, regardless of whether this is true or not; a tactic used to coerce military women into dating, behaving more femininely, etc.

En banc—the entire court; when an appeal is heard "en banc," all members of the court are present, rather than merely a quorum, as is often the case.

Enlisted—term used to include both male and female members of the Army below the grade of an officer or warrant officer; enlisted personnel.

GLBT—gay, lesbian, bisexual, transgender.

Judicial review—the power of a court to adjudicate the constitutionality of the laws of a government.

MOS—military occupational specialty; category assigned to a particular occupational position (e.g., military police = 31B).

Non-commissioned officer—enlisted person holding a rank (e.g., Sergeant) for which qualities of leadership are expected; a leadership position held by appointment or promotion, not commission.

Plaintiff—person who brings suit in a court of law.

Propensity—inclination or tendency toward a specific behavior or behaviors.

Rebuttable presumption—under "Don't Ask, Don't Tell," the accused has the right to counter, or rebut, a presumption of homosexuality; unlike non-military law where proving guilt typically lies with the accusing party; the rebuttable presumption puts the burden of proving innocence on the defendant; further complicating matters is the need to prove the future negative—that is, prove that you will not do something in the future.

Retention—keeping military personnel in military service; "recruitment and retention."

Separation/separated—all-inclusive term which is applied to personnel actions resulting from release from active duty, discharge, retirement, dismissal, resignation, dropped from the rolls, or death.

SLDN—Servicemembers Legal Defense Network; their mission describes the organization as "a national, non-profit legal services, watchdog and policy organization dedicated to ending discrimination against and harassment of military personnel affected by 'Don't Ask, Don't Tell' and related forms of intolerance."

Sodomy—addressed in Article 125 of the Uniform Code of Military Justice; includes oral and anal sex with another person, regardless of sex.

UCMJ—Uniform Code of Military Justice; Congressional code of military law.

Unit cohesion—working together as a team; presumed by many to be required for the accomplishment of a unit's mission; the primary rationale for prohibiting the military service of openly gay and lesbian persons.

Witch hunt—though typically used in reference to lesbians, an investigation to identify gay and lesbian service members; often accomplished through intimidation and illegal actions.

Annotated Bibliography

There are far many more books and articles addressing gays and lesbians in the military than I have included here. I have not included any of the many fine biographies, autobiographies, or oral history volumes. I have also not included many of the exceptional pieces of legal scholarship that continue to appear. Rather, I have selected some of those writings I believe most relevant to a broad understanding of the issues. For a more extensive list of resources, see the Michael D. Palm Center Web site, www.palmcenter.org.

Articles

Alexander, Sharon E. Debbage (2004). "A Ban by Any Other Name: Ten Years of 'Don't Ask, Don't Tell.';" 21 *Hofstra Lab. and Emp. L.J.*, 403. This article provides a brief history and describes the mandates of "Don't Ask, Don't Tell." Published as part of the symposium, "Don't Ask, Don't Tell: 10 Years Later," this article is particularly valuable for its provision of an accessible overview of relevant legal issues.

Belkin, Aaron (2001). "The Pentagon's Gay Ban Is Not Based on Military Necessity." *Journal of Homosexuality* 41, 103–130. During the 1993 Congressional debates, unit cohesion was the primary rationale for prohibiting gays and lesbians from serving openly in the U.S. military. It was argued that performance and morale would decline if gays and lesbians were allowed to serve. In this article Belkin asserts that the evidence used to support this position lacks validity. Under his analysis the unit cohesion rationale falls short, as does the larger discriminatory policy.

——— (2003). "Don't Ask, Don't Tell: Is the Gay Ban Based on Military Necessity?" *Parameters: U.S. Army War College Quarterly* 33, 108–119. This article reports the results of studies examining the effect of lifting gay bans in foreign militaries. The Center for the Study of Sexual Minorities in the Military (CSSMM), now the Michael D. Palm Center, looked at Australia, Great Britain, Canada, and Israel. These countries were chosen because all have lifted bans against the wishes of their military and share cultural similarities with the United States. Great Britain is of particular interest because their policy had been used to support the arguments of those in the United States opposed to allowing gay and lesbian service members to serve openly.

Belkin, Aaron and Melissa Levitt (2001). "Homosexuality and the Israel Defense Forces; Did Lifting the Gay Ban Undermine Military Performance?" *Armed Forces and Society* 27, 541–566. This article examines whether Israel's decision to include homosexual service members in its military led to any changes in performance. The authors consider this an example of lifting the gay ban in a "high stakes security context." This analysis is particularly significant because the Israel Defense Forces are considered elite and the country has been engaged in over half a century of continuous military conflict.

Belkin, Aaron and Melissa Sheridan Embser-Herbert (2002). "A Modest Proposal: Privacy as a Rationale for Excluding Gays and Lesbians from the U.S. Military." *International Security* 27, 178–187. As unit cohesion became a less convincing rationale for prohibiting the open military service of gays and lesbians, attention turned to the argument that the presence of openly gay and lesbian service members would violate the privacy of heterosexual service members. The authors conclude that lifting the ban would not detract from heterosexual privacy. They also explain how the ban itself actually serves to systematically invade the privacy of heterosexual, as well as homosexual, service members. They argue that those who advocate for heterosexual privacy should support lifting the ban.

Evans, Rhonda L. (2002). "U.S. Military Policies Concerning Homosexuals: Development, Implementation and Outcomes." *Law and Sexuality* 11, 113–191. This article considers the development of U.S. policies restricting the service of gay men and lesbians and the rationales used to support these policies. The author analyzes various data on gay and lesbian service members and their effect on military operations. The article includes four case studies of service members who challenged the military's ban while continuing to serve.

Frank, Nathaniel (2000). "What's Love Got to Do with It? The Real Story of Military Sociology and 'Don't Ask, Don't Tell.'" *Lingua Franca* 10(7), 71–79, 81. This article focuses on Charles Moskos, self-described "architect" of "Don't Ask, Don't Tell," and the role of social science, particularly sociology, in research on the policy. It further provides a nice overview of the history of the policy.

Gilreath, Shannon. "Sexually Speaking: 'Don't Ask, Don't Tell' and the First Amendment after *Lawrence v. Texas*," 14 Duke J. of Gender L. & Pol'y 953, May 2007. This article argues that "Don't Ask, Don't Tell" is unconstitutional because it violates the First Amendment guarantees of free speech and freedom of expression. Part I examines the First Amendment implications of the policy, pointing out the fact that "Don't Ask, Don't Tell" purports to be focusing on conduct, not speech. Part II explains why the tradition of deferring to military decision making does not save the policy. Part III explains why it is appropriate that the policy be evaluated under heightened First Amendment review. And, Part IV finds that, in addition to failing heightened scrutiny, the defenses also fail rational basis review.

Kier, Elizabeth (1998). "Homosexuals in the U.S. Military: Open Integration and Combat Effectiveness." *International Security* 23, 5–39. The author analyzes the issue of integrating gays and lesbians into the military and the effect this action would have on the organization. She points out that the individual abilities of the service members are not in question. Rather, the debate revolves around unit cohesion and overall military effectiveness. The author provides an overview of military effectiveness and unit cohesion, and goes on to challenge two ideas that form the basis of the unit cohesion rationale. The first of these ideas is that unit cohesion is actually essential to military effectiveness. The second is that allowing openly gay and lesbian service members would undermine unit cohesion. She uses studies of racial and gender integration in the U.S. military as well as the integration of gays into foreign militaries to prove that segregated groups can be integrated with no cost in terms of effectiveness.

Osburn, C. Dixon (1995). "A Policy in Desperate Search of a Rationale: The Military's Policy on Lesbians, Gays, and Bisexuals." *University of Missouri-Kansas City Law Review* 64(1), 199–236. This article examines the constitutionality of "Don't Ask, Don't Tell" under the Equal Protection Clause. The author concludes that even under the most deferential standard that courts sometimes afford the military, the policy cannot withstand Equal Protection review.

Books

Belkin, Aaron and Geoffrey Bateman (Eds.) (2003). *Don't Ask, Don't Tell: Debating the Gay Ban in the Military*. Boulder, CO: Lynne Rienner Publishers. The murder of private first-class Barry Winchell set the stage for the Center for the Study of Sexual Minorities in the Military's December 2000 conference titled "Don't Ask, Don't Tell: Is the Gay Ban Based on Military Necessity or Prejudice?" Five of the chapters in this book are "edited transcripts" from the conference, with topics ranging from the costs of the ban to its impact on individual service members to analyzing foreign military experiences. The book also contains chapters on the history of gay and lesbian service members' participation in the military and personal testimonials from service members.

Berube, Allan (1990). *Coming Out Under Fire: The History of Gay Men and Women in World War Two*. New York: The Free Press. Based on ten years of research that included interviews with gay and lesbian veterans and examinations of government documents and wartime letters, the author describes World War II as both an awakening for gays and lesbians and a catalyst for antigay reactions after the war. Berube details everything from the screening process that supposedly excluded gays to the discharge system to the redefining of homosexuality as a medical problem by military officials.

Halley, Janet (1999). *Don't*. Durham, NC: Duke University Press. In this book, the author argues that "Don't Ask, Don't Tell" is a misnomer for the U.S. military policy. Halley details the steps that led to the creation of the law and ultimately the claim of regulating status, not conduct. She argues that the policy places all service members, regardless of their sexual orientation, in a precarious situation of self-monitoring behavior and that the policy should be found unconstitutional.

Herek, Gregory M. and Aaron Belkin (2005). "Sexual Orientation and Military Service: Prospects for Organizational and Individual Change in the United States," in *Military Life: The Psychology of Serving in Peace and Combat*, Thomas W. Britt, Amy B. Adler, and Carl Andrew Castro (Eds.). Westport, CT: Praeger Security International. This book provides an historical overview of how homosexuality has been understood in the United States and its armed forces. The authors critique contemporary rationales for excluding gay men and lesbians from the military, discuss social and psychological issues relevant to the organizational and individual changes that might follow the elimination of "Don't Ask, Don't Tell," and conclude with suggestions for future research

Herek, Gregory M., Jared B. Jobe, and Ralph M. Carney (Eds.) (1996). *Out in Force: Sexual Orientation in the U.S. Military*. Chicago: University of Chicago Press. This book presents fifteen chapters authored by social science scholars on sexual orientation and the military. These authorities discuss the military and sexuality and address questions about the possible effects of integrating the military.

Lehring, Gary L. (2003). *Officially Gay: The Political Construction of Sexuality by the U.S. Military*. Philadelphia, PA: Temple University Press. This book describes the military's attempt to identify and exclude gays and lesbians, tracing how the military has historically constructed definitions of homosexual identity. The author argues that this process made possible greater regulation and scrutiny of gays and lesbians, both within and outside of the military, while also helping to create a gay and lesbian political movement and shaping the direction of that movement.

Rimmerman, Craig A. (Ed.) (1996). *Gay Rights, Military Wrongs: Political Perspectives on Lesbians and Gays in the Military*. New York: Garland Publishing, Inc. This book contains chapters looking at issues surrounding the military service of openly gay and lesbian people. Topics include foreign militaries ending their gay bans, "witch hunts" for lesbian service members, and the parallels between racial integration of the military and the gay ban.

Scott, Wilbur J. and Sandra Carson Stanley (1994). *Gays and Lesbians in the Military: Issues, Concerns, and Contrasts*. New York: Aldine de Gruyter. This book contains seventeen chapters on various aspects of sexual orientation and military service, and all but one of these was written for this text specifically. The work includes chapters that give context and background to the issue as well as those that highlight the division of views on the topic. There is a section devoted to contrasting the gay ban to policies directed at women; another section looks at the experiences of foreign militaries. A final section addresses policy implications. This volume is particularly interesting because it was solicited after Clinton announced his intent to lift the ban on gay and lesbian service members, but was published in 1994, prior to the opportunity to observe the implementation of the new policy.

Shawer, Lois (1995). *And the Flag Was Still There: Straight People, Gay People, and Sexuality in the U.S. Military*. New York: Harrington Park Press. This book addresses the relationship between the military, sexuality, and modesty. The author cites the U.S. military culture as particularly damaging to sexual identity. It contains a wealth of information about sexual identity in the military context.

Shilts, Randy (1993). *Conduct Unbecoming: Gays & Lesbians in the U.S. Military*. New York: Fawcett Columbine. This book is considered, by many, the definitive work on gays and lesbians in the military, post–World War II and pre–"Don't Ask, Don't Tell." Shilts interviewed service members of all levels and branches of the military in addition to analyzing thousands of documents. The author provides a comprehensive history of gays and lesbians in the military and details the persecution they have faced.

Index

About the Author

MELISSA SHERIDAN EMBSER-HERBERT, a veteran of the U.S. Army and Army Reserve, is Professor and Chair, Department of Sociology at Hamline University in Saint Paul, Minnesota. Her publications include *Camouflage Isn't Only for Combat: Gender, Sexuality, and Women in the Military* and "Changes in Latitudes, Changes in Attitudes: Is There a Role for Canadian Jurisprudence in Ending Discrimination in the U.S. Military?"